EDUCATED FOR FREEDOM

JAMES McCUNE SMITH

HENRY HIGHLAND GARNET

EDUCATED

for

FREEDOM

~ *The Incredible Story of* ~
TWO FUGITIVE SCHOOLBOYS
Who Grew Up to Change a Nation

ANNA MAE DUANE

NEW YORK UNIVERSITY PRESS
New York

NEW YORK UNIVERSITY PRESS
New York
www.nyupress.org

First published in paperback in 2022

References to Internet websites (URLs) were accurate at the time of writing.
Neither the author nor New York University Press is responsible for URLs
that may have expired or changed since the manuscript was prepared.

Library of Congress Cataloging-in-Publication Data
Names: Duane, Anna Mae, 1968– author.
Title: Educated for freedom : the incredible story of two fugitive schoolboys
who grew up to change a nation / Anna Mae Duane.
Description: New York : New York University Press, [2020] |
Includes bibliographical references and index. |
Summary: "Educated for Freedom" explores the story of two fugitive schoolboys
who grew up to change a nation"— Provided by publisher.
Identifiers: LCCN 2019006871 | ISBN 9781479847471 (cloth) |
ISBN 9781479816712 (pb)
Subjects: LCSH: Garnet, Henry Highland, 1815–1882. | Smith, James McCune, 1813–1865. |
African Americans—Colonization—Africa—History—19th century. | African Americans—
Cultural assimilation—History—19th century. | Antislavery movements—United
States—History. | New-York African Free-School—History. | American Colonization
Society—History. | Slavery—United States—History—19th century. | Free blacks—United
States—History—19th century. | African American intellectuals—Biography.
Classification: LCC E449 .D835 2019 | DDC 306.3/620973—dc23
LC record available at https://lccn.loc.gov/2019006871

New York University Press books are printed on acid-free paper, and their binding materials
are chosen for strength and durability. We strive to use environmentally responsible
suppliers and materials to the greatest extent possible in publishing our books.

Manufactured in the United States of America

10 9 8 7 6 5 4 3 2 1

Also available as an ebook

CONTENTS

Rose with Thorns, artist unknown. New-York Historical Society & Museum, New-York African Free-School Records, vol. 4.

Introduction

WHEN a fourteen-year-old Black girl took her place at the front of the Mulberry Street New York African Free School (NYAFS),[1] she had already done the impossible. In 1822, when slavery was still legal in New York, and the nation was two generations away from the Emancipation Proclamation, Margaret Odle had graduated at the top of her class.[2] And she had stiff competition: the New York African Free Schools would produce brilliant leaders in medicine, politics, and the arts, including the first African American to earn an MD and the first Black man to perform *Othello* on the London stage. When Margaret looked out at the audience who had come to the NYAFS to witness the student performances, she would have seen a mix of white and Black faces, her fellow schoolmates among them, ready to applaud her accomplishments. We know that her brother was in the audience, probably joined by her family and other members of the community. In addition to the familiar faces of benefactors and local community members, white journalists were there, as they were nearly every year. They watched carefully, eager to file the children's success (or failure) as evidence in the ongoing experiment testing Black children's ability to master the trappings of freedom. Finally, as Margaret's eyes scanned the crowd, they would have fallen upon her teacher, Charles C. Andrews, a white Englishman who served as the schoolmaster at the school for over twenty years. It was Charles Andrews, not Margaret, who had written the speech she was about to give.

When she finally spoke, Margaret told the story of a Black child caught between a promising future and a traumatic past. Her speech began with a hopeful look towards a future of equality, citing her own accomplishments as proof that such a future was, in fact, possible. She needed "only to point you to those specimens," she told the crowd, "and remind you of the exercises this day exhibited before you to demonstrate a truth." That truth, she insisted, was that Black people could, through education, grow into full, mature citizenship. Yes, the "African race" had "long been . . . held in a state, the most degrading to humanity," she explained to the crowd. But they were "nevertheless, endowed by the same almighty power that made us all, with intellectual capacities, not inferior to any of the greater human family."[3]

Yet even as she looked forward to a future made possible by her own education, the hopeful world in which she stood seemed to dissolve. Margaret's speech suddenly immersed her—and the crowd—in a very different reality. Pausing in her recitation, she looked "round on my school mates" and soon observed "one among them who excites my most tender solicitudes." "It is my Brother," she told the crowd. Looking at her sibling, she did not see the freedom that was promised to both of them. Rather, she imagined that she saw him on the auction block. Moved by the horror of the vision, she spoke of her grief in this alternate reality. "Oh!" she exclaimed, "if I were called to part with you as some poor girls have, to part with their equally dear kindred, and each of us (like them) to be forcibly conveyed away into wretched slavery never to see each other again . . ." In that moment, the school, the proud community members, the liberal reporters, all fell away before slavery's world-destroying power. Almost as soon as the horror raised its head in the schoolroom, Margaret banished it, telling herself and the crowd that here, in the house of learning, time moves forward, not backward. "I must forbear," she told herself, looking back out at the group of well-wishers, her brother among them. "Thank heaven it is not, no it is not the case with us."[4] She ended her speech by reminding her brother to study hard and to listen to his teachers. Nonetheless, this look forward to her brother's future remains haunted by her vision of the slave block. Her tale of progress had been broken in the middle, the rift in her story filled with a past that cannot be left behind. Slavery in this speech works as a force of gravity, perhaps allowing a naive child to think she can jump high enough to escape, but always, always pulling the aspirant back to earth, tethering her to a landscape where youth, old age, and everything in between became indistinguishable in the fog of endless bondage.

This book is about the lessons conveyed by Margaret's speech and taught for generations to Black children in a New York City school. It focuses on two schoolboys educated at Margaret's school who absorbed those lessons, and who, in their struggle to transcend them, changed the nation they lived in.[5] James McCune Smith and Henry Highland Garnet achieved unprecedented honors in a world that believed Black people were irredeemably inferior. As the sons of enslaved mothers, these schoolboy friends would meet Revolutionary War heroes, travel the world, publish in medical journals, and speak before crowds of cheering thousands. Through their work in medicine, literature, public service, political activism, and the ministry, they showed others how to reject the false choices they themselves had been taught at school: that Black people must either embrace a cheerful exile abroad or accept a living death in the United States. Their work, and that of the Black activist community they helped to lead, influenced how the United States could imagine a way to grow out of its slave past.

As two Black children who came of age and came into freedom as the country itself matured from a slave nation to federal emancipation, James McCune Smith and Henry Highland Garnet illustrate how powerfully narratives about Black children's capacity for growth influenced the national debate about slavery's future. The school where they met—and where these narratives were tested for public scrutiny—was the focus of intense local, national, and even international attention. That school, part of the New York African Free School system, was first created in 1787 by a group that included Alexander Hamilton and John Jay, two founding fathers still flush with optimism about freedom's power to transform the country. That optimism had worn thin by the time Garnet and Smith graduated in the late 1820s, even as New York moved towards ending slavery throughout the state in 1827. The students literally had to fight their way through the city streets to get to class, continually harassed by poor white New Yorkers who felt excluded from the progress that these students seemed able to access.

But it was not just prejudice from outsiders that tore the school apart. The school's white teachers and trustees found themselves unable to prepare their students for a future as citizens. In truth, they simply could not imagine what that future would look like. Black parents were especially outraged by the schoolmaster's belief that Black children could never grow into full maturity in the United States, and thus needed to "return" to Africa. Indeed, by the 1830s, almost all the school's administrators had aligned themselves with the American Colonization Society, an organization that argued that emancipation could only be achieved through exile, that somehow America's future was doomed unless the descendants of slaves went "back" to the scene of the historical crime, resetting the clock on America's original sin. The lives of both Smith and Garnet would be shaped by the powerful story that the American Colonization Society told—that Black people were somehow lost in American time, but could grow into maturity if they returned to Africa as colonizers. Only by returning to an origin first stolen from their African ancestors, and then imposed on American-born Black people, the story ran, could Black children ever hope to grow up and assume the respect and responsibility accorded to adults.

The conflicting stories the NYAFS rehearsed about the future of Black children was part of a nationwide conversation anxiously considering how Americans would be able to "grow up." As the nation emerged from the War of 1812—largely considered the second war of independence from Mother England—Americans increasingly embraced the idea of the nation as a promising youth moving towards maturity. Yet even as Americans embraced youth as a political symbol, they scrambled to write laws reinforcing the dividing lines between the adult citizen and the child subject. To take just one example, the years between 1790 and 1840 saw a decided shift in what Americans deemed a prerequisite for full citizenship. In the eighteenth century, men had to own property to be able to vote, but by 1840, most states felt that it was age, not wealth, that should be the determining factor in voting eligibility.[6] While voting laws throughout the young country differed in many respects, they all agreed that adulthood—defined as turning twenty-one—was required to access political power. This legal investment in a certain kind of adulthood (almost always defined as white and male) was just one part of a growing tapestry of narratives about development that would include medical, scientific, economic, and political theories that rendered progress the ultimate good. Those who were considered unable to develop along particular timelines were doomed to a life of childlike dependence. In short, nineteenth-century debates about the very nature of political power would, again and again, compare disempowered populations to children in order to justify their exclusion from a sovereignty that was solely the realm of adults.[7]

The bias against children was reinforced by narratives that relegated Black people to a permanent state of immaturity, forever unable to access the responsibilities of citizenship. That bias continues to shape our understanding of how freedom was imagined and established in the nineteenth century. We have long listened carefully to the enfranchised men who wrote the legislation that pushed the nation towards war and, eventually, legal guarantees of abolition. This book participates in the ongoing work of engaging how African Americans themselves—men, women, and children—conceived of the freedom they fought to inhabit.[8] The lives of James McCune Smith and Henry Highland Garnet provide two remarkable responses to a political question that shaped their generation: how to imagine and secure a Black child's liberation.

As Smith and Garnet argued—sometimes bitterly—over how Black people could possibly grow up in a nation that sought to render them perpetual children, they laid the groundwork for Black political and intellectual thought for generations to come. They emerge in these pages both as friends and as rivals. They had widely different temperaments, and left decidedly divergent paths through the archive that shapes the format of the chapters that follow, and the personalities that we glimpse within them. James McCune Smith, a believer in institutions and in the collaborations that could build them, is an elusive presence, even as his name appears on dozens of erudite and important documents. Naturally self-effacing, Smith once imagined himself as the descendent of a "coral insect . . . longing to work beneath the tide in a super-structure."[9] For him, the work of supporting a larger whole would include introducing Frederick Douglass's life story, expanding the educational possibilities at the Colored Orphan Asylum, and writing loving portraits of everyday Black life.

The documents generated by Garnet's work testify to his infectious charisma, even as the records themselves are often a chronicle of conflict. Where Smith sought to methodically set building blocks in place, Garnet often sought to burn the whole house down. He changed his mind often, reflecting the tumultuous nature of the nation he lived in. His speeches were incendiary, and his political philosophy volatile and provocative. Much of what we know of him emerges from the words—sometimes admiring, often exasperated—of friends and rivals seeking to come to terms with his formidable rhetorical and political skill. The format of the book attends to the separate paths of these two leaders by alternating focus between Smith's and Garnet's early years for the first section of the book. The last two chapters bring the schoolboy friends back together as they faced the cataclysmic events of the Civil War, the 1863 Draft Riots, and the crafting of the Thirteenth Amendment.

Not surprisingly, both men disagreed about the possibility of progress and the best way to achieve it in the United States. Smith, a star student who achieved success and stability as the first African American to earn an MD, would remain passionately opposed to the arguments made by the American Colonization Society throughout his life. He rejected the premise that Black children needed to orphan themselves from America in order to achieve the equality America promised. For much of his career, Smith would draw upon his scientific training to rewrite the pessimistic narrative that posed African exile as the only viable future for Black people. He used medical and statistical methods to refute arguments of Black pathology that showed up everywhere, from US census reports to autopsies performed on orphans. As head physician of the New York Colored Orphan Asylum, he held up Black children's physical health and academic prowess to prove racial equality. By the eve of the Civil War, Smith's faith in the ability of factual evidence to disrupt racism had been profoundly shaken. The man who had dedicated his life to healing argued that if abolitionists could not move hearts and minds, they would have to resort to violence. Yet he always believed that progress would come, if only Black people would fight for it on American soil. For Smith, choosing exile from the United States was nothing less than surrender.

Henry Highland Garnet had a markedly different relationship to exile, perhaps because he spent his life searching for stable ground, only to have it repeatedly torn from under his feet. From the moment he ran away from slavery as a nine-year-old child, he had to look over his shoulder in fear. When he was just fourteen, he returned to his family's home one evening to find the rooms ransacked, his family hunted down by agents eager to sell them back into slavery. Garnet's response to this horror foreshadowed his life as a rebel and as an activist. Faced with the potential loss of his family and grave danger to himself, he grabbed a knife and took to the streets, hoping to confront his family's tormentors. Throughout his life, Garnet would run towards a fight, no matter the consequences. And fights would follow him wherever he went. As a minister and famous orator, Garnet gave speeches that would gather audiences of hundreds, even thousands, of rapt listeners. The content of those speeches—some of which were too controversial for immediate publication—urged Black resistance, even as they portrayed the United States as a landscape full of ghosts. In prose that echoed the gothic writers he had admired as a young man, Garnet described the United States as haunted by specters of

Black ancestors lamenting a cycle of injustice endlessly repeating itself. Eventually, his despondence at the nation's lack of progress led him to believe that African Americans needed to settle in West Africa—a belief that would render him an outcast among his old schoolmates.

As they rose to the top of their respective fields, Garnet and Smith would join a conversation about the nature of freedom alongside some of the nation's leading cultural and political figures.[10] As gifted writers, they were inspired by—and contributed to—emerging literary conversations. Smith, for instance, used the imagery he found in Melville's *Moby-Dick* to make the case for dogged persistence in the antislavery cause. Garnet, for his part, drew inspiration from the Byronic hero, both in prose and in personal demeanor. Both men tangled with pro-colonizationist politicians like Senator Henry Clay, and had pointed conversations with radical abolitionist John Brown about the role of violence in the struggle. Frederick Douglass emerges as an important character in this story, as he spent years working alongside both men. He had a close friendship with Smith, deepened by engaging editorial collaborations. When it came to Henry Highland Garnet, Douglass would often swing from admiration to attack and then back again within a matter of weeks. Many considered Henry Highland Garnet a contender for the most eloquent Black orator of the time, a title Douglass coveted; the two ambitious men clashed often on matters both personal and political.

When Garnet declared himself in favor of African colonization, Smith and Douglass were some of his loudest critics. Smith felt that Garnet's work closely resembled the mission of the hated American Colonization Society, whose proponents had filled their school days with lessons about how Black children had no future in the United States. Both words and fists would fly between the opposing camps, even as the nation itself split apart along two irreconcilable visions of the country's future. In the midst of this acrimony, the spring of 1863 would remind Smith and Garnet that they had all too much in common. While the Civil War raged on, and Lincoln moved towards rendering slavery illegal throughout the nation, white prejudice revealed just how little Black "freedom" could mean.

The story ends with the two New York African Free School friends coming together for one final collaboration. When the Thirteenth Amendment was finally on the road to being ratified, Congress requested a speech from Henry Highland Garnet, "the most eloquent Black man in America." When it was time to publish his words, Garnet wanted just one man to write the introduction to his life and work: James McCune Smith. The historic document reveals how deeply the men had influenced one another. Garnet's fire had shaped Smith's belief that progress could not come without bloodshed. For his part, Garnet would recalibrate his colonizationist plans to align with the hopes of his old friend Dr. Smith, who had always believed that progress was possible in the United States. After Smith passed away in 1865, Garnet would dedicate the next twenty years of his life to educating Black youth above and below the Mason-Dixon Line. He would, however, die on the African soil he had spent much of his life dreaming about but had never actually seen.

In telling this story, I have chosen to depart from standard biographical practice, in which one moves quickly from a subject's childhood in order to attend to the historian's "proper focus"—the politically significant work that the subject engaged in as an adult. *Educated for Freedom* braids the personal with the political, the needs of a child with the demands of a citizen, to reflect how deeply intertwined these ideas were in the way slavery was being defined, attacked, and defended in the antebellum United States. Each chapter of the book features a document taken from the schoolwork of students at the school Garnet and Smith attended as children, creating an ongoing conversation between the issues they navigated as children and the work they pursued as adults. Rather than featuring their remarkable childhood as an interesting side note, *Educated for Freedom* traces the importance of children— imagined and actual—throughout the lives of both men, with much of the story crystallizing around moments when their "adult" work in medicine, science, and politics was shaped by the Black children in their lives. Sometimes those children were strangers, sometimes they were weary fugitives, and sometimes, they were their own flesh and blood. These children emerge from a range of documents—newspapers, orphan asylum records, the letters of their grieving fathers. Although they have rarely appeared in the history books, these young people were anything but marginal to the lives of these men who so deeply influenced the antislavery debate, and by that debate's outcome, have helped create the nation we live in today. By refusing separations between my subjects' work as schoolchildren and their work as activists, *Educated for Freedom* recasts the well-worn narrative of Black abolitionism primarily as a demand for political manhood. This book tells a different story, in which Black leaders sought to create alternate paths to freedom that discarded—or at least redrew—the usual dividing lines between child and adult, Black and white.

In addition to recovering the work of two understudied African American leaders, this study also provides new insight into how deeply slavery, colonialism, and capitalism were intertwined in the first half of the nineteenth century—and how savvy many abolitionists were about the odds of disentangling these threads. The very school Garnet and Smith attended was organized around a system devoted to producing, and dispersing, reliable labor across the world. Administrators boasted that both the system and the students it produced could be exported to faraway climes with consistent results. While analyzing the mutually constitutive connections between slavery and capitalism is a relatively recent trend in twenty-first-century scholarship, *Educated for Freedom* demonstrates that Black abolitionists had recognized—and resisted—this relationship as early as the 1840s.[11]

The questions that plagued Smith and Garnet remain relevant today. The notion that somehow Black bodies are doomed—stuck on a historical wheel that keeps returning them to the same place—has powerful resonance in the twenty-first century, as the country continues to re-enact bitter divisions over the role of race in remembering our history and imagining our future.[12] Current educational and legal approaches to children of color are not free from the longstanding idea that somehow Black children have inherited an inability to leave the past.[13] By looking to—and learning from—nineteenth-century children as they navigated their school's problematic lessons to forge new possibilities for Black people in the United States and abroad, this book asks us to think of how powerfully children operate within the racial stories this country has told, and continues to tell. This work is necessary if we are to fully comprehend the nineteenth century, when the majority of the US population was under eighteen, and to better understand our own moment, when so many American children are excluded from the promises the future should offer.

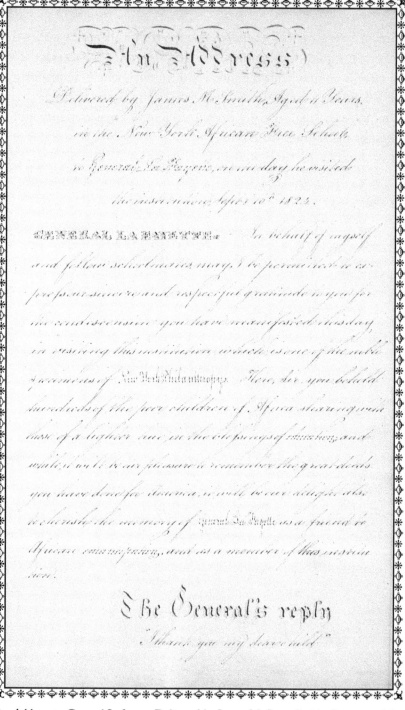

An Address to General Lafayette Delivered by James McCune Smith. Courtesy of the New-York Historical Society.

CHAPTER I

The Star Student as Specimen
(CIRCA 1822–1837)

W HEN James McCune Smith woke up on September 10, 1824, he must have been nervous. True, he had been a star student at the New York African Free School for the past two years. In the collection of exemplary student work compiled by schoolmaster Charles C. Andrews, Smith's work shows up more than that of any other student. This was not the first time young James performed before an audience. Far from it. But certainly little could have prepared this young boy, poised at the precipice between slavery and freedom, for his encounter with General Marquis de Lafayette, an international celebrity whose US visit sparked wild enthusiasm across the nation.[1] Having the opportunity to address this living Revolutionary War legend was a remarkable honor for any American, but for the poor Black child of an enslaved mother, it was an almost unfathomable opportunity. A symbol of the most liberatory aspects of the Revolutionary War, the still-dashing Lafayette generated remarkable crowds throughout his 1824 tour. Cities vied for his presence, scrambling to finish construction projects impressive enough to entice the famous war hero to visit. Both the vice president in New York and the president himself in DC invited Lafayette to stay with them. Everywhere he went, the general met crowds of adoring Americans, many of whom—like Walt Whitman—would recount their memory of the grand tour years later.[2]

In many ways Lafayette's presence allowed ghostly aspects of America's national story to put on weight and flesh, even as much of the Revolutionary War generation died off. Wherever Lafayette visited, memories of the departed, and the meaning of the revolution that defined them, became literally inscribed in stone. Nothing less than Philadelphia's Hall of Independence—the site of the signing of the Declaration—was refurbished and renamed to provide a fitting place to receive the returning hero.[3] Now, it seemed, the nation was ready to put the finishing touches on the first chapter in its history and begin in earnest on the next installment.[4] The symbolism of the meeting that day in the New York African Free School would have been lost on no one—a poor Black eleven-year-old boy welcoming a legendary elder figure of American liberty. The archive itself reflects an awareness of how significant this moment was. In the NYAFS records, there are very few redundancies. Often student samples are bunched together on one page, as if to save precious space. But there are no less than three full-length copies of James McCune Smith's "Address to Lafayette" contained among those pages. The care with which the copies were created and preserved makes it clear that everyone at the school that day knew that they were participating in a history-making moment.

On that celebrated day in September, the eleven-year-old James McCune Smith found himself confronting the tortuously intractable contrasts he would spend his life trying to resolve. The son of a formerly enslaved mother, he stood before a Revolutionary War hero who had fought for freedom, but who had come to lament how unevenly that freedom was distributed. "I would never have drawn my sword in the cause of America," Lafayette reportedly declared, "if I could have conceived that thereby I was founding a land of slavery."[5] As the best and the brightest among those who lived in the shadow of slavery, young James stood at a precipice yawning between potential and failed promise. He would either illustrate the great capacity for equality, or he would become yet another specimen of insufficiency, a perpetual child who could never lay claim to the rights of a United States citizen.

If anyone could tip the scales towards equality, it was this brilliant young student. Later remembered as a child who "worked the Blacksmith's bellows with one hand, [while] he held a Latin grammar in the other," Smith learned early on to deploy his own intellect to win—and keep—the approval of benefactors.[6] He thoroughly enjoyed his time at school, where he succeeded at just about everything he attempted. For an ambitious young student like Smith, the Mulberry Street school was a haven, an escape route, a path to the promised land of achievement. His attachment to this school, to the city, and to the friends and family that filled his schoolboy days would remain profound throughout his life.

Many of his classmates went on to remarkable careers, and Smith was undoubtedly the most careful historian of the school and of his schoolmates' childhoods there. As an adult, he would write about Henry Highland Garnet's, Ira Aldridge's, and Philip Bell's school days with obvious affection.[7] As for himself, he believed that the New York African Free School was responsible for the path his life would take. "In all cases," Smith would write in 1865, "the school-house, and schoolboy days settle the permanent characteristics, establish the level, gauge the relative, mental and moral power of the man in after life; especially it was so in this school."[8] A man who spent much of his political and scientific career working to discover the laws of cause and effect, Smith saw his own schoolboy days as a root cause of his intellect and character.

The school he attended was, by all accounts, remarkable. If historians have been tempted to read the first fifty years of US history much like a novel in which we can chart the development of a national character, the New York African Free School system offers a different way of reading the era, one in which Americans were encouraged to embrace their role as a moving piece in a global system. Founded in the flush of postrevolutionary optimism by New York's founding fathers in the late eighteenth century, the school embraced the popular Lancasterian system of education by 1808, when Charles Andrews became schoolmaster. Rather than depending on the intense relationship between master and

Emblem of Education, Henry Hill. New-York Historical Society & Museum, New-York African Free-School Records.

student that had characterized schooling for much of the late eighteenth century, Joseph Lancaster offered a startling innovation: he distributed the work of teaching among the students themselves. Older children continually quizzed the others in small groups, and, if the younger students performed well, they earned the chance to become instructors (often called "monitors") themselves. If they wanted to keep their coveted status as leaders, they would have to consistently outperform other students. There were elaborate systems of verbal and visual cues to keep things running smoothly, along with a series of rewards and punishments. These innovations were certainly cost-effective—one teacher could now oversee hundreds of students. They also changed the dynamics of education in which the schoolmaster was the sole guardian of true education.[9]

Through the Lancasterian system that educated them, the students at the New York African Free School were told to imagine themselves as interchangeable parts in a machine. As the school increasingly embraced the ideas of the American Colonization Society (ACS), administrators would tell their young charges that they could easily exchange an American future in the United States for a colonial future in Africa and still participate in the machinery of uplift. By colonizing Africa, the argument ran, Black youth would be able to rewrite a history that threatened the United States' ability to properly grow up. Instead, by going "back," these children would provide a historical do-over. ACS rhetoric depicted the African American colonization of Africa as a way to reenact and ultimately redeem American colonization. Indeed, one of the first ships headed towards the African colony was nicknamed the "Mayflower of Liberia."[10]

The NYAFS's embrace of both the Lancasterian educational system and the American Colonization Society's vision was—at least in part—a response to the bleak prospects for its students' future. Even as northern states began to enact gradual manumission laws, the gravitational pull of slavery was so strong that it threatened to keep the nation walking in circles. In 1824, young James McCune Smith stood before Lafayette as a prodigy among prodigies. For the rest of his life, he would try to demonstrate that he was not the exception that proved the rule. For even as he was able to access an education no other African American had yet received, his single achievement set the struggles of his classmates into sharp relief. His beloved school may have given the students the tools they needed to inhabit freedom, but it also provided an increasingly strident series of lessons warning that they would never be able to truly achieve it.

Indeed, even as he shook Lafayette's hand, or wowed reporters from national newspapers, James McCune Smith grew up on the precipice of disaster. As the son of a self-emancipated[11] slave woman, he would have been well aware of the dangers that roaming slave catchers and kidnappers posed for any Black children unlucky enough to get caught up in one of their gambits.[12] In a few years a group of slave catchers would come calling at his friend Henry Highland Garnet's home, disrupting the family's peace for years to come. Such events shook the entire community. Everyone knew that each morning's walk to school involved navigating a host of threats.

Still, James McCune Smith had warm memories of his childhood school and of his schoolmaster, Charles Andrews. In Smith's memory, Andrews was a passionate advocate for his students, and sought to cultivate their individual aptitudes. "Without being, in the modern, sense, an abolitionist," Andrews was, in Smith's words, "in true sympathy with his scholars in their desire to advance." The schoolmaster "taught his boys and girls to look upward; to believe themselves capable of accomplishing as much as any others could, and to regard the higher walks of life as within their reach."[13] Andrews took a personal interest in individual children, working to "find out what a boy was good for—in other words, the bent of the child; and having once ascertained this, he would spare no pains to cultivate such bent with untiring industry." The stakes, everyone knew, were high. "Mr. Andrews felt, and often said, that the character of the race was in the keeping of his scholars, and that they must exert themselves to maintain it."[14] In other words, one student's success or failure served as a specimen that others would hold up for study, and from which they would draw broad, and often unfair, conclusions. It was a lesson Smith would never forget.

To cultivate his students' talents, Andrews created what he called the Class of Merit, which was "composed of such boys, as are the best behaved, and most advanced in their learning." Considering that young James was singled out for every other honor the school could bestow, it seems likely that he was a member of this illustrious club, proudly sporting the engraved medal that was given to all members of this particular class. In Smith's memory, even moments of discipline and punishment became instances of comradery and affection between teachers and students. Years later, in correspondence with one of his schoolmates, he recalled one boy who had played truant the day before, and knew he would probably be paddled for his transgression. The boy "came to school duly prepared by extra pantaloons to undergo the usual flagellation." The plan might have worked "had it not been for an unfortunate layer of paper, which betrayed an unusual sound to Charley Andrew's [*sic*] quick ear as the rattan went wop!" In response, Andrews stripped off the extra garment, and "laid on with a mischievous vigor which brought from the boy a hundred exclamations of 'Oh! Oh! Oh! Mr. Andrews I'll never! Oh! Mr. Andrews, and finally, *dear Mr. Andrews! My dear Mr. Andrews!*"[15] Both the teacher and the surrounding students dissolved into laughter. Andrews, unable to recover his stern demeanor, returned the truant to his studies.

Yet even as Andrews invested in his students' potential, he grew increasingly convinced that such potential would be squandered in a country that would never let them advance. In 1830, Andrews published *The History of the African Free Schools*—a hodgepodge compilation that reproduced exceptional student work, rave reviews from visiting press, and, incongruously, tales of student frustration and failure. Sandwiched between advice on manners and a note to parents, Andrews included the story of Isaac, a student who graduated within a year of James McCune Smith. This young man, Andrews relates, "left this school with a respectable education, and an irreproachable character." Yet the best work he could find was as a blacksmith. When that business floundered, the young man found himself unemployed and faced with a veritable wall of discrimination blocking his way forward. He looked for work, but "every place that appeared suitable to his object was closed against him because he was black." At last, he found a friend who offered to hire him at a factory, but the benefactor soon had to rescind the proposal because his employees refused to work with a Black man. "When the lad was informed of this," Andrews tells us, the young man realized that there would be no future for him in the United States. Far "from uttering a word of angry disappointment, he resolved to leave the country and go to the Colony of Liberia."[16] The same fate, Andrews implied, awaited all of his students, no matter what academic credentials they might be able to accrue.

As James McCune Smith, Henry Highland Garnet, and their remarkable class prepared to graduate, they faced the happy prospect of living in a state finally free of slavery's grasp, thanks to New York State's 1827 manumission law. But the men in charge of their education saw little future for them in New York City. In 1826, New York Manumission Society delegates had put forth resolutions that the American Anti-slavery Convention should advocate *both* for the "gradual, but certain, extinguishment of slavery" *and* for "the transportation of the whole coloured population, now held in bondage, to the coast of Africa, or the island of St. Domingo."[17] Those sentiments were made manifest at the Mulberry Street school both in the curriculum and in the students they chose to admit. In 1828, the NYAFS struck a deal with the American Colonization Society to train two Black students, Cecil Ashman and Washington Davis, in Lancasterian pedagogy, but only if they promised to apply their education across the ocean as Liberian schoolteachers. In 1829, when John B. Russwurm, coeditor of *Freedom's Journal*, a Black newspaper that frequently sang the praises of the NYAFS, decided to go to Liberia, Charles Andrews offered to instruct him in school administration.[18] The more enamored the administration became with the idea of colonization, the more the community resisted the idea. The inability of administrators to accept and work towards Black parents' vision of their children's future would prove the school's downfall.

A few years after Smith and his classmates graduated and had moved on to new endeavors, a parent-led boycott would shut down their childhood school, and cost Charles Andrews his job.[19] In a largely unnoted moment in early Black activism—a moment that almost certainly had mothers at the forefront—the largely impoverished and disenfranchised community of NYAFS parents forced the hands of the elite members of the New York Manumission Society.[20] They declared that they simply would not send their children to a school to be taught that their only hope lay in colonizing Africa. The school was forced to accept their demands. "It was with regret," the minutes record, that "the Board felt itself bound to accept his [Charles C. Andrews'] resignation from the great decline in the number of scholars and the prejudice now existing against him among the coloured people."[21]

Their community's initial success would come at a cost. Stung by the rebuke of Black people who unapologetically insisted that their children be educated for lives of freedom in the United States, the Manumission Society withdrew its support of the school altogether. By 1833, the NYMS's forty-year oversight of the New York African Free Schools would come to an end, and with it the resources that had helped students like James McCune Smith to flourish. The school would become part of the New York public school system, where it would receive far less attention from the city's elite. The lesson was clear. If Black parents, and particularly Black women, were going to assert control over their children's future, they would do so without the help of the city patriarchs.

For current and future students, the lack of support would bring them to the brink of the same fate that had met Isaac, the talented student who had been forced to emigrate. Because so many of the city's leading lights felt that colonization was the only reasonable option for educated Black people, there were depressingly few options for any of James McCune Smith's graduating cohort to further their education, or even to utilize what they had already learned at the NYAFS. Smith's classmates Henry Highland Garnet, Alexander Crummell, Thomas Sidney, and others would spend the next several years scrambling to gain further education where they could, only to find the institutions that would take them in defunded or physically attacked. James McCune Smith too found his way blocked initially. He applied to both a medical school in Geneva,

New York, and to Columbia College in New York City. In both cases, he was turned down "on account of his complexion."[22] It was not the first time an African American man had applied to Columbia only to be turned away. John Brown, a Black man who had already been studying medicine in New York City, had been refused admission to examinations at Columbia, unless he promised to take his medical degree—and himself—to Liberia afterwards. Refusing the insulting offer, Dr. Brown went to work in the public schools, where he fought exclusionary rules that prevented "colored men from becoming the instructors of our offspring."[23] Frustrated, Brown left the public school system in 1839. He would be dead by 1840. There was little reason to hope for better for any the NYAFS schoolmates.

But James McCune Smith, the boy lucky enough to be chosen to address Lafayette, would be fortunate once again. Just as parents were shutting down the school because the schoolmaster thought colonization was the only way out of the dead end Black children faced, Smith was preparing for an elite education abroad. The Reverend Peter Williams, himself an alumnus of the New York African Free School, had been tutoring Smith in languages, and, along with the larger community, raised funds to send the promising young student abroad to study medicine at the University of Glasgow, an institution that had boasted prominent men among its faculty and alumni, including Adam Smith and Edmund Burke. It would be an honor for a young American man of any race to win admission to such a prestigious university, and to study at a global center of learning. For a fatherless son of an enslaved mother in the 1830s, it was an almost unimaginable achievement. Smith felt both excitement and trepidation as he packed his belongings to head to a new land. In one respect, he was following the implicit script he had been given at the New York African Free School—he had taken his education out of the country in order to prosper. Much of the reading he had done in those Mulberry Street classrooms—like much of the reading given to young Americans all over the country—depicted leaving home as a necessary and often exciting adventure through which a young man would find his fortune. On the other hand, he keenly felt his separation from home, particularly from his beloved mother, and lamented that his education would require exile.[24]

Portrait of Benjamin Franklin by James McCune Smith, 1826. New-York Historical
Society & Museum, New-York African Free-School Records, vol. 4.

As James McCune Smith's own schoolwork testifies, Ben Franklin was among the most prominent exemplars the New York African Free School held up to extol the advantages of American wanderlust. Franklin, after all, had left home, and a legal indenture, to follow his dreams. The founding father would not have been much older than Smith when he headed to England to further his career as a printer, a fact that would not have been lost on such an assiduous student of history. Franklin was not the NYAFS's only lesson in success wrought through travel. In 1830, Abigail Mott published a book created explicitly for the students at the New York African Free School that adapted the well-known slave narrative of Olaudah Equiano, notably changing the title to render Equiano's tale of kidnapping and enslavement a story of his "Life and Adventures."[25] In the version of the story the school preferred, Equiano's early enslavement was only one aspect of a story that ended happily, largely because the protagonist was not afraid to travel until he found a location where he could thrive.

As Smith headed across the seas to England, he had much in common with both of the men whose lives were held up as exemplars at the NYAFS. As a brilliant student who had known both slavery and indenture, Smith must have been excited by the radical change offered by visiting a free nation. And surely, the distinction in the stories of Equiano and Franklin would not have been lost on him. Although both men had formative experiences both in England and in the United States, they would make very different choices about where they would create a national affiliation. For Franklin, freedom would eventually be defined as disentangling himself—and the new nation—from the English empire to proudly declare himself an American. For Equiano, freedom only came when he left the United States altogether and laid claim to the status of an Englishman.

Smith—perhaps inspired by these adventures—kept a journal recording his impressions of his sea journey and time abroad.[26] And like Ben Franklin, Smith would publish his record of his youthful journey only once he had already achieved some success, so that others might emulate him. The *Colored American*, the newspaper that would eventually publish the excerpts, introduced Smith's memoirs with a flourish worthy of any founding father: the editors felt sure that their readers would be "instructed and highly entertained" by the words of "one of our most worthy and beloved young brethren," endowed with "all the eminent talents and moral worth" that could be furnished to an individual.[27]

The journal reveals Smith's keen awareness of the two competing stories his Atlantic journey conjured for a Black man—one of self-making adventure like Franklin's and the other of self-obliterating loss like Equiano's. While he does not mention slave ships explicitly in his journal, the specter of the Middle Passage ghosts Smith's impressions, rendering what one might expect to be the excited observations of an adventurous young man instead a document chronicling the terrors of loss. Revealing an acuity for character portraits, Smith describes several fellow passengers, none so interesting as Longwood, the man with "a fine blue eye" who talked endlessly of his exploits on the "Ivory Coast of Africa," where he executed "Manchurian like feats of daring." Longwood's colonial adventure tales anticipate the sort of storytelling that would later make Henry Morton Stanley one of the most famous men in the world.[28] Here was a man who had gained money and reputation from African trade, a man who, in the hands of another writer, might have been portrayed as a bold explorer whose theft of African property was something to be admired. Smith would probably have viewed Longwood as a two-sided coin. Certainly, he would have seen in him a perpetrator of racial injustice and an inheritor of slavery's brutal riches. But, at least in the narratives of influential whites—including his beloved schoolmaster—Longwood was also a possible role model. For several years before he met this man with a "fine blue eye," Smith had been taught that Africa offered the possibility of both wealth and advancement for promising Black youth.

Smith's description of Longwood ultimately paints him neither as victor nor villain, but as a man consumed by his past sins. The traveler is rich, but emaciated; he has ample wealth but no inner resources. Longwood had been engaged in "nobody knew what sort of traffic in the neighborhood of Liberia, where, according to his own account, he made a fortune and lost his health." In a moment that provides a glimpse of his own worst fears, Smith depicts this wealthy colonizer as the victim in a gothic scene of living death. Longwood liked to portray himself as a man of action when talking to other passengers, but Smith saw him as a man morally and creatively paralyzed. He described how Longwood sat "before his escritoire, pen in hand, nearly an hour," seemingly stock still. When a passenger happened to enter the cabin, "he read aloud the fruit of his labor," which had come to nothing more than "the following sentence: 'Of all poverty that of mind is the most deplorable.'" For the brilliant and ambitious Smith, witnessing how the effects of Longwood's life of plunder had left him mired in a profound "poverty of mind" made a powerful impression. In a manner that anticipates the preoccupations of Edgar Allan Poe and Nathaniel Hawthorne, Smith wrote a scene that casts Longwood as a morose and doomed sinner, whom guilt has robbed of flexibility or hope, leaving him only with an obsessive return to guilty "adventures."

While Smith's journal of the trip over was rather gloomy—he describes at great length the gruesome fate of a cholera victim on board—he found ample sunshine once he landed on British soil. Much of the abolitionism of his childhood placed England at the center of the antislavery universe. As a child he had thrilled to the exuberant parades celebrating antislavery victories, waving and cheering as banners celebrating British abolitionists Wilberforce and Clarkson were held high.[29] Now, he was about to step foot on the ground he had been long taught to treat as hallowed. "I am free!" he declared after disembarking the *Caledonia* and walking the Liverpool wharf. "I could embrace the soil on which I now live, since it yields not only to all who dwell, but to all who may come to it, a greater amount of rational liberty than is secured to man in any other portion of the globe."[30]

For this exceptionally bright young man—already schooled in Latin and Greek and a devotee of the classics—that freedom was as intellectual as it was political. Having had to balance manual labor and schoolwork all his life, dodging the racist insults of white boys as he made his way to class, he now found himself in the land of Chaucer and Milton, at leisure to fully participate in the life of the mind with his peers. He reveled in the refined atmosphere, and took no small pleasure in the fact that his old friend and schoolmate, Ira Aldridge, had taken England by storm through his masterful performances of Shakespeare. Aldridge was the first African American—indeed the first American of any race—to perform *Othello* in London.[31] Smith's old schoolmate was actually performing in London when Smith stopped in Liverpool on his way to Glasgow, but Smith was able to spend an amicable afternoon with Aldridge's wife, Margaret Gill, a white woman from Yorkshire.

As he strolled through a picturesque cemetery with this charming Englishwoman, discussing his schoolmate's London performances, Smith was giddy with the possibilities this new land seemed to offer. He was moved by the "sublime and beautiful objects" before him, a stark contrast from the gritty Five Points neighborhood that had been his only home. Here, a man could flourish—one needed no further evidence than the success of Ira Aldridge, "whose fine genius" would "have withered beneath the sickly glare of" America's "pseudo-republican sun." Even imagining another American with him while he contemplated such sublimity seemed a jarring prospect to this ambitious medical student. "Fancy Byron," he wrote, taking in a beautiful waterfall, in a "tete a tete with the calculating Yankee," who would view a site of stunning natural splendor and have nothing to say but "'Gosh! What a mighty fine water privilege!'" Indeed, in nearly any comparison between Great Britain and America, Smith found his home country sorely lacking.[32]

After a month in Liverpool and environs, Smith left for Glasgow and the beginning of the school year. Every new college student is nervous on the first day of classes, but for Smith the anxiety was multiplied by the fact that he was about to attempt what no other African American had ever done—earn a medical degree. He recalled feeling like "a young and friendless exile" as he entered the hallowed halls of the University of Glasgow. But unlike his New York classmates Henry Highland Garnet and Alexander Crummell, back home, who would be forced from their classrooms at the end of a torch or a gun, Smith found a warm welcome among his new classmates and teachers. He embarked on a rigorous course of study that included courses in Latin and Greek literature, logic, and moral and natural philosophy. His scientific studies included courses in botany, surgery, anatomy, and chemistry. The young Smith spent time among the specimens of geology and natural history that came to Glasgow when the Hunterian Museum had been transferred there in 1807. The university had an impressively large collection of anatomical specimens, which in both their variety and their abundance confirmed both universality among human beings (all humans had the same organs, and were subject to illness) and diversity (anatomy could be wonderfully unique, even if dysfunctional). Finally, he served a twelve-month clerkship, probably performed at the Royal Infirmary. He moved masterfully through his studies, progressing from his BA to his MD in five years.[33] In 1837, he became the first Black American in the world to have earned a medical degree, and he had done so, with honors, at one of Europe's great universities.

While Smith was expanding the boundaries of what was possible for an African American student in Glasgow, the educational options for Black youth in New York City continued to shrink. In the absence of moral or financial support for either the New York African Free School or the few other options for further educating the school's graduates, Smith's classmates scrambled to try to further themselves. In 1833, they helped create the Phoenix Society, which offered everything from lectures to poetry readings to fundamental instruction in reading and writing. Henry Highland Garnet—a classmate who matched Smith in ambition and surpassed him in oratorical brilliance—both supported and benefited from the community that the society engendered. The society had big plans to expand its endeavors in the city to include a manual labor school, and it had managed to gather some support. Local abolitionist William Turpin had left instructions that, upon his death, over one thousand dollars be distributed "for the purpose of educating colored youth."[34] For the members of the Phoenix Society, this bequest meant that the community could work to address the need for higher education of the children who graduated from the African Free Schools, thereby picking up where the New York Manumission

Society had so precipitously left off. Although Turpin's will did not explicitly mention the Phoenix Society, because he had served on its board, all felt sure that when the time came, that money would be used to build a community-run school. In the meantime, they made do. Henry Highland Garnet, Alexander Crummell, Thomas Sidney, James Fields, and others all scrambled to further their education in bits and pieces.

In truth, being able to attend school at all was a luxury many Black children could not afford. For many Black orphans—children whose parents were either dead or unable to care for them—their very survival was an uncertain proposition. While there were private orphanages for white children in the city, including one set up in 1805 by Elizabeth Schuyler Hamilton, Black children were sent to the almshouse, a Dickensian institution that lumped together the poor, the criminal, and the disabled. The unfortunate white children who were housed there were often housed separately from adults, and received a rudimentary education. No such care was taken with Black children, who were lumped in with adult inmates.[35]

The white abolitionist and philanthropist class in New York still wanted to help Black children, but, as the recent debacle over the colonizationist leanings of the New York African Free School had demonstrated, they preferred that support be accepted without question or critique from Black adults. Exactly such an opportunity arose on a spring day in 1834. While James McCune Smith was studying for upcoming exams in Scotland, Anna Shotwell was out for a stroll with her niece, Mary Murray, in New York City. Mary, like her aunt, had been raised in a house where benevolence towards the Black community was practiced with paternalistic zeal. Her father, William Shotwell, had been at the original meeting in Simmon's Inn on January 25, 1785, where a group of some of New York's most powerful men decided that they would take collective action on behalf of the city's Black residents, a commitment that ultimately resulted in the founding of the first New York African Free School.[36] Mary's grandfather, John Murray Jr., had long been the treasurer of the New York Manumission

Society, and thus the treasurer for the New York African Free Schools. It had been John's considerable charm and influence among elite New Yorkers that had raised funds for the schoolhouse built on 1820 on Mulberry Street—the very building where James McCune Smith, Henry Highland Garnet, and their classmates would compete for honors and applause.

When the two women looked up from their chat on this particular day, they found themselves stopped by a sight their own childhoods had taught them required a response. According to a historical account of the event, as the two women passed one building, their eyes fell upon two Black children described as "dirty, unkempt, but rather engaging in appearance." In a moment that encompassed both compassion and condescension, Miss Shotwell stopped to pat one of the children on the head. Seeing "a buxom woman" looking down on the scene from a window above, she called and asked if the two urchins were her children. The woman explained that they were orphans whom she was trying to keep from the clutches of the almshouse. Shotwell and Murray provided some money to this unnamed Black woman, telling her to buy the children new clothes. This small act of charity revealed a proliferation of need. When Shotwell and Murray returned a few days later, they found not two children, but six! Clearly the woman knew how to stretch a dollar. She had taken the money given to buy clothes for two children, and extended those funds to feed and shelter four more.

In many ways, this resourceful "buxom woman" was a founder of the New York Colored Orphan Asylum, although her name is lost to history. Shotwell and Murray worked tirelessly to follow her lead and take in as many orphans as they could. Mary was only eighteen at the time, while her aunt was twenty-eight. In an age when demure modesty was considered a white woman's greatest asset, Mary and Anna "battered upon the doors of the municipal offices" trying to raise funds, explaining to the officials that "they were only storing up trouble for themselves if they did not find homes, education and a chance for self-respecting employment for hapless negro boys and girls."[37] Their appeals fell on deaf ears. City officials felt no need to allot public money to care for

Black children. Pulling together what funding they could, they opened what would come to be called the Colored Orphan Asylum in William Shotwell's home in November 1836.[38] It is unclear how much James McCune Smith knew about these developments as he finished his studies in Glasgow; he certainly could not have known the profound effect Shotwell's and Murray's spring walk would have on his own future.

Shortly after graduation at the University of Glasgow, Smith left for Paris, where he did additional clinical work. The city charmed him, as it had so many others. Like the traveling adventurers he had read so much about, this New York City boy had traveled, been tested, and succeeded. If he was tempted to continue his life among the cosmopolitan friends he had gained, he did not succumb to that desire. His studies done, he began to make preparations to return home. Perhaps, he might have told himself, race relations had progressed in ways that would make it easier to be a Black man in that city. If he had indulged any of those hopes, he would lose those illusions as soon as he attempted to book a ticket back across the Atlantic, for he was summarily refused passage aboard the ship *Canonicus* by its captain. It was a humiliation that enraged his friends on both sides of the Atlantic.[39]

Furious on behalf of their colleague, sympathetic faculty and alumni of the University of Glasgow invited Smith back one last time for an event created both to honor their friend and to "express contempt of a prejudice so pitiful, and so unworthy of rational beings." In an assembly that manifested the loyalty and respect Smith would inspire throughout his life, the august group raised their glasses to "an esteemed friend" and "a talented former student," whose intellect was complemented by the "most engaging and amiable moral and social qualities." The Scotsmen had hoped—much like Smith's benefactors back home—that Smith's remarkable achievements would refute any assertions that somehow Black men were incapable of reaching the highest rungs of professional and intellectual accomplishment. They were shocked to find that the "manner in which those talents had been appreciated here" had not "gone far to shame his countrymen out of a prejudice so unjust." If this first harsh refusal was any indication, Smith's power as an

Engraving of James McCune Smith by Patrick Reason. Collection of the New-York Historical Society.

example of future possibility had shockingly limited utility back in the United States.

We do not have any images of James McCune Smith that capture him as a student in Glasgow, but a surviving portrait of him in later life offers a fascinating study of this brilliant man who had an ambivalent relationship to the spotlight. Even as his likeness is captured by his friend and former classmate Patrick Reason, Smith looks away from the viewer's gaze, as if eager to move on to another topic of conversation. His response to the effusive praise of his Scottish friends and classmates reveals this same tendency to change the subject away from himself. After acknowledging his friends' outpouring of support, Smith quickly asserted that while he both pitied the disrespectful captain and forgave the keen insult towards himself, he took umbrage with Captain's Bigley's disrespect towards Scotland itself. If "this great country" had bestowed him with high honors, how could America declare that he was not good enough to enter its borders? Yet, in spite of the humiliation that seemed to await the now-respected doctor, James McCune Smith did not waver in his resolve to return, even as his heart sank at the prospect of the "many insults, which I go, perhaps to meet in my country." He promised his friends that their kindness and the freedom he had enjoyed during his time in Glasgow would sustain him in the trials to come. He then bid them adieu. Having found another passage back, he sailed back to the country that saw no future for him.

Or, to be more precise, he returned to a nation whose white inhabitants could not imagine a future for such a brilliant Black man. For the African American community he had left behind, James McCune Smith was a conquering hero, who would lead other youth to greatness through his prodigious example. The nine-year-old boy who had been chosen to represent the Black community's admiration for the gallant Lafayette now returned to enthusiastic applause from those who saw him, once again, as a shining emblem of the best the community had to offer. A reception was held for him upon his return to New York, organized and attended by his old friends, mentors, and schoolmates. Charles Reason, who had attended the New York African Free School at roughly the same time as Henry Highland Garnet and James McCune Smith, duly recorded the day's events. Ransom F. Wake and John J. Zuille, both of whom would serve as teachers and administrators at the successor to the New York African Free School, were featured speakers, clearly bursting with pride over the success of one of their own. They hoped that his work would help lead the way for others. "Dr. Smith," an editorial in *Colored American* declared, "and all other young men, alike situated, are public property. Whatever of talent, of learning, and moral worth there be among us, we shall take the liberty of serving up, for the benefit of our brethren, whenever, and wherever they come in our way. All that is great or excellent, in colored men, is our coin, and should be made to tell to the best advantage, in the cause of colored men."

At the gathering at a large lecture room in New York, the pact between Smith and a community that prized him as "their coin" was made explicit. Black New Yorkers exulted in Smith's sterling reputation in Europe, as well as "his close connexion and familiar intimacy with the genius of Literature." Most important, they were moved by his loyalty to his childhood community. They were honored, they told Smith, by how admirably "you have represented the character and intellectual capabilities of those with whom you are proud to be identified." They cheered the young physician for having "sacrificed valuable considerations abroad, in order that you might return to your native land" to assist the Black community "in living down prejudice, Satan's prime minister," in the United States. The young doctor's choice to return from the glittering capitals of Europe was, for the crowd before him, a triumph over "slavery, prejudice, and colonization."[40]

Coming to the podium while his schoolboy friends cheered and clapped, Dr. Smith solemnly took up the mantle bestowed on him as the "public property" of a desperate and maligned people. He accepted their congratulations as proof that he had "not entirely failed in the endeavor to do my duty." He grieved the time that his studies had taken away from friends and family, but also expressed gratitude for the welcome he had received at Glasgow. Unlike so many of his friends, when Smith had entered a hall of learning as "a young and friendless exile," he was "received and treated as a brother and an equal."[41] He knew his good fortune was not something to be cherished as an individual accomplishment, but was a treasure he was bound to share. He vowed then, before the crowd of well-wishers, "to remain in my native land, and to spare no effort, and withhold no sacrifice in the doing all that I can for the elevation of the American people—of the whole people, without regard to caste or condition."[42]

His commitment to fight on behalf of all Americans was striking testimony to a belief in interracial collaboration born of the powerful friendships he had made abroad.[43] He believed, he told the crowd, that all the nation's "inhabitants are essentially one and the same in their interest. What is weal to one is weal to all, and what is woe to one is woe to all." His time in Scotland had taught him that a genuine pursuit of reason, of learning, and of beauty had the power to overcome the false doctrine of prejudice. For him, both Black and white Americans could, and would, work together, on American soil, to progress towards the freedom that the whole world seemed to be inevitably moving towards. His guiding principle had always been "to obtain education at every sacrifice and every hazard, and to apply such education to the good of our common country." Now, home at last, he assured the crowd that he would spend the rest of his life standing where he was rooted, fiercely determined to spend every bit of social equity he had on their behalf.

He wasted no time getting to work. He immersed himself in the intellectual and political life of the city, reconnecting with old schoolmates. He supported a plan created by Highland Garnet and other NYAFS alumni to advocate for Black suffrage.[44] His professional reputation grew steadily. Just a few months after his return, Smith was invited to speak at the Philadelphia Library Company—one of Benjamin Franklin's famous investments in his own community—where he was awarded an honorary membership. He also spoke against the errors of phrenology, a practice that tied intellectual and moral traits to certain physical features. By the new year, he had set up a medical practice and pharmacy on 151 Reade Street, where he treated both Black and white patients. He seemed well on his way to joining the medical and scientific community with which he was so eminently qualified to converse.[45]

But as he set about applying his education "to the good of our common country," the chances of other Black children gaining a similar education were slimmer than they had been when Smith had begun his own studies at the New York African Free School. The Phoenix Society had been working assiduously to fill the gap left by the New York Manumission Society's abandoning of the New York African Free Schools. But in the months after Smith's return, it became clear that the white abolitionist establishment would turn its back on that endeavor as well.[46] In the same year that Smith returned to New York with his medical degree, the money Black New Yorkers thought would help support future prodigies—over eleven hundred dollars generated from the sale of stock—was designated to go to the newly formed Colored Orphan Asylum, which had been struggling for funding since its beginnings back in 1834. Whereas the Phoenix Society provided services for both children and those seeking higher education, in 1837, the asylum primarily served children whose age hovered around four years.

The supporters of the Phoenix Society, itself a sort of alumni club of the New York African Free Schools, felt shocked and betrayed.[47] Samuel Cornish, the editor of the *Colored American* and former agent for the NYAFS, was furious. While the benevolent work the orphanage performed for small children was no doubt admirable, Samuel Cornish wrote in an impassioned editorial, it was a far cry from actually educating Black youth. The asylum provided food and clothing, but nothing that would allow these children to do much more than subsist until they aged out and were apprenticed as domestic or manual laborers. On the other hand, Cornish insisted, the Phoenix Society was already running several schools, for both children and adults, and was thus the natural choice to expand Black education in the state.[48] But Cornish's pleas went unheard. While the managers of the Colored Orphan Asylum eventually, "out of sympathy," bestowed four hundred dollars to the Phoenix Society, the blow was struck. The society would never achieve its goals. "What has become of the Phoenix Society?" asked one reader of the *Colored American* in 1838. Cornish's terse answer asks for help he knew he was unlikely to receive. "The Phoenix Society," he responded, "is still existing and wants aid."[49]

Since his return in the fall of 1837, Smith had worked closely with Cornish, and would in fact take over his editorship in 1840. So surely the young physician had noted these developments with concern. But at least at first, he kept his misgivings to himself. If the powers that be—many of whom had been responsible for his own early education—had decided that saving young orphan children was more urgent than educating older youth, then he did not feel obliged to publicly weigh in.

But soon it became clear that "saving" was hardly an apt description of what was happening to the young children under the auspices of the Colored Orphan Asylum. Under the care of physician Dr. MacDonald, who subscribed to the colonizationist belief that Black children's racial inheritance would keep them from ever truly thriving on American soil, nine children—out of the asylum's sixty-four occupants—died within the span of twelve months. To add insult to injury, the physician's report blamed the staggering loss on the children's Blackness. The primary reasons for these untimely deaths, Dr. MacDonald asserted, were the "peculiar constitution and condition of the colored race," in which the children were "the offspring of unhealthy parents."[50] In other words, he depicted these dead orphans as specimens of inferiority, grim evidence that Black children were inherently unfit to grow up in the free city of New York.

James McCune Smith, the soft-spoken, dutiful son of both Manumission Society benefactors and the city's Black founding fathers, was livid. In a January issue of the *Colored American*, with his name now on the masthead as a coeditor, Smith reprinted the asylum physician's report in full. Then, in an article dripping with both sarcasm and references to erudite European medical journals, he methodically dismantled the white colonizationist doctor's assertions, one by one. He pointed out that far from dying at higher rates from the diseases attributed to the young children under Dr. MacDonald's care, Black children generally had much lower mortality rates from tuberculosis (popularly known as "the consumption"), scrofula, and other ailments that MacDonald had sought to blame on racially transmitted weakness. After scrupulously citing sources illustrating Black children's relative hardiness, Smith derided the weak excuse that the children under the doctor's care had succumbed to the "peculiar constitution and condition of the colored race." Instead, he insisted, "the conclusion is inevitable on the Doctor's own principles, that the colored race is best fitted by nature to endure the climate of

New York." If somehow the children failed to flourish in the city, "it cannot be the result of any 'peculiarity of constitution,' but rather of that . . . hell-born prejudice which shuts out from its proper sphere the patriotic intellect of colored men, in crushing whom the state suicidally destroys the hardiest frames with which she is blessed."[51]

James McCune Smith had found reason to be optimistic upon his first return to his hometown in the fall of 1837. He had declared at his welcome ceremony that after "three weeks in the land of prejudice," he had "not yet been sensible of the fact."[52] Now, two years later, in the freezing January of 1839, he could not avoid facing the prejudice that came not just for him but for any future he might hope to have. Amidst the flurry of medical citations and mortality statistics, the young, as yet childless Smith conjured up an imaginary scene in which his own future, his own children, would be threatened by the racist quackery that he saw at work at the asylum. "Dear, dear Doctor," he declared, his tone honey-sweet, with a sharp bitterness underneath. If "providence should ever bless us with a small family, and a hopeful little one becomes sick, we shall certainly employ you as the most *satisfactory* man in the profession. If the child recovers, you will be able to show that you have snatched it from the very jaws of death, but if you kill—No, if the patient dies, you will smother our grief in wonderment that it did not die nine times instead of one." Smith's mocking invocation of the doctor as a killer—a "slip" that he immediately corrects—probably gave voice to some of the worst anxieties of the Black community. The doctor's use of colonizationist logic—in which Black people were doomed to wither on American soil—to explain away the deaths of Black children could be read as an ominous portent. If people of African descent would not go "home" of their own accord, what actions would white people shrug off in order to fulfill a vision of a nation in which Black people were either slaves or nonexistent?

Dr. Smith followed his accusatory barb with an assurance that he had no personal "feeling of malevolence" towards the asylum's doctor. But he was adamant that the doctor's report be recognized for the tripe that it was, utterly debunked by "statements in figures 'which cannot lie.'" For Smith, such factual statements administer "a rebuke more stern than" any that could be written by an individual author. Indeed, the young doctor seemed as hurt by the bad science as he was by the racism that generated such erroneous assertions. It was "with painful feelings," he told the readers of the *Colored American*, that he had sat down to write a response to such scurrilous lies published by an alleged man of science. "Next to our Maker," Smith revered "Science as the clearest manifestation of his law." In that divinely ordered law, Smith had anticipated deliverance. He had hoped for much from science. Although "born in penury, nursed by persecution, we have fondly dreamed that science would ever rear her head far above the buzz of popular applause, or the clash of conflicting opinion in the moral world." It was with an "anguish that springs from a blasted hope that we view this first, however flimsy, attempt to demean her to the contemptible office of ministering to public prejudices."[53]

It was unlikely that this was the first attempt that Smith encountered in which science was demeaned in the employ of prejudice, but it would be far from the last. His belief in the power of facts to overcome prejudice would be tested in the years to come. He had taken a profound risk, in his first year back on American soil, in calling out a respected doctor at an institution favored by the very abolitionist circles that—a few years earlier—had held him up as an example of what Black children could accomplish. But the female managers of the asylum proved more capable of hearing criticism from Black leaders than their male relatives and friends, at least when it came to this educated young doctor. While the asylum would retain many of its colonizationist ties throughout the next generation, they would—albeit nearly ten years later—hire James McCune Smith as the institution's physician. In that capacity, he would draw upon all he knew to shepherd New York City's most vulnerable Black children through the "anguish that springs" from the "hell-born prejudice" he had chosen to come to live amongst, and fight against, for the rest of his days.

Man with Dogs. New-York Historical Society & Museum, New-York African Free-School Records, vol. 4.

CHAPTER 2

Shifting Ground, Lost Parents, Uprooted Schools
(CIRCA 1822–1840)

W E do not know which student at the New York African Free School drew this colorful image of a hunter, strolling down a hill with his two faithful canine companions. Whoever it was had a knack for detail.[1] The hunter's jaunty cap, with a spray of red feathers, bespeaks an artist's eye for color. The texture and hue of the hunter's satchel, his pants, and the dry grass beneath his feet create a coherent, orderly composition. Overall, this child's drawing would fit well in a collection of British pastorals, depicting an English gentleman's wealth, leisure, and comfort in the great outdoors. For British viewers, the image would probably evoke an easy familiarity.

For Henry Highland Garnet, such an image might have been familiar, but would have evoked anything but ease. As a child who had recently run away from the Maryland slave plantation where he had been born, he would have been much less likely to identify with the trappings accrued around this aristocratic hunter—the unfettered access to the countryside, the agility with a gun, and the helpful dogs. Garnet's sympathy would always lie with those being hunted, those who would spend their lives staring back at white men with guns.

For much of Garnet's life, including his time at the Mulberry Street New York African Free School, being free and being hunted were two sides of the same coin. A fugitive slave from the age of nine, he would spend his youth looking over his shoulder, waiting for the men with guns to claim their "property." That initial decision to leave the plantation, in Garnet's telling, had been his mother's. Once she had heard rumors of the family being separated by sale, Elizabeth Garnet declared that running away was the only option: "We can but die should we fail," Henry recalled her declaring. "Let us make the attempt."[2] As childhood friend Alexander Crummell recalled years later, Elizabeth Garnet was a "most comely and beautiful woman" who possessed the "very soul of fun, wit, frolic, and laughter." When considering where Garnet had received the "readiness, humor, intellectual fire, steadiness of character and strong native thought" that so characterized him, Crummell asserted that these traits were "especially the gift of that good mother."[3] For his part, Henry Highland Garnet praised the "boldness and energy" of his mother and her brave decision to lead the family out of slavery. Such confidence and courage were qualities she clearly bestowed upon her son, who would, throughout his life, place dignity above safety, walking into any fight offered with his head held high.[4]

Once the family had made it to free territory, Garnet's father officially broke the paternalistic links to their former enslavers by changing the names of every member of the family, both as a means of avoiding capture and as a self-administered baptism into a life of freedom. No longer would the family answer to the name of Trusty—a surname bestowed by their former enslavers. They were now the Garnets, the name given to themselves.[5] Eventually, they would make their way to New York City, moving next door to community pillar Boston Crummell and his family. Garnet would enroll, along with the Crummells' young son Alexander, in New York African Free School #2, where both boys would get to know James McCune Smith, among other students. Alexander and Henry became fast friends, probably walking to school together through the often rough streets of Lower Manhattan. Alexander Crummell, like his friend Garnet, was destined to change the face of abolitionism, working tirelessly throughout his life, much of it dedicated to the idea of African settlement.[6] Crummell would live the longest of any of the schoolboys, long enough to meet W. E. B. Du Bois. Upon meeting Crummell, Du Bois was struck by the momentous changes the older man had personally witnessed. Crummell was, Du Bois wrote, a man who was "born with the Missouri Compromise and lay a-dying amid the echoes of Manila and El Caney [both sites of colonial conquest and strife, in the Philippines and Cuba, respectively]."[7] Instinctively, Du Bois recollected, "I bowed before this man, as one bows before the prophets of the world." Crummell, for his part, was always in awe of Garnet's strength, and was moved by the fundamental kindness he saw at the heart of Garnet's personality. "There are two words," Crummell wrote, that "will serve to delineate [Garnet's] character—LARGENESS and SWEETNESS."[8] James McCune Smith, whose relationship with Garnet would be more tempestuous than Crummell's, discerned quite a bit of salt along with young Henry's sweetness. At school, he was "quite the opposite of the nice, good, quiet little fellow," Smith recalled, "in whose mouth 'butter wouldn't melt.'"[9] It is tempting to think that Smith's wry description of who Garnet was not—nice, good, quiet—was also a self-deprecating remembrance of his own childhood as a star student who did not ruffle feathers.

Garnet would grow up to be an imposing physical presence, eventually reaching a height of nearly six feet, with a complexion of what one onlooker described as "unmitigated blackness." From his earliest days, he commanded any room he entered.[10] It is not surprising that many of his close friends and later biographers insisted that he was descended from African royalty, the grandson of a Mandingo chief stolen from his native land.[11] He certainly possessed a warrior's relish for combat, and a nobleman's sense of the respect he was owed. Uninterested in receiving praise for obedience, Garnet soon displayed his knack for leadership, and a passion for resistance. Shortly after his arrival at the NYAFS, he began organizing his schoolmates into political units, making plans for a future in which they would lead those left behind in slavery into a new era. Both Crummell and Garnet were part of a company of schoolmates in New York ranging from ages thirteen to sixteen, who would gather to plan future political action. Together, they resolved that they would refuse to celebrate the Fourth of July as long as slavery existed. Instead, the schoolboys would meet among themselves "on that day, and the time was devoted to planning schemes for the freeing and upbuilding of our race."

They also declared that "when we had educated ourselves we would go South, start an insurrection and free our brethren in bondage." "Garnet," Crummell recalled, "was a leader in these rash but noble resolves."[12]

The young Garnet's choice to boycott the Fourth of July showed a keen awareness of the yawning disjunction between the promise of that day and the reality Black people experienced. Independence Day was, in its declaration of both national birth and colonial rebellion, a particularly powerful version of the story of self-orphaning that would become so important to America's story about itself.[13] Every new July Fourth brought a celebration of a nation that was repeatedly remade, since the country itself was physically and conceptually different from the blueprint created in 1776. Indeed, in the rapidly evolving events of the first half of the nineteenth century, the nation celebrated on July Fourth of one year could look significantly different from the nation Americans had celebrated just the year before. For Garnet, the promises embedded in the Declaration of Independence—and the celebration of those promises—rendered his own reality surreal. How could one celebrate independence in a country that held four million of its own inhabitants in lifelong slavery? "I am not included within the pale of this glorious anniversary," Frederick Douglass told a crowd gathered to celebrate the Fourth of July in 1852. "Your high independence only reveals the immeasurable distance between us. . . . The rich inheritance of justice, liberty, prosperity and independence, bequeathed by your fathers, is shared by you, not by me. . . . This Fourth [of] July is *yours*, not *mine*. *You* may rejoice, *I* must mourn."[14] Garnet and his schoolmates keenly felt this chasm between their experience and the nation's nearly thirty years before Douglass's famous speech. As children, they knew that their stories simply did not fit within the celebratory narrative of the nation's birth and growth. Their orphanhood—both from their own history, and from the nation where they were born—could not be accommodated in this yearly celebration of the rebellious colonial son who insists on claiming a home of his own.

The young Garnet would learn an especially painful lesson about how far short his story fell from the Fourth of July myth one fateful evening. On his return home from one of several stints as a cabin boy on sea voyages that might well have appealed to a young man's sense of adventure, Garnet walked into a void.[15] At fourteen years old, he disembarked from the ship to find his beloved family—his mother, father, and sister—gone. Slave catchers had knocked on the door, forever disrupting the peace the family had imagined New York City might hold for them.

Until this moment, the teleology of Garnet's life—paralleling the story of the slave narrative—had been one of liberating mobility. He had moved northward from slavery to freedom, from a perpetual childhood to the prospect of a dignified and self-determined adulthood, from uncharted, unmarked time to a clear and orderly progression of hours, days, grades, apprenticeships, meetings, and elections. Movement north had allowed his father to establish himself as a member of the community, and young Henry had already distinguished himself at the New York African Free School. Now, with this violation of his family's home, he was cast adrift, with slavery's strong gravity towing him slowly, but surely, back to its flat landscape of endless, undistinguishable labor.

Taking place two years after New York had instituted statewide manumission, the slave catchers' attack at the Garnets' house proved that slavery's ghosts were never far away. Even in a free state, slavery had the power to collapse both time and space, insisting that no matter how far you might run, you were going to wind up in the same place. As James McCune Smith would later recall, on the night the slave catchers came calling, the Garnets' quiet family evening was suddenly, terrifyingly indiscernible from a dogged pursuit on a slave plantation: "His [Garnet's] father, in escaping from them had leaped from the roof of the two-story house, . . . his mother had barely eluded their grasp." Alexander Crummell had seen the whole event unfold from his vantage point in a nearby dwelling. He stood spellbound, he recounted, watching Garnet's father make the "fearful leap" across the chasm between two buildings. "How he escaped without breaking both neck and legs is a mystery to this day," Crummell would write nearly seventy years after it happened.[16] While the father was able to escape the slave catchers' clutches, Garnet's sister was not quite so lucky. She was arrested and tried as a "fugitive from labor." According to Garnet's recollection, that arrest took place at school—almost certainly the New York African Free School.[17] If so, she would not have been the only child literally pulled from her schoolroom to be deposited in a jail cell. The American Anti-Slavery Society's report of 1834 recounts the story of "a little boy, by the name of Henry Scott," who "was taken from one of the public schools of this city, where he had been placed by his father" and "was thrown into prison," where the child soon became ill from exposure.[18] Henry's sister, Eliza, also spent time in prison before being brought before city recorder Richard Riker, who ultimately accepted her defense: "She proved a residence in the city of New York at the very time when the witnesses for the prosecution swore that she was in Maryland a slave."[19] As the family's very narrow escape proved, a stranger's assertion could collapse New York City into the landscape of a Maryland plantation. You may think you are in one place and time, but if white people decide otherwise, the ground beneath your feet would be torn away without a second thought.

The fear of the kidnapper afflicted every Black family in New York City, regardless of their legal status. Long after slavery was rendered illegal in New York, slave traders would seek to make an easy profit by stealing freed people and selling them down south. Abolitionists had a name for the slave catchers who roamed the streets, and the court officials who would enable their success by ruling in their favor: the Kidnapping Club.[20] James McCune Smith recalled the "one-horse buggies" carrying "wretches in abundance who would snatch up a colored child and run down to Virginia and make a handsome sum by the operation."[21] Every day that Henry Highland Garnet, Alexander Crummell, James McCune Smith, and other schoolmates walked the streets, they carried with them the terror that they themselves could be "snatched" or, as in Garnet's case, that they would make it home only to find their family gone, themselves unceremoniously orphaned by slavery's emissaries.

When the teenaged Garnet received the news of what had happened to his family, he could not stand still. Without a home, his family either in hiding or in jail, young Henry reacted by running headlong into the fight. "He was roused almost to madness," James McCune Smith would later recall. "With the little money he had he purchased a large clasp-knife, openly carried it in his hand and wandered up and down Broadway, waiting and hoping for the assault of the men-hunters."[22] This restless courage would never leave Garnet, ultimately leading him to travel three continents looking for a home that could not be torn from him.

In this case, however, his passionate response to the temporary orphaning caused by this attack resulted in a longer, more painful isolation. Shaken by their own near escape, and frightened by Henry's rash actions, the family sent the boy away to an apprenticeship on a farm on Long Island, a veritable world away from the close-knit community he had enjoyed in Lower Manhattan.[23] According to his friends, the experience of being forced from his family home changed him forever. James McCune Smith credited that fateful night as the impetus for Garnet's adult career: "It seared his soul with an undying hatred of slavery," he later related, and "touched his lips with that anti-slavery fervor and eloquence which has never gone out."[24] Although little is known about Garnet's experience as an apprentice in Long Island, we do know that during his time there he sustained a grave injury to his leg that would cause him much suffering for the rest of his life. Eventually, as an adult, he would have to undergo the injured leg's amputation, an unbearably painful prospect in an era without reliable anesthetic.

Garnet had lost at least two homes by the time he was fourteen— one in slavery, and one in freedom. Once he aged out of the New York African Free School, he would spend years trying to find an educational home. Unlike his more fortunate friend James McCune Smith, Garnet had neither the backing nor the invitation to head overseas to pursue his studies. So he remained in the United States, seeking a path forward. As he sought higher education and eventual employment, he would instead find promises, opportunities, and even entire institutions ripped away like a tablecloth snapped up by an amateur magician. During these very same years when James McCune Smith was immersing himself in his studies at Glasgow, winning admiration and honors, Garnet, injured and indigent, found himself in a cruel labyrinth that kept placing him back where he started.

Garnet's experience was far more common than that of his more fortunate classmate. After the New York Manumission Society had withdrawn its support for the New York African Free Schools over the colonization boycott, prospects for any Black student seeking higher learning were bleak indeed. Many whites seemed utterly incapable of thinking of a Black future that extended beyond early adolescence. Smith, looking back on his schooldays, remembered wryly that when he and his classmates were children, "the education of the Black man was considered complete by his white friends when he reached the sentence of the Primers of those days which began with 'No man—.'" At that moment, progressive time came to a stop for Black students. Further instruction then ceased, his education was complete, he graduated, truly— "NO man."[25]

Garnet, like others in New York City, including classmates Alexander Crummell, Thomas Sidney, and others, was anxious to find educational opportunities that would usher him into the adulthood that white educators felt was beyond his reach. Even when the young men took on the mantle of instructors, however, onlookers saw children at play. Garnet and others created a literary association in which young adults worked to "extend the great interests of religion, virtue and literature" to young men and boys of color.[26] As a token of the great esteem in which the community held William Lloyd Garrison, the firebrand white abolitionist, they named the association the Garrison Literary and Benevolent Association. The first meeting took place in a public school, but the gathering of around 150 young people was told that it would have to drop the controversial Garrison name if they wanted to use public facilities. The group decided to move their meeting rather than relinquish the name of a man they so admired.[27]

Garnet, as a young man of about nineteen years of age, took it upon himself to tell Garrison of this society, which was "formed for mutual assistance and mental improvement" and was "composed of boys from 4 to 20 years of age."[28] Garrison's gushing response reinforced the idea that Black education was a quaint performance enacted by appealing children. He took to the *Liberator* to "express the delighted emotions which fill my breast, arising from the token of gratitude and esteem proffered to me. . . . As I hope to be in the midst of this worthy little band, in the course of a few days, and shall therefore have an opportunity to tell them my feelings and express to them my thanks, they will excuse my brevity at the present time."[29] Garrison, as both Garnet and Frederick Douglass would later realize to their sorrow, was often most comfortable inhabiting a paternal role, evidenced here by his reveling in the "affection" of a "worthy little band" of plucky Black children. Although there is no evidence that Garnet bristled at Garrison's patronizing characterization of his literary society in 1834, his patience for paternalizing assurances would wear thin as he increasingly found himself at the receiving end of broken promises made by well-meaning white patriarchs.

To be fair, Garrison was not alone in his inability to fully imagine a thriving educational system that would usher Black children into adulthood. Throughout the 1820s and for the first years of the 1830s, Black education and African colonization were considered to be mutually constitutive by most of the leaders of the abolitionist movement. To take just one example, the wealthy white abolitionist Arthur Tappan had, at first, fully subscribed to the prevailing logic that the future of African American people could only lie in Africa. As a founding member of the African Education Society, he sought to "prepare, by suitable education, young persons of color for usefulness in Africa."[30] From the start, however, these initiatives had met resistance from the Black community.[31] *Freedom's Journal*, the first African American newspaper, started in New York City in 1827 by John Russwurm and Samuel Cornish—who also worked as an NYAFS agent—often ran pro-education and anticolonization stories in the same issue. The paper was only published for two years. But even in that short time, having Black voices speaking in the press—largely against colonizationism—helped to showcase the resistance many within the community felt towards the idea.

Yet, by the end of its short-lived run, even the editors of a paper professing to speak for the Black community were divided over colonization. *Freedom's Journal* was determined to include arguments both for and against colonization, and it seemed that some of the pro-colonization arguments stuck with editor John Russwurm. He left New York for Liberia in 1829 and remained in Africa until his death. Russwurm's defection was a powerful testament to how strong the pull of colonization was, and would remain, throughout much of the nineteenth century. Nonetheless, the strongly stated opposition by a majority of free Black people, articulated in *Freedom's Journal* and in other venues, did much to convince white abolitionists that the colonization scheme was fatally flawed. By the mid-1830s, at the insistence of the Black communities they professed to be championing, high-profile white abolitionists William Lloyd Garrison, Arthur Tappan, and others had all changed their minds about the efficacy of colonization schemes.[32]

Yet even as African American parents and children demanded the decolonization of their schools, the pace of change was slow. The still-powerful notion that the only way a Black child could access the higher realms of learning and responsibility would be to go "back" to Africa kept the options for a brilliant young man like Garnet maddeningly limited. Realizing that little help would be forthcoming to allow Black youth to step forward into higher education, and the higher professions that accompanied it, leaders of New York's Black community set about creating their own organizations, ranging from reading groups (like the Garrison Literary and Benevolent Association) to fledgling colleges. Garnet was a passionate participant in many of them. Along with good friends and former NYAFS schoolmates Alexander Crummell and George T. Downing, Garnet attended the Canal Street High School for a time. Boston Crummell (Alexander's father) and Peter Williams (James McCune Smith's mentor) were instrumental in starting the school.[33] Garnet would become a leading member of and participant in the Phoenix Society, where he found space to share intellectual and political ambitions with like-minded Black people, including his cousin Samuel Ringgold Ward, and former schoolmates Charles Reason and Patrick Reason.[34]

As hard as Garnet's community worked to create stopgap measures for higher education, everyone knew that much more needed to be done. In 1831, organizers gathered at the second National Convention of Colored People in Philadelphia to plan a path forward. The convention's work revolved around two intertwined goals—to resist the growing movement to push freed Blacks out of the country and to establish schools of higher education that would admit Black youth.[35] Among the other business of this meeting, a college for Black students in New Haven was proposed, and the proposal passed. It was a remarkable moment—this new school, advocates hoped, would emerge as a bold strike against the current trend of educating Black children only to prepare them to colonize their own distantly imagined "homeland."

And on that point—but nothing else—New Haven residents agreed. At a town meeting held to discuss the school, opponents argued that to establish Black colleges on US soil would deal a killing blow to the logic of the American Colonization Society. To their mind, such a school would also, in a strange stretch of logic, turn the entire United States back into a colony itself, subject to the whims of foreign forces. Townspeople declared that a school designed to educate "the colored population of the United States, the West Indies, and other countries adjacent" would constitute "an unwarantable [sic] and dangerous inter-ference with the internal concerns of other States" and thus, "ought to be discouraged."[36] Overwhelming resistance from New Haven officials foiled the plan before it ever truly began, as anxious whites painted fear-ful pictures in which educated Black people emerged as an invading force, proving "totally ruinous to the city." The presence of Black students, they predicted, would have the "certain effect" of lowering the town's "public morals."[37] The college never moved past the proposal stage.

In the face of such staunch resistance to a new college in New Haven, organizers, including New York African Free School associates Samuel Cornish and Peter Williams Jr., turned their sights to a new possibility. Prudence Crandall, who had been running a girls' school in Canterbury, Connecticut, had proposed admitting Black girls to her "Female Academy." Again, there were town meetings held about this develop-ment, and again, the language filling the hall seemed more appropriate to a plan for international war than a discussion of the roster at a local girls' school. Local lawyer and devoted colonizationist Andrew Judson was particularly fond of imagining the school as an invading force that needed to be defended against by beleaguered Connecticut residents. "Should Miss C attempt to cross their lines for the purpose of establish-ing a negro school," he declared, "every one of these voters would ar-range themselves upon it."[38] The line Judson wanted to draw in the sand rendered race and nation one and the same—Black students from places like New York and New Hampshire were, by definition, alien invaders. Judson insisted that "they had a law which would prevent that school from going into operation, the law that related to the introduction of foreigners."[39] Judson's rhetoric was supported by many in the meeting, including one Dr. Harris, who, William Lloyd Garrison disdainfully recorded, was "a life member of the American Colonization Society."[40]

For Judson, as for many pro-colonizationists, there were only two choices for the nation's future—either Black people would leave for Africa upon reaching adulthood, or America itself would become hopelessly Africanized. The concept of African American education was a direct threat to the logic that would render Black children and youth forever mired in a realm outside the nation, incapable of accessing the progress that was increasingly central to that nation's idea of itself. If the school was allowed to continue, he declared, "the obvious tendency . . . would be, to collect within the town of Canterbury, large numbers of persons from other States, whose characters and habits might be various and unknown to us," thereby rendering "insecure the persons, property, and reputations of our citizens." This incursion, the school's opponents insisted, would de-Americanize New England itself: "We might ask the citizens of *any town* in New-England, wherever situated, would it be well for *that town* to admit the Blacks from slave States, or other States, to an unlimited extent? Once open this door, and New-England will become the Liberia of America!!"[41] As Samuel May would later recall, Judson argued that "we are not merely opposed to the establishment of that school in Canterbury; we mean there shall not be such a school set up anywhere in our State. The colored people never can rise from their menial condition in our country; they ought not to be permitted to rise here. They are an inferior race of beings, and never can or ought to be recognized as the equals of the whites." Black people were, for Judson, forever an aberration on US soil. "Africa is the place for them. I am in favor of the Colonization scheme."[42]

Indeed, the school's very existence would become a referendum on whether or not Black people could ever be considered Americans or would be forever relegated to a dangerous foreign status. On May 24, 1833, the town's general assembly enacted the so-called Black Law, which made it illegal for any Black student "who is not an inhabitant of any town in this state" to attend school, or indeed, even to board at someone else's home in the hope of gaining the residency that would allow the student to eventually attend school. By August of that year, Crandall was arrested for violating this law. In response, her lawyers argued that the Black Law was unconstitutional. They would lose that battle. Judges sided with arguments like Judson's, which declared that if the court lets "principles [of Black residency] be once established by the judiciary, the consequences will inevitably destroy the government itself, and this American nation—this nation of white men, may be taken from us, and given to the African race!"[43]

In September of 1834, Prudence Crandall's school was vandalized. The mob approached the building with heavy clubs and iron bars. The attackers struck at the windows, smashing over ninety panes of glass, leaving the school's interior exposed to further harm. This assault, coming after a summer that had featured several acts of aggression against Crandall and her students, was the final straw. Neither Crandall nor her students felt it was safe to stay, and the school ceased operations.[44] At least one of those students, however, would be moving on to yet another school. Julia Williams, originally of South Carolina, refused to relinquish her quest for education. Undaunted by the violence she had already encountered, she would sign up to study at the newly erected Noyes Academy, where she would make lifelong alliances.

As Connecticut panicked over Black students they imagined as foreign invaders on American shores, New York smoldered with white resentment of Black achievements within city limits. As the summer heat began to bear down on the city in 1834, that resentment exploded into violence, and Henry Highland Garnet once again saw the ground he stood upon crack open beneath his feet. Although it is always difficult to pin down the precise catalyst that initiates a riot, at least some accounts relate that the trouble began when Black people dared to include themselves in Fourth of July celebrations. On this particular Independence Day, it seems, an integrated group of marchers came out to celebrate the 1827 emancipation of New York slaves.[45] Reportedly on the same day, NYAFS advocate Samuel Cornish, who had worked with Arthur Tappan on seeking to create Black schools in Connecticut, had the audacity to sit next to his white colleague in a public gathering.

In any case, by the end of the day, and for several nights afterwards, New York City was transformed into a battlefield. In the flames that followed, many of the landmarks of Garnet's childhood were destroyed as the city devolved into chaos. Hundreds, if not thousands, of rioters faced off with authorities in protracted clashes. In one newspaper account, authorities on horseback were forced to retreat, outnumbered by the mob outside a church on Spring Street. Once they had regained the street, rioters set to work creating obstructions to keep the police at bay. As one newspaper relates, "The mob erected a strong barrier, composed of carts, and pieces of timber, across the street." When the cavalry returned to Spring Street with reinforcements, the mounted men "charged at full gallop at the barriers," losing several horses to the assault.[46] They were not the only losses. Peter Williams's beloved St. Philip's Church—spiritual home to the community Garnet had come to call his own—was completely destroyed, as well as the Society for African Mutual Relief, the Chatham Street Chapel, the "African school house on Orange Street," and other sites of abolitionist and educational activity. Leonard Street, the same street where Garnet's home had been ransacked by slave catchers in 1829, was ravaged once again by whites determined to stop the progress they felt Black New Yorkers were making.[47]

On the very same day that would usher in such destruction in New York, hundreds of miles away in a small New Hampshire town, July Fourth was being appropriated as a day of hope—one that would forever shape Garnet's prospects. On July Fourth, 1834, a charter was granted in Canaan, New Hampshire, to Samuel Noyes, George Kimball, Nathaniel Currier, George Walworth, and John H. Harris, as incorporators of Noyes Academy, the successor to the failed dream of a Black college in New Haven. These founders, deciding to build the school "upon the principles of the Declaration of Independence," announced that the school would be open to all, regardless of color.[48] Newspaper accounts note that "fourteen colored students" signed up immediately. Among that fourteen were three students from New York City: Henry Highland Garnet, and NYAFS schoolmates Alexander Crummell and Thomas Sidney.

Garnet, Crummell, and Sidney were already proficient scholars and writers in comparison with many white youths their age, but nonetheless, they were immediately advertised as an experiment by Noyes Academy administrators. In the days leading up to the college's opening, the trustees of Noyes sold their idea to the public as an act of research that would facilitate future plans for the nation. The administrators believed that Black youth were capable of being educated, but they were open to being proven wrong: "If however we are mistaken in supposing, that they possess such capacity; if, as some assert, they are naturally and irremediably stupid, and incorrigibly vicious, then the experiment we propose will prove this fact; and will in any event furnish valuable data, upon which the excited patriotism and piety of the land may predicate suitable measures in time to come, or may relapse into undisturbed repose, and forever forbear to form designs upon this agitating subject."[49] Here, as at the New York African Free School, Black students were held up as specimens that could stand in for the abilities of their race, even as the "data" they supplied seemed destined to be discounted, only to be requested again and again. Regardless, Garnet and his school friends jumped at the opportunity to attend the Noyes Academy. Any chance was worth taking.

Unlike James McCune Smith's relatively smooth departure aboard a transatlantic vessel, Garnet's journey to his college was filled with pain and hardship. As they made their way from New York to New Hampshire, Garnet, Crummell, and Sidney were often forced to ride on the outside of coaches, and on the open decks of ships. Night after night, they had to forage for themselves because they could not gain admittance to an inn. These hardships were particularly difficult for Garnet to endure. In constant pain from his injured leg, he would grow increasingly ill as the journey progressed. "I can never forget his sufferings," Crummell wrote years later, "sufferings from pain, sufferings from cold and exposure, sufferings from thirst and hunger, sufferings from taunt and insult at every village and town, and ofttimes at every farm house, as we rode, mounted upon the top of the coach, through all this long journey."[50] Yet, there was hope that this suffering would reap rewards—that Garnet, like many a brave young adventurer before him, would find his fortune through his travels. Although he had a much more serpentine path than his old schoolmate James McCune Smith, Garnet was finally, through his own persistence and the persistence of the Black community, arriving to claim a higher education. For a short while, it looked as if Garnet might actually be making progress in his own personal coming-of-age story. The three dauntless students finally arrived at school, and enrolled in classes. Here, as in New York, Garnet's formidable charisma pushed him to the center of attention: he quickly emerged as a gifted public speaker and as a poet. Garnet kept a common-place book during his time in Canaan, "in which were gathered many of the fine effusions of his muse, sweet and tender poems, which he used to read as class compositions."[51] Sadly, the book, and his poems, have not been recovered.

As a teenager attending the New York African Free School, Garnet had vowed to boycott celebrations of Independence Day, and to spend that time instead working to free enslaved people, for whom the lofty sentiments of the Declaration were a particularly cruel joke. On July 4, 1835, one year after the Black celebrations of July Fourth had set off riots that had destroyed so much of the architecture of Garnet's New York childhood, Garnet would find himself called upon to give a July Fourth oration to a white audience. It was quite an honor for a young student, and he jumped at the challenge. He, Alexander Crummell, and Thomas Sidney accompanied school trustee George Kimball to an antislavery gathering in a town a short distance away from the Noyes Academy. The New York African Free School had rendered Garnet quite familiar with standing in front of a mixed-race audience, knowing his body and his bearing would bear testimony to the possibilities of Black talent. Now, as a young man of nineteen, he caused a sensation, both for what he said and for how he looked. The onlooker writing for Garrison's *Liberator* described Garnet as possessing "full unmitigated, unalleviated, unpardonable blackness" and noted that the young man was "crippled with severe lameness." Garnet made an intellectual as well as a physical impression, as onlookers found him "an enlightened and refined scholar, a writer and speaker of touching beauty."[52]

His classmates Thomas Sidney—"an orphan literally as well as by caste"—and Alexander Crummell—"sable as Toussaint"—also gave speeches. None of the young men's speeches, unfortunately, have been preserved in the historical record. From coverage of the event, however, it is quite clear that Garnet made a powerful impression. He spoke of his own enslaved childhood, so far removed from this hall in Plymouth, New Hampshire, filled with white people celebrating freedom. He lamented that the Fourth of July did not hold the meaning for him that it did for his audience—and mourned the "contrast of his own feelings with those proper to the joyous day." Although he stood in a free state, expanding the boundaries of what it was possible for a young Black man to achieve, he could not help but feel constrained by the slavery that had dominated his early childhood. An onlooker reported that "when he told of the objects that met his earliest vision and shed natural tears at the remembrance of his own and his parents' bondage I found many moistened eyes in the audience besides my own."[53]

If Garnet knew what was happening back in Canaan that night, his tears would have been bitter ones indeed. On the same day that he was making his New England debut in public speaking, and one year—to the day—after the brutal riots that destroyed so much of his childhood landscape, a crowd of angry townspeople was gathering outside the Noyes Academy, threatening to demolish it.[54] As had been the case in Connecticut, fearful New Hampshire whites had spurred themselves to a panic with dire predictions that the "village was to be overrun with negroes from the South" and, further, that "the slaves were coming here to line the streets with their huts, and to inundate the industrious town with paupers and vagabonds." Hundreds of men amassed outside the academy to stop the alleged colonization of their town by an international throng of Black people.[55]

They would be initially repelled by a magistrate who, recognizing many members of the mob, called out the men by name and warned them of legal repercussions if they followed through on their violent threats. But the town's animosity grew along with the summer heat. On August 10, the mob had gathered again. This time, they brought a remarkable set of companions. Local accounts relate that the rioters yoked no less than ninety oxen to a Noyes Academy building. After much straining in the August sun, the building groaned, coming off its foundation entirely.

Seemingly unsatisfied with simply destroying the building, the mob drove the oxen and their burden into a swamp about a half-mile from its original site. The vandals spent two days, Alexander Crummell recalled, "accomplishing their miserable work." Students holed up in the nearby boarding house, hoping for the best, fearing the worst.

With no prospect of protection coming, students feared for their lives, watching to see how far the mob would go, and what, if anything, would stop them from turning their attack on property to an attack on the students themselves. When the assault began, Garnet had been laid low by a prolonged illness. Weak with a high fever, suffering from intense pain from his injured (and probably infected) leg, Garnet was in a particularly vulnerable position if worse came to worst. Ill as he was, he resolved, as he always would, to fight to the last. Neither "sickness, nor infirmity, nor the howling of the mob could subdue his fiery spirit," James McCune Smith would write of the event years later. Garnet used his confinement to spend "most of the day in casting bullets in anticipation of the attack." And sure enough, "at about eleven o'clock at night the tramp of horses was heard approaching," and "one rapid rider passed the house and fired at it." Garnet, faced once again with violence against his home, "quickly replied by a discharge from a double-barreled shotgun which blazed away through the window. At once the hills, for many a mile around, reverberated with the sound. Lights were seen in scores of houses on every side, and the towns and villages near and far were in a state of great excitement."[56] One can imagine how Henry Highland Garnet's bold act of self-defense was interpreted by those who already believed that their town was being colonized by dark "foreign" forces. "But that musket shot by Garnet," Crummell asserted, "doubtless saved our lives. The cowardly ruffians dared not to attack us." Even as they had stayed the hands of the mob, they were unable to reestablish their ruined school, or to remain in a town capable of such violence against their isolated outpost. They were told to leave within two weeks, so they began to pack their things. As they climbed into the coach to go home, their dreams once again dashed, the townspeople made sure to let them know that they should never come back. "When we left," Crummell recalled, "the mob assembled on the outskirts of the village and fired a field piece, charged with powder, at our wagon."[57]

Once again, the Fourth of July had served as a tragically stark reminder of how far Garnet stood from the promises celebrated on that day. For at least the third time in his young life, Garnet had endured the physical and mental terrors of running from white people, whose violence seemed determined to pull him inexorably back to the void of slavery and death. This time, the trip home nearly killed Garnet. Once he and his friends finally made their way back to New York City, he was confined to bed rest for two months.[58] If he had seen himself as the hero in a story in which a bright young man sets out to seek his fortune, he was now confronted with a very different ending: a youth restricted to a sickbed, immobilized and indigent.

Knocked down by hatred and violence, Garnet would soon get up to fight another day. In 1836, Garnet found a new opportunity to study at the Oneida Institute, which had recently come under the supervision of Beriah Green, a firebrand abolitionist who would go on to form the Liberty Party—the first political party devoted entirely to the abolition of slavery. Green insisted on admitting both Black and white students to his new school. Once word got out, Garnet rejoined his old traveling companions and together the three young men chose to stake their claim to being schoolmates once again. Together Garnet, Thomas Sidney, and Alexander Crummell enrolled in the school. This time, no one would force them to leave.

As with every other accomplishment in Garnet's young life, his success at the Oneida Institute would not come easily. The Oneida Institute required that every student engage in at least three hours of "muscular labor" every day. The requirement was partially the result of Beriah Green's belief that students engaging in mental toil would find "relaxation, refreshment, and delight in giving a portion of their time and strength to agricultural efforts or mechanical pursuits."[59] It was also, undeniably, a necessity for a school in dire financial straits, made worse by both the Presbyterian Education Society and the American Education Society removing Oneida from the list of schools they were willing to support. Allegedly that support had been withdrawn because of low academic standards: under Green's leadership, students were taught Hebrew, rather than Latin, a decision many found scandalous. For his part, Beriah Green was quick to point out that this rejection came shortly after his announcement that he would accept Black students. For Green, the "eager and indecent haste" to "force us to terms" was a response to the "position we had taken in support of the cause of Human Rights."[60] In any case, the school's tightened financial situation made the labor of the students a necessity as well as a virtue.

As James McCune Smith was finishing his studies in Scotland and preparing himself for a career in New York City, Garnet was, once again, starting over. Because he suffered from near constant pain from his leg injury, and was subject to what seemed to be recurrent infections, the Oneida schedule must have been particularly grueling. Students rose before dawn, attended chapel, went to classes, and then put in several hours of hard labor in the hot sun. But, as he had everywhere else, Garnet quickly emerged as a leader. His room was, in the words of schoolmate Crummell, "the central point of attraction." Other Oneida students would gather there each evening while Garnet "sick and racked with pain as he was," would "rise above physical ailment and delight us, hour after hour, with the choicest gems of eloquence and poetry."[61]

Garnet was reunited with one other former classmate at Oneida: Julia Williams. She had been expelled from Prudence Crandall's school and then enrolled at the Noyes Academy, only to be expelled with Garnet and the other Black students. Undaunted, she enrolled at the Oneida Institute. There her friendship with Garnet would deepen into something more. Both Julia and Henry had come from the South, and they had both fought hard for their education. Julia's fierce intellect and her consistent bravery won Garnet's admiration early on. Soon, he was smitten. As he wrote blushingly to Alexander Crummell, he found Julia a "lovely being. . . . A Good Christian, and a scholar. Did I think myself worthy I don't know but I should venture my bark upon the stream."[62] He would, eventually, venture to ask for her hand in marriage—although it would take some time before they were wed, in no small part because she was teaching in Boston. They were married in 1841, and they would work, teach, and travel together for the next thirty years.

Garnet would occasionally visit New York City on breaks from the Oneida Institute, and kept in scrupulous touch with his old acquaintances. On his trips home, he visited old friends and participated in Phoenix Society gatherings. The financial crash of 1837 brought another wave of difficulties for his community. New York was hit particularly hard by the panic, putting pressure on already stressed resources. On one trip home, Garnet wrote to Crummell, reporting dutifully on his visits to his friend's family, where the news seemed to be all bad. It was, he relayed, "very hard times in New York."[63] He warned Crummell that he would "find things much altered when you come home."[64] Yet the city still had its pleasures. As one of the rising stars of the Black community, Garnet found himself in demand among both the social and the literary set, a fact he seemed to enjoy immensely. "I am quite popular among the people," he told Crummell, "and were I not so well acquainted with the honesty of the world there would be some danger of being puffed up. I [am] called the poet, and often solicited to write."[65]

And write he did, as well as lead political gatherings. One particularly momentous meeting made a deep impression on James McCune Smith, newly back in New York after receiving his medical degree in Scotland. Garnet, along with other NYAFS schoolmates George T. Downing and Charles Reason, came together to organize a writing campaign to win the right of Black men to vote. While Smith is not listed as one of the committee members, he would later recall his attendance at the meeting.[66] Together, the assembled group swore to continue to support one another and the cause until universal male suffrage was achieved. This was at least the second instance of Garnet inspiring his schoolmates to take a lifelong vow—a testament to the power of his charisma over a group of ambitious and talented young men.

During the late '30s and early 1840s, Garnet's influence over his cohort grew unabated. Indeed, Garnet made his presence felt on the New York scene even when he was not around. One newspaper account of an 1837 gathering of the Phoenix Society relates that Garnet's friend and classmate Thomas Sidney read an original poem by Garnet, "Alonzo," aloud to the society, apparently because Garnet was unavailable to attend the meeting himself.[67] Biographer Joel Schor suggests that Garnet's piece was probably inspired by a poem written by Matthew Lewis, included in the gothic blockbuster *The Monk*. In Lewis's poem, a knight in "sable armor" returns from beyond the grave to exact revenge for a broken promise:

> "Behold me, Thou false one! Behold me!" He cried;
> "Remember Alonzo the Brave!
> God grants, that to punish thy falsehood and pride
> My Ghost at thy marriage should sit by thy side,
> Should tax thee with perjury, claim thee as Bride
> And bear thee away to the Grave!"

> Thus saying, his arms round the Lady He wound,
> While loudly She shrieked in dismay;
> Then sunk with his prey through the wide-yawning ground,
> Nor ever again was Fair Imogine found,
> Or the spectre who bore her away.[68]

Although we cannot know how much Garnet's "Alonzo" shared with Lewis's version, the gothic horror of the past coming to steal away the promise of the present was a subject that preoccupied Garnet throughout his life. In 1838, the past would repeat once again, as yet another intellectual home was pulled off its foundations, and the Phoenix Society withered after its promised funding was diverted to the white-run Colored Orphan Asylum. By the time Garnet graduated from the Oneida Institute in 1839, his repeated displacements had intensified his desire for a home, and lessened his belief that he would ever find one that would not require a prolonged fight to claim as his own.

His studies at the institute had immersed him into a deep past—he studied both Hebrew and Greek, spending hours immersed in the biblical timescape.[69] As he evolved as a political speaker, he would often portray the United States as a place haunted by competing notions of the past and its influence on the present. In some of Garnet's speeches, the past emerges as a place full of the rich—but lost—possibility that he had learned about through study of ancient times. In others, the past provides stepping stones upon which one could progress to further maturity and wisdom, a story borne out by his own hard-won movement from fugitive slave to college graduate. But his brushes with slave catchers and angry mobs had also taught him to distrust the fable of progress. He knew well how quickly slavery's violence and prejudice could resurface, no matter how much time had passed or how much work had been done. In many of Garnet's writings, the past roams as a predator: gaunt and hungry, a wolf always at the door.

Garnet had the opportunity to showcase his oratorical talent on the national stage when his old headmaster at Oneida Institute invited him to speak at an anniversary celebration of the American Anti-Slavery Society. The event was held in New York City in 1840, and it was a great honor for the young Garnet to be on the program. Standing before a mixed audience that included, among others, his childhood hero William Lloyd Garrison, Garnet invoked slavery's ability to twist time. In Garnet's hands, the anniversary celebration was recast as a funeral dirge, as African Americans found themselves precisely in the same spot, year after year. He began with ancestral claims to land and to history: "In consideration of the toils of our fathers in both wars," he insisted, "we claim the right of American citizenship." Yet, in Garnet's vision, their past investment in the nation, and the dividends those investments should yield in the present, soon dissipate into smoke:

We claim it, but shall we ever enjoy it. Our ancestors fought and bled for it, but I will leave it with this assembly to decide whether they fought and bled as wise men or as fools. They have gone to their rest, many of them with their brows all marked with wounds received in fighting the battles of Liberty, while their backs were furrowed by the cruel scourge. Unfortunate men! They knew not that their children were to be immolated upon the altars of slavery—altars erected upon their very graves. They little thought that the Power against which they were fighting would one day emancipate all its slaves, while their own country would master

all her power, and make her mightiest effort to blow out the few scatter-
ing stars that linger in the horizon of their posterity's hopes.[70]

His particular education had taught Garnet that history was a rigged game,
in which one would be led backwards no matter which path one chose.

That was not the only gathering Garnet would attend in 1840. Garnet's
childhood friends Samuel Ringgold Ward, Charles Reason, and others organized a Convention of Colored People to be held that same
year. Back at the 1831 convention, a committee of white abolitionists—
William Lloyd Garrison, Simeon Jocelyn, and Arthur Tappan—had led
the charge for proposing and promoting the (ultimately doomed) Black
college in New Haven.[71] In 1840, Black men set the agenda and popu-
lated the committees. White supporters were still welcomed, but it was
Black men who would lead. And, Garnet made immediately clear, he
was quite sure of the direction that leadership should take. His growing reputation for eloquence made him a natural choice to chair the
committee charged with writing and presenting the convention's address.
Garnet opened his remark with a call to radical action, gleaned from a
favorite poet, Lord Byron.

> Hereditary bondsmen, know ye not,
> Who would be free, themselves must strike the blow![72]

It is not difficult to see why Garnet would have found Byron's battle
cry resonant. In the stanza from which Garnet's epigraph is excerpted,
the narrator looks to the future to resurrect a past that had been un-
justly interred. "Who shall lead thy scatter'd children forth," Byron's
narrator asks, and "long accustom'd bondage uncreate?" He laments
the "hopeless warriors of a willing doom" and asks when we shall ever
see a "gallant spirit" who shall "resume . . . , and call thee from the
tomb?"[73]

Childe Harold's Pilgrimage (1812–1818), the poem that first made Byron
famous, follows the restless wanderings of the protagonist, who moves
through countries, through time, and through lovers with poetic restless-
ness. By appropriating the entitlement, the heredity, and, yes, even the

uncontrolled passion Byron's poetic identity evoked, Garnet found an imaginative space that could take some pleasure in the situation forced upon African Americans. Rather than digging deeper into a soil that would never be his, Byron's *Childe Harold* created art from the endless longing for a home. In Byron's work, a lack of groundedness initiates a poetic journey, rather than a fruitless wandering. This was a different sort of control—of kind of self-possession that might, and actually probably would, lead to tragedy, but that still had a sense of nobility to it. By citing Byron's call for rebellion, Garnet offers the possibility of pleasure, if not progress, in the pathless wood.

For his part, Garnet would find himself torn between the extremes that Byron had come to represent. He himself manifested a Byronic passion for liberty, a passion that often led to reckless action.[74] Like Byron, Garnet would both thrill and repel those around him, who looked on with admiring trepidation at his uncompromising vision. As he moved from his role as student to embark on an adult career, that vision led him to reject the New York African Free School's early lessons, which had urged Black children to embrace colonial wandering in order to heal slavery's brutal rupture from family and culture. In a country that celebrated the Fourth of July's collective act of self-orphaning, the young Garnet demanded that children claim justice on behalf of their wronged parents.

As he moved into his own as a minister, as a husband, as a father, and as a political leader, he would continually refuse any future that insisted he relinquish the past, although his thoughts about colonialism would change profoundly. The deep conviction of his inherent dignity and his absolute refusal to cede ground when he felt in the right made Garnet both a Byronic figure and a natural leader. But his willingness to rise up at any perceived insult would at times render him an outcast, even among those whose cause he shared. The next phase of his life would not only alienate him from much of the white abolitionist establishment, but would find him excoriated by schoolboy friends, including James McCune Smith, whose alliance with Frederick Douglass set the stage for these two emerging leaders to become bitter opponents on the issue of what future Black people should embrace.

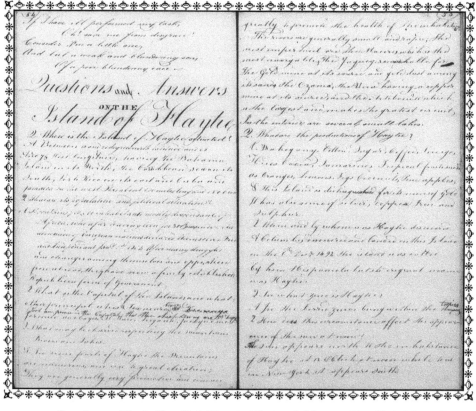

Questions on Haytie. New-York Historical Society & Museum, New-York African Free-School Records, circa 1825, vol. 3.

CHAPTER 3

Orphans, Data, and the American Story
(CIRCA 1837–1850)

———————————————∾———————————————

T HE work of at least two students jostles for space on a single page of the New York African Free School records. In this case, we do not know the name of the children who stood on stage and said the words so carefully recorded, in a penmanship designed to impress. But whoever they were, it is safe to say that they would have been anxious about their public appearances. Every student knew that impressing the onlookers was essential to the school's reputation.

One of the performances—and clearly one of the highlights of the day—was an oral exam in which a student answered very particular questions about "The Island of Haytie." "Where is the island of Haytie located?" inquired the schoolmaster. The student didn't hesitate: "Between 18 and 20 degrees latitude and 68 and 75 degrees West longitude, having the Bahama Island to its North and the Caribbean Sea to its South."

The child who answered with such alacrity had probably put in some sleepless nights committing these facts to memory. As the examination continued, the level of detail required only grew. The student in the hot seat provided answers about the position of the Haitian sun at noon, and correctly named the two days of the year when the sun would appear directly above Port au Prince. The records do not note a sigh of relief when the examination was over, but the student certainly would have been entitled to it. A wrong answer on stage would have been far more than a personal embarrassment. It would be an indictment of the entire project of the NYAFS, where the performances of individuals were held up as specimens that could reveal the essential nature of the group. This Examination Day, like all the others, brought in an audience of newspaper reporters, parents, trustees, and members of the public, all watching attentively to see what the students could do.

Squeezed at the top of the page detailing this successful quiz on Haitian geography was a poem crackling with anxiety about the possibility of failing to live up to the expectations of Examination Day. In light of the intense pressure to ace the performance, this other snippet of student work crammed in the corner might be read as a hushed stage whisper, reminding the nervous examinant of exactly how much was at stake.

> If I have ill performed my task;
>   Oh! save me from disgrace!
> Consider I'm a little one,
> And but a weak and blundering son
>   Of a poor, blundering race.[1]

James McCune Smith would have been twelve years old at the probable date of this public quiz. He had been the star student of previous demonstrations, so it is not impossible that he was the geography whiz held up as testimony to the strong minds formed by the NYAFS's rigorous curriculum. Whether or not he had been personally chosen to be the student taking this particular quiz, fifteen years after this examination Smith was still doing the same sort of work that his eager classmates had performed on Mulberry Street that day: proving that Black children could grow into productive citizens. As an educated doctor in New York City, Smith drew on his scientific training and his personal accomplishments not simply to heal the bodies of members of his community but also to prove that those bodies were not emblems of doom. When, in

1839, he had responded to the Colored Orphan Asylum's physician's report attributing Black children's deaths to the "weakness" transmitted by Black parents, he had begun—whether he had intended to or not—a career in which he provided counterevidence to the increasingly popular set of theories arguing that Black people would remain forever frozen in a primitive time. As a child, he was himself a specimen of Black excellence, and now, as a highly educated man, he was called upon to provide data to refute the fantasies that the American Colonization Society had found so compelling—the pseudoscientific belief that Black people were constitutionally unable to live well in a free climate.

One of Smith's first public speeches in New York City, given at the Philomethan Hall in 1837, drew on medical knowledge to insist that Black bodies were no less suited for democracy than white ones. More specifically, he attacked phrenology—a branch of inquiry that posited that the shape of a skull provided irrefutable facts about an individual's personality and cognitive ability. In the hands of phrenologists, the body—especially the Black body—was a text from which all future potential could be deciphered. For Smith, the work of phrenologists was a perversion of science, and he took the stage determined to prove that fact. The young doctor impressed the crowd with his "modest demeanor," which, along with "the ease of his address" and "the facility of his elocution," combined to win "the favor of his audience."[2] Like the men whose theories he wished to refute, Dr. Smith used skulls in his demonstration. He was no stranger to using props in a public speech designed to make the case that Black people were equal to whites— for much of his young life, he himself had been the prop, standing on stage, showing onlookers how fully he had absorbed his lessons. Now, after years of training, he was the teacher, holding skulls in front of the crowd to make the case that any differences between the bodies of white and Black people were irrelevant. Moving smoothly from science to religion, Smith warned his audience that phrenology was blasphemous, arguing that its "dogmas" had "a tendency to lead the mind into skepticism, in relation to the doctrines of Christianity, by their incapacity of agreement with the peculiarities of revealed religion."[3]

In other words, phrenologists' insistence on an inherent, ancient set of differences between Black and white races was an implicit argument for "polygenesis," or the theory that God had, in fact, created multiple races. According to this blasphemous theory, humans did not all descend from Adam, but rather occupied separate branches of the biblical family tree.

In 1840, the Bible notwithstanding, the US government published a mountain of data designed to support the theory of inborn, irreversible racial inequality. More specifically, the census statistics seemed to demonstrate that freedom was literally toxic to Black bodies. The report's (soon wholly disproven) data indicated that the further north African Americans lived, the more likely they were to become mentally insane, or physically disabled, or, in many cases, both. The further the census takers went into the slave South, on the other hand, the healthier African Americans were reported to be. One startled physician, trying to account for the shocking figures, suggested that slavery must have had "a wonderful influence" by freeing its subjects of adult "responsibilities which the free, self-thinking and self-acting enjoy and sustain." The enslaved actually enjoyed better health, the argument ran, precisely because they were denied "the liabilities and dangers of active self direction."[4] At the same time when Henry Highland Garnet was giving speeches that painted the past as a force that stalked Black people, the US census created a portrait in which a free future would exterminate the race altogether. As one commentator suggested, the census indicated that Black people simply had not grown into the necessary maturity for freedom. It would require "many successive generations," he argued, before people of African descent could handle the "difficult task of self-direction, amidst the dangerous temptations and ardent rivalries of civilized life."[5] Black people needed to grow up, but, white commentators agreed, it would take "generations," if not centuries, for the permanently childlike race to move forward.

Secretary of State John Calhoun, one of slavery's most ardent supporters, found in this data proof of his most deeply held beliefs. In a letter decrying what he saw as England's meddlesome antislavery advocacy, Calhoun pointed to the "census and other authentic documents" to "show that, in all instances in which the States have changed the former relation between the two races, the condition of the African, instead of being improved, has become worse." Black bodies were tuned for perpetual servitude, he argued. Any disturbance of that balance led them to sink into "vice and pauperism, accompanied by the bodily and mental inflictions incident thereto—deafness, blindness, insanity, and idiocy—to a degree without example." Calhoun went on to argue that in states that had "retained the ancient relation between" slave and master, Black people "have improved greatly in every respect—in number, comfort, intelligence, and morals." He then directs the reader to a list of "facts" gleaned from the census and other sources to illustrate his point.[6]

Clearly enamored with the power of scientific fact to support his proslavery agenda, Calhoun turned to the former counsel general of Egypt, George Gliddon, whose recent lecture tour featuring the "Panorama of the Nile" had helped fuel a fascination with all things Egyptian throughout the mid-nineteenth century. Gliddon, in turn, recommended that Calhoun read the work of Samuel Morton. If the census counted and evaluated every individual to make a collective case for the allegedly stunted growth of Black people, Morton worked the case from the other angle. His studies demonstrated how one person—or, to be more precise, one skull, one specimen—could stand in for multitudes of human lives. Morton publicly asserted that he was no phrenologist, preferring to consider himself a craniologist. As far as James McCune Smith and other antiracist onlookers were concerned, however, the distinction made little difference. Like phrenologists, Morton looked at the shapes of skulls to make pronouncements about irrefutable racial differences in which Black people seemed trapped in perpetual immaturity, unable ever to progress out of the servitude they had inherited.

In Samuel Morton's 1844 *Crania Aegyptica*, chronology collapsed as the specimen functioned as a historical crystal ball in which past, present, and future tell the same story: "Complexion, features, and expression, these and every other attribute of the race are depicted precisely as we are accustomed to see them in our daily walks: indeed, were we to judge by the drawings alone, we might suppose them to have been executed but yesterday: and yet some of these vivid delineations are really three thousand five hundred years old!"[7] Even centuries of racial intermarriage, Morton noted, were unable to change the balance between Black and white. "While nature kindly endeavors to wash out the stain," Morton writes of racial mixing, "every caravan from the South or West pours in a new supply of slaves and restores the blackening element."[8] Blackness, in Morton's view, will always end exactly where it started.

Slavery, too, seems impervious to time. Morton notes in *Crania Aegyptica* that "the attendant circumstances of this inhuman traffic appear to have been much the same in ancient as in modern times." No matter where one stood in history, slavery presented the same picture. "It is curious," Morton mused, "to observe that Arrian, who wrote in the second century, gives three thousand as the number of Negroes annually brought down the Nile in his time." Now, Morton asserted that "Madden, writing in our own day, . . . sixteen hundred years later than Arrian, estimates the present number in nearly the same words." Not only is the practice of slavery an ever-changing same, but the proportions themselves seem to represent a historical mean, which nature will continually reassert, like water leveling back after a pebble unsettles the surface.[9] In light of this "evidence," it would not take much imagination to extrapolate—as Calhoun and others certainly did—that the 1840 census, rather than providing new revelations, was merely another reiteration of the data contained in the skulls of Africans who died over three thousand years earlier.[10]

If Black children at the New York African Free School had been held up as specimens of Black potential, Morton's iteration of the Black specimen foreclosed any possibility for the change and progress that childhood was supposed to possess.[11] At James McCune Smith's school, teachers had held up the stories of successful orphans to teach students the benefits of breaking from history. But in the hands of Morton—and of men like Calhoun, who cited him—the specimen *is* history, offering a solidity that defies change for centuries. The 1840 census, coming so soon after the Colored Orphan Asylum's physician's

1838 report attributing orphan deaths to their inferior racial makeup, offered yet another blow to Smith's hopes that data would be able to undo the irrational work of prejudice. He did not abandon the fight, however. He offered a powerfully erudite refutation of the census's erroneous numbers. Smith authored "A Dissertation on the Influence of Climate on Longevity," which was offered for consideration to medical faculty at Harvard University and later published.[12] The young doctor also turned to newspapers and lectures to correct the twisted chronologies of the census and the "science" that supported it. Time, he insisted, was not static. Race relations were not set in stone, but could, and would, evolve.

As he continued to build his career throughout the 1840s, Smith put all of his intellectual force into demonstrating that present action could, in fact, change future outcomes. "How shall we enquire into the future?" he asked in an 1843 speech, "The Destiny of the People of Color." With "what line and rule shall we step beyond the bounds of the present and read with an intelligent eye the 'fate of men and empires?'" The answer, or "the rule," for the young physician, was "announced in a simple proposition of cause and effect. 'What hath been will be,' or like causes under like circumstances will cause like effects." In a world where forward progress was often derailed by chaos and violence, Smith's scientific mind took refuge in the power of study to provide guidelines on how to shape future results. For him, an investment in analyzing the past to plan for a better future was "the very basis of all our belief, all our hope." The law of cause and effect was, Smith wrote, "the very essence of that *Faith* in the stability of things, without which life would be made of dismal, because uncertain, anticipation."[13]

By the 1840s Henry Highland Garnet was lamenting the uncertain future facing Black children who were unable to redeem the struggles of their ancestors. James McCune Smith spent much of the decade investing in a future in which the children of those silenced ancestors would be able to advance in their native land. Admittedly, that progress could be maddeningly slow, but Smith believed that if the seeds were planted the tree would grow, even if it took centuries to bear fruit. "It may be," he mused in an 1841 lecture, "that we, and even those who come immediately after us, shall not perceive the benefits nor enjoy the good which our patience, under long suffering and contumely, must work out—but what then?" Henry Highland Garnet's speeches of the era raise precisely this question, warning that the unremunerated dead would haunt the present, twisting it back in on itself as injustice continued unabated. For James McCune Smith, the correct response to the present's disregard for the past was patience, not despair. "Harmodious and Aristogiton lived not to see Athens free," Smith reminded his listeners who had come to hear about the "Destiny of the People of Color." Those "who fell at Marathon beheld not from mortal eyes their country safe from the relentless clutches of a foreign foe; Toussaint L'Ouverture saw not his own Haiti free from foreign rule." But, Smith insisted, even those who might not see the end in sight had to look to further horizons, and trust to the legacies their work would engender, for history now revealed that "all these glorious events were necessarily linked with the labors of those brave and virtuous men, and therefore as inseparable from their destinies as is the light of the day from the rising of the sun."[14] Smith's turn to astronomy here is not an accident; he often saw political time in cosmic terms. Only by drawing on a scale akin to geologic time could he find a way to chart progress for Black people in America.

Science's reliance on facts and figures, on neat rows of evidence rendered in numerical tables, offered, for Smith, the only way to throw down a marker on the otherwise imperceptible progress towards justice. In ways that anticipated W. E. B. Du Bois's reliance on statistics to make racial arguments, Smith would gather an army of numbers to dispute the vague arguments of prejudice.[15] "Figures," Smith wrote, "cannot be charged with fanaticism. Like the everlasting hills, they give cold, silent evidence, unmoved by the clouds and shadows of whatever present may surround them."[16] For this physician, and for the experts he sought to correct, rendering individual souls within a statistic's "cold, silent, evidence" made them more—not less—human.

Calculations could render even the bloody, chaotic work of revolution as manageable—or at least as understandable—as a mathematics equation. When speaking on the Haitian Revolution, Smith sought to replace the popular recounting of the atrocities committed by the rebellious enslaved with a dispassionate, statistics-laden accounting of cause and effect. To take just one example of the stories that circulated about the alleged savagery of the Haitians, Bryan Edwards's *History . . . of the West Indies* recounted an attack on a pregnant white woman that involved her mutilation and her unborn infant "thrown to the hogs."[17] While whites had attributed such violence to Black people's inherent barbarity, Smith insisted that Haiti's bloodletting could be attributed to a series of bad policy decisions. If those decisions were repeated, one could expect similar results. If avoided, then a better outcome could be expected. Like everything else, political upheaval was brought about through small actions that accrete through the generations: "Revolutions," he wrote, "are the sudden developments of the slow and scarcely perceptible changes wrought by the conservative power of his destiny over the evils which afflict man in his social state." Rather than evidence of barbarity or unpredictability, the Haitian Revolution was a site of valuable data, a "field from which [one] may gather truths beneficial to the human race." The bloodier the deeds, the more "extraordinary" the events, Smith insisted, "the greater should be [the scientist's] care in dispassionately analyzing the events which constitute its history."[18] And in this case, an analysis of events laid the blame at the feet of the enslavers, and the laws that supported the white supremacy that had enabled their reign. By its unjust treatment of the free Black population in Haiti, Smith argued, authorities, in effect, took "bread out of their own children's mouth and gave it to strangers," replacing it with the "hatred of children who for bread received a stone."[19] Although Smith did not explicitly make the connection to US politics, the inference was not hard to discern: if the United States continued to turn its back on its Black children, continued to render them outcasts within their own country, there would, with the unerring certainty of a mathematical proof, be a similarly bloody result.

In the midst of scientific debate over what future the United States' Black children could possibly access, a living specimen entered the scene. In the late 1840s the counselor of South Africa, Isaac Chase, returned to the United States bringing an orphaned African youth, soon to be known as "Henry the Little Bushman." A New Hampshire native and the owner of two whaling ships, Isaac Chase was captivated by the tales he heard from an acquaintance who had visited the Cape of Good Hope. After hearing his friend the sea captain's stories of adventure, Chase became determined not only to live in Africa but to act as a pioneer for American interests there. After petitioning the highest powers in Washington, he secured the position of the first American counselor to South Africa. Chase's decision to raise a family there rendered him an object of political and scientific interest. How would white children fare, many wondered, in a climate that seemed to engender barbarism? Newspaper accounts upon Chase's return to the United States paid homage to the "accomplished family, reared almost from its infancy in that distant clime." The reporters' interest in the white children who had grown to accomplishment in such an alien climate paled in comparison to the fascination generated by the additional youth that Chase had in tow. "He has brought along with him," accounts related, "a *lusus naturae* of the African race, of the tribe called Bosjesman or Bushman."[20]

Chase's "*lusus naturae*" (translation: freak of nature) was called Henry the Bushman by everyone in the United States, including James McCune Smith. One account lists his "Forest name," or birth name, as Omo, but it seems no American felt obligated to call him that.[21] According to Chase, he received Omo from "the hands of a trader." The trader had come into the area after a brutal tribal battle. As he traversed the miles, he related, he was overwhelmed by the "many dead bodies being constantly in view." Then something caught his eye—whether it was a sudden movement or a dying moan we do not know. The trader approached one of the bodies and "found that life still remained in the boy Henry." He gathered the youth from the dusty ground, placed him into his wagon, and brought him to his living quarters. After nursing the boy back to health, he brought him to Counselor Chase, asking him to take charge of the youth. By the time Henry/Omo came to the United States as a "possession" of Isaac Chase, he had spent four or five years with the Chase family, during which Chase had attempted to educate the lad: "I have succeeded in teaching him to speak the English language," he told the Lyceum of Natural History, but "with great trouble."[22] Although he found Omo "somewhat stubborn and disobedient," he assured his audience that he had "thus far succeeded in subduing him without once inflicting the smallest chastisement."[23]

From the outset, onlookers were eager to cast the young African as a data point about the Black body's place in time, as well as its place in the progression from animal to primitive man to democratic citizen. One newspaper account spoke warmly of the time when Omo "lived as a pet in the family of Mr. Chase." Omo was short—about four feet tall. His slight form, paired with his youth, rendered him a particularly powerful specimen for those who sought to link Africanness with perpetual childhood. His age was always a point of contention, as commenters vacillated between his likely age of seventeen or eighteen—putting him at the cusp of manhood—and the childish age of six or seven that both his small stature and his African features seemed to indicate. As the press would invariably report, Omo's time with Mr. Chase and his children had not enabled either his body or his mind to emerge from the amber of a permanent childhood, resistant to the sort of progress that Chase's African counselorship was designed to promote. "Mr. Chase," the *New-Hampshire Gazette* related, "supposes him to be seventeen years old." However, the reporter remarked, Omo "has the playful simplicity of a child of six or seven years."[24] Slave children had long been denied knowledge of their birth age to make them fit with a narrative casting them as either younger or older, depending on the market's needs. Omo's age was adjusted to support another narrative—one of perpetual Black childishness.

Although he would be studied by many, poked and prodded by dozens, the records tell us almost nothing about Omo as a person, rather than as a specimen. Despite Chase's boast that he had taught Omo to speak English, the archive has preserved very little of Omo's words in any language. So we cannot know how he felt about being a visitor at the White House—a particular distinction for a person of African descent, nearly fifteen years before Frederick Douglass would be allowed to enter the building to meet with Lincoln. Did he perceive it as an honor? Or just as one more trial to be endured? We do know that he seemed intrigued by the opulence of the White House drawing room. He walked around, stopping to admire a full-length portrait of George Washington, and taking in the texture of damask curtains.[25] Shortly into his visit, he was met by Elizabeth Hamilton, the widow of Alexander, who, among his many other accomplishments, had been a founding member of the group that had created the New York African Free School.

Perhaps Mrs. Hamilton was particularly interested in Omo's story because of his orphan status. She had been an advocate for orphans since shortly after her husband's death and, together with Isabella Graham and her daughter Johanna Bethune, had helped to found the Orphan Asylum Society. That organization, like all other private orphanages in the city, did not take in Black children, a deficit that Anna Shotwell and Mary Murray had sought to address when they founded New York's Colored Orphan Asylum in 1836. Upon seeing him in the grand setting of the White House, Mrs. Hamilton approached Omo with politeness, extending her hand in greeting. Omo refused the gesture and turned away. An onlooker suggested that Omo's rejection of Eliza Hamilton's hand was due not to "fear or disgust" but to a wish to "avoid without offending." Perhaps he interpreted her gesture as invasive, and so sought to avoid contact. Mrs. Hamilton, unfailingly polite, sought to engage Omo in conversation, an overture that yielded one of the few records of Omo's own words. She asked him how he liked America. He looked at her, shivered, and replied, "Too cold."[26]

When Omo turned away from Elizabeth Hamilton's proffered hand, he did so with the recent memory of white hands that, unlike the gracious Eliza's, would not take no for an answer. His incongruous visit to the White House came only after he had passed through two other profoundly American performance spaces: the medical theater and the freak show. For much of the nineteenth century, the freak and the specimen were two sides of a coin crafted to pay homage to an ideal against which all others could be judged and, if found wanting, dismissed. Omo's time in the United States provides a case study in how easily a person, once cast as a specimen, could find his or her time divided between a circus tent and a medical examination room.[27] In both cases, the body is isolated, stared at as a text telling a story of pathology that reaffirms the alleged superiority of the onlooker.

Omo's appearance in the United States came a generation after another globally famous African "specimen." In 1810, Sarah Baartman, a young woman from South Africa, was put on display in London, where onlookers lined up for hours to look at her reportedly large buttocks and genitalia. The text that Sarah Baartman's body conveyed was one of voracious, excessive Black female sexuality, a narrative that served to support the idea that European bodies were inherently more civilized. This narrative also served to excuse white male predations on Black women, whose appetites were allegedly made manifest and undeniable by the measurements scientists incessantly took of Baartman's body. Abolitionists objected to her display and degrading treatment, but they were unable to free her from her handlers. Once she was taken to France and put on display by the animal trainer to whom she had been sold, her situation deteriorated, as she became an object of interest—not just to leering customers but to men of scientific stature. George Cuvier took particular interest in the sexualized story he read in her physiology. His credentials turned the coarse language of street hawkers into the Latinate phrases of a scientist studying a specimen, but in the end his relentless staring did much the same work. And as with many other specimens studied by medical students across the Atlantic world, Baartman's value did not change when she died. She was dissected by George Cuvier, and her body parts were put on display in French museums, until 1974, when her skeleton was finally taken down in response to protests. Her body would remain in French custody, however, until 2002, when, after years of legal wrangling, it was returned to South Africa.

Omo, or "Henry the little Bushman"—like the "Hottentot Venus"—was also named in a way that telegraphed his exoticness, and was also rendered a text by the curious, scientific stares at his body. Shortly after his arrival in the United States, Omo was put on display in Boston, where he was held up to the general public as an emblem of African backwardness. In Omo's coerced performances, as in the 1840 census, the logic of the specimen bends both time and space around the Black body, somehow always returning it "home," to slavery, no matter how many miles and years are traversed. In this case, in the free city of Boston, an African youth found his body held up as a commodity, assessed, if not for immediate labor, then for evidence that his race was suited for nothing else. One newspaper described Omo as an "evidently connecting link between the animal and rational works of the great Creator." Certainly he received a treatment similar to that of slaves subject to the auction block, as one report describes him "weeping" while several "spectators . . . were pulling his hair, feeling his head and poking his ribs." Omo, the report relates, was "so much aggrieved by the interrogatory of a gentlemen, who asked him if he was not a humbug, that he began weeping, and displayed a keen sense of insult."[28]

After his time in Boston, Omo had been brought to the Philadelphia Academy of Natural Sciences,[29] where he was examined by Samuel George Morton. Morton, was, of course, the author of *Crania Aegyptica*, whose theories were used to support the very assertions of the 1840 census that James McCune Smith had struggled mightily to disprove. Morton had made his name by examining skulls that allegedly provided "proof" that Black people were incapable of progress. Now, presented with an African youth whose body functioned as a sign of perpetual, unmoving childhood, Morton was no doubt delighted to examine a living person who could support his theories. And sure enough, Morton found Omo—whom he called Henry—to represent a perfect specimen of a seemingly unchanging race. He noted with some satisfaction that "the boy's head corresponds, in most of its developments, to those of two Hottentot skulls in Dr. M.'s collection, sent him by Mr. John Watson, of Cape Town." He made a point of connecting his specimen to the famous Sarah Baartman when he described "a prominence at or near the top of the sacrum . . . which would appear to be the osseous frame-work of that fatty cushion which is of proverbial occurrence in the Hottentot women."[30] In other words, both Omo's head and his bottom marked him as an iteration of a frozen history.

After his sojourn from the freak show to the medical theater to the White House, the next, and last, stop in Omo's tour of the United States was a home for the homeless: the New York Colored Orphan Asylum. This same institution had occupied James McCune Smith's time almost from the moment he had returned to the United States, medical degree in hand. Initially an outsider critiquing the head physician's racist accounts of orphans' deaths, he had worked for years to support the organization through medical advice and fundraising. By the time of Omo's arrival, Smith occupied the role of head physician. Surely, there was much that Smith found familiar at the asylum, overseen by many from the same circle of reformers who had supported the New York African Free School. And as at the African Free School, the asylum children were held up as specimens proving the capacity of the race to learn, to move forward, to grow up successfully in a nation that had little patience for stragglers. The annual reports of the institution were testaments to the benevolence of white benefactors, and to the children's exemplary progress. In 1849, the asylum's annual report asserted that no one "can read this interesting story of the benefits bestowed on these helpless children, without feelings of strong approbation of the management of this charity, and of gratified benevolence for the happy condition of the subjects of its charge. The good effects of their physical training can be seen at a glance by every transient visitor at the asylum, and their intellectual improvement by those who examine the school's rooms."[31]

By taking in Omo, the asylum effectively changed his story: once he was placed in the asylum's rigorous regimen of improvement, there was hope that he could represent change, rather than confirm the essential primitiveness that Samuel George Morton thought surely resided in his "Hottentot" physique. On display in Boston and Philadelphia, Omo was largely indistinguishable from a fossil—a walking endorsement of the permanence of racial distinction. Morton's examination of Omo in Philadelphia had, not surprisingly, been restricted solely to the youth's physical attributes, with no attempt to discern what emotional or intellectual capacities might be lurking inside. While Morton admitted that "the mental and moral questions connected with the history of this youth, possess an extreme interest," he himself showed no interest in exploring those moral questions. Now James McCune Smith would be in charge of leading precisely such inquiries into Omo's—whom he, too, called Henry the Bushman—interior state. At seventeen or eighteen years of age, Omo would have been the oldest "child" in residence at the institution by far: more than half the inmates were under eight years of age, and most were apprenticed out at around age twelve.[32]

Shortly after his arrival, Omo was featured at a public gathering at the asylum, presided over by James McCune Smith, now serving the dual role of instructor and master of ceremonies, charged with explaining Omo's existence to a crowd fascinated by the figure of permanent childhood he had come to represent. It is tempting to imagine that Dr. Smith, even as he prepared to speak as a respected medical authority, must have felt himself to be stuck in his own version of perpetual childhood. After all, twenty years earlier, he had played a role not dissimilar to the one assigned to Omo. Now this former star student of the New York African Free School, a child whose intellect was held up as proof of the possibility of racial progress, found himself standing on stage showcasing another Black youth to demonstrate the same lesson. Like the images on Egyptian structures, like the numbers of slaves coming down the Nile, Omo was held up as the moral of the same story James McCune Smith himself had been written into as a child. He was the specimen that demonstrated whether or not progress was possible, the protagonist in a story that, every time it needed to be reiterated, became more proof against the thesis it was supposed to promote. In other words, the need to continually showcase "promising" children twenty years after Smith and his cohort had made good on that promise meant that no one was moving forward. Rather, this parade of showcased Black children was just retreading the same ground. Perhaps it was his frustration with the difficulty of removing Black children from this fossilized position that led Smith to turn his sights to antiquity. He began his remarks to the crowd gathered that day by recounting the exploits of an English explorer who, "seized with a desire to excavate . . . finally penetrates deeply into the earth, to find that the glory of *Ninevah* is disclosed before him!"

The lucky explorer finds that "gorgeous figures made by the Assyrian workmen 3,000 years ago, are unveiled to his enraptured vision." "This traveler," Smith remarked, "was filled with and urged on by the spirit of the Past."

As he addressed the assembled crowd that day at the asylum, Dr. Smith then asked his audience to consider some much more recent history: "Some twelve or thirteen years ago, some ladies of this city, more struck with the deep degradation of a portion of its children . . . literally made excavations in the mud and mire of murky cellars, and brought to the light of day the living images you see before you; full of life, full of hope, full of energies." The orphans arrayed on stage—which perhaps someone like Morton might want to equate with artifacts dug up by the civilized travelers—were, Smith insisted, nothing like the stone statues that had lain dormant in Ninevah. No, these children were "being rightly directed to help roll on the flood of light and life, liberty and civilization which God has entrusted to the hands of the American people." The work of the Colored Orphan Asylum, Smith insisted, is "endowed with the spirit of the Present." And into this present, Smith introduces Omo, as Henry the Little Bushman, "a living specimen." He, like nearly everyone else who discusses Omo, begins with an analysis of his body. Now, however, Smith offers a description that counters the attempts of Samuel George Morton and others to render this African youth the very template of an inferior race. Rather than betraying a primitive mind, Smith points out, Omo's "head is well formed" and his "facial angle not only excels that of the Caucasian, but equals that which the Greeks gave Jupiter." Yet as long as Omo's merits were being determined by the shape of his skull, he remained trapped in the role of specimen—all that was changed was the lesson to be drawn from it. Smith's assertions that Omo's head rendered him an admirable—rather than a backwards—example of character did little to refute the logic that character itself could be identified through the body.[33]

But even as Smith cites the logic of the specimen by evoking ancient artifacts and analyzing the dimensions of Omo's skull, he unsettles that logic as well. For Dr. Smith's introduction of Omo does substantially differ from the framing of his schoolmates' performances twenty years earlier. At the New York African Free School, students were expected to read scripts to illustrate their fitness for education and development. But the audience got no such performance at the Colored Orphan Asylum. As far as we can tell from the records of that day's events, Omo did not perform at all. There is no recording of words that he spoke. There are no poems, or skits, or skillfully drawn maps. Instead, James McCune Smith offered the audience, in a word, nothing. At the point in the speech when he might be expected to turn to Henry/Omo and urge him to showcase his capacity for progress, Smith turns to the audience and tells a different story. "To-day," he said, "I asked Henry if he remembered his native language; a few clicks of the tongue, such as we would express pity with, were his reply: and I felt how utterly an orphan he is, when he could not interpret their meaning."[34]

It is precisely at this moment of miscomprehension, I would suggest, that Dr. Smith prevents the audience before him, the future readers of the newspaper account, and himself as an adult and a medical authority, from reading Omo as an example. He does not showcase the youth's words as the pin that holds down the unlucky specimen, solidifying the meaning we can attribute to it. Omo, as someone who is privy to a meaning that eludes the doctor interrogating him, is not the Black child as fossil, trapped in time as a mosquito might be held in amber, unable to evolve. Nor is he the Enlightenment child the New York African Free School meant to celebrate, who, if he were only able to orphan himself from his unlucky inheritance and given the right tutelage, would be able to grow in any direction.

Instead, Smith insists on leaving us with a meaning we cannot decipher. The scientist so enamored with the explanatory power of figures, of studies, and, yes, of specimens, ends his speech with what twenty-first-century theorist Saidiya Hartman has called "narrative restraint"—a stance she believes might be the most ethical means of engaging the experience of those who are denied the opportunity to fully speak for themselves. For Hartman, the "refusal to fill in the gaps and provide closure" is an act of homage, as is the "imperative to respect Black noise—the shrieks, the moans, the nonsense, and the opacity, which are always in excess of legibility and of the law."[35] James McCune Smith makes no effort to translate Omo's "noise," the "clicks of the tongue" carried over the seas from Africa. Rather, Smith feels—and asks his audience to feel—how utterly an orphan Omo is, and not just because the youth is so far from home. Omo has been continually un-homed by narratives that demand that a Black child function as a specimen, that he embody a story in which time continually loops back on itself even as he is required to act as if progress is possible. In asking us to feel "how utterly an orphan he is," James McCune Smith was not simply trying to counter the racist narratives of Morton and others. Instead, he creates a space—a present—in which narrative fails altogether. His refusal to elucidate the mystery Omo presents here opens a space in which the past is not something to be reiterated, refuted, or rehabilitated. Instead, Omo's body holds meanings that resist adult, logical, scientific explanation— the very sort of explanation into which Smith had invested much of his life and all of his hope.

Dr. James McCune Smith introduced Omo to the New York public in February of 1849. In August of that same year, he found himself once again explaining Omo's significance to an audience interested in the ability of Black orphans to progress. Cholera swept the city in the summer of 1849, and the Colored Orphan Asylum was hit hard. Twenty-four children were sent home, shipped out to any relatives or friends who could shelter them until the worst of the epidemic had spent its fury. Omo, having no home to go to, was the first to die. As with every moment of his life in the United States, Omo's death was read as a text that could add to the evidence for or against Black children's ability to grow and thrive in a free climate. For some, Omo's early death could be read, as had the deaths of the asylum's inmates ten years earlier, as a testament to a weakness endemic to the "peculiar constitution and condition of the colored race." Their early deaths were primed to be read as yet another data point indicating that people of African descent could handle neither a northern climate nor the freedom that accompanied it.[36]

For their part, both the female managers of the institution and James McCune Smith took special care to frame Omo's/Henry's death as evidence that he did indeed belong in the free city of New York. The first account, by an unattributed manager, places Omo in a long literary tradition in which a pious child dies a "good death," sure of heavenly recompense for his sufferings on earth. This initial account—probably written by one of the asylum's female managers—sought to place Omo's early death outside the realm of statistics that had preoccupied both Smith and Morton. Instead, she chose to place his short life in a narrative of angelic childhood death that nineteenth-century readers would find familiar and comforting. Depicting the death of children as evidence of their piety—and thus their likely entry into heaven—had been a staple of American literature since James Janeway's 1671 *Token for Children* had been a bestseller in colonial nurseries. In story after story, *Token* depicted children as young as eight years old who, through their remarkably pious behavior, served as examples of God's redemption. Take, for example, the story of Sarah Hawley, an eight-year-old who was so moved by one sermon that she immediately embarked on a path of exemplary behavior ("she abhorred lying" and "allowed herself in no known sin") accompanied by passionate praying and weeping.[37] After some worry about whether or not she was indeed headed for heaven, and a good deal of praying for "some token for good" so that "she might go off in triumph," Sarah dies enraptured by the sights of heaven, her death a comfort to all believers who witness it.

While the model made its appearance in the United States in the seventeenth century, the nineteenth century elevated the angelic child sufferer as a cultural touchstone. Two years after Omo's death, the nation would be transfixed by the fictional death of Little Eva, the centerpiece of the antislavery masterpiece *Uncle Tom's Cabin*. Literary critics have noted that Eva's Christlike submission to death, caused in no small part by her proximity to the great sins of slavery, offered white readers a way to connect a familiar grief—the loss of a child—with the griefs of the enslaved. As readers wept for Eva, they shared an emotional connection with Uncle Tom and the other Black characters, who suffered their own losses.

The depictions of deaths at the Orphan Asylum, as related by the female managers, shared much with this centuries-old script of the child's "good death." "'Will you forgive me, for being so naughty and giving you so much trouble?'" related one child in the asylum records, "'for,' said she, 'I am going to die tonight.'" Like Stowe's snow-white Little Eva, this dying Black child sought to gather loved ones as she sought redemption. In *Uncle Tom's Cabin*, Eva's deathbed is surrounded by dozens, eagerly accepting locks of her lovely hair as gifts. Like Eva, the dying child at the Colored Orphan Asylum desired one last meeting with members of her community. She asked her caretaker to "please send for all the children? I want to bid them good-by."[38]

The depiction of Omo's/Henry's death also sought to place him within the familiar comforts of the good death narrative. "The first victim to the disease was Henry, our interesting little Bushman," the account relates. True to form, Henry's lapse into illness is preceded by a religious conversion. "During the religious meetings held by the children last winter," the records relate, "our poor little Bushman showed much anxiety to be instructed how to pray." Yet, once again, even in a narrative calculated to create a sympathetic bond between the educated New York reader and the "little Bushman," a gulf of incomprehension opens. While Omo/Henry wanted to learn to pray, the other students would often find him weeping, because "he could not pray, he could only say 'Our Father.'" "He was a remarkably innocent and guileless boy," we are told. He had a deep sense of "humility" that, coupled with a Christian "sense of innate depravity," led him to worry about his own salvation. At the end, the account relates, Omo "expressed to the matron great doubts of his safety when drawing near to the close of life."[39]

Omo's doubt-ridden, fear-filled end, marred by inability to connect to a God who seems a long way off, presents a jarring diversion from the usual denouement of the child experiencing a good death. At the moment of her passing, Little Eva looks into the great beyond and exclaims, "O! love,—joy,—peace!"[40] Omo's account has no such assurances. But even as he is denied the child's good death, he is depicted as childlike until the very end. According to the asylum reports, Omo begged for the comfort of a playmate—a "favorite little boy" because, like a preliterate child, his inability to read and recite prayers adequately kept him from divine comforts. For Omo, it seems, the best that even sympathetic white Americans could imagine for him was a fictional, infantilized childhood.

James McCune Smith's physician's report follows immediately after the sentimental account of Omo's death, and opens with a detached account of the facts. "Henry, the Bushman," Smith wrote, "who had narrowly escaped with life from a violent and protracted dysentery, in August 1848, was the first victim [of the cholera epidemic]. His illness lasted twelve hours." Smith had refused to dissect Henry's mental capacities for the original audience of onlookers in February 1849. Now, in August, his scalpel cut where his interview could not, as he reported the results of the autopsy performed on the youth. "A post-mortem revealed a frame of the most perfect symmetry," Smith relates. Implicitly refuting the theory—dating at least as far back as Thomas Jefferson's *Notes on the State of Virginia*—that people of African descent were particularly vulnerable to pulmonary ailments, Smith took pains to identify that Omo's left "lung was with difficulty separated from the thoracic walls," but attributed the problem to his early life in Africa, rather to breathing New York's cold, free air.[41] As if he were still haunted by how utterly an orphan Omo had appeared to him, Smith wrote of all the children at the asylum as exiles, far from any home that would truly welcome them. "Our habits and institutions have made the difference of colour," he wrote in the asylum's report, "a line of separation, and these little orphans are almost as strangers in a strange land among us."[42] Perhaps Dr. Smith, who had sought to spend his life residing comfortably in the predictable land of scientific analysis, found himself feeling stranded as well. Confronted with Omo's suffering, Smith had come to a place where the logic of the specimen could not adequately represent the reality before him.

In the years to come, both the managers of the asylum and Dr. Smith worked tirelessly to create a space where the "little orphans" under their care would no longer remain strangers, a home in which they would find a path of belonging in their native land. Shortly after the cholera epidemic, Smith led an effort, along with the managers of the asylum, to create a place where Black children could thrive in their journey to a productive childhood. Throughout the 1850s, the improvements to the asylum were impressive, including the addition of a well-appointed hospital wing. James McCune Smith was heavily involved in much of the necessary planning and fundraising.

Through it all, he would continue to gain stature among his own community as he sought tirelessly to promote useful collaborations with both white and Black institutions. On one notable occasion, Smith was asked to give an address before "a thousand Sunday school teachers" who had come from Boston to consult with New York City teachers. The teachers were gathered, along with other distinguished guests and thousands of assembled children, at the splendid Crystal Palace on Forty-Second Street between Fifth and Sixth Avenues, roughly across the street from the Colored Orphan Asylum's location on Fifth Avenue between Forty-Second and Forty-Third Streets. There, in one of the architectural wonders of the city, a stone's throw from the institution devoted to the care of Black children to whom he had devoted much of his life, James McCune Smith listened to the applause as he, a Black man, was heralded as an honored guest and as an expert. Looking out at the thousands of white faces, he saw his own charges standing among them. The asylum's children were probably thrilled by the pomp of the day, the splendor of the building, and the sight of their physician, himself a fatherless New Yorker, standing in a place of honor amidst the steel and glass. In an era in which Black children were rendered, in James McCune Smith's words, "strangers in a strange land," to be included among this huge gathering of white children and their teachers must have felt, at least for the day, like inclusion, if not equality.

The gathering at the Crystal Palace occurred six years after the event where, just across the street, Smith had given a speech at the Colored Orphan Asylum to introduce "the Little Bushman" as a specimen for white people to examine. Now, on this sparkling Tuesday morning, the distinguished scientist and physician rose to speak, and "gave an interesting sketch of the history and progress of the institution" where he had spent so much of his professional and political energy. The asylum children looked up at their physician with a mix of admiration and pride. The accomplished man who had begun life in a position quite similar to their own probably offered hope that there would soon be a time when

Black success would be an expectation, rather than an anomaly. But that day would not be today. As soon as James McCune Smith sat down, a newspaper reported, "Mr. Hoyt, of Boston, the chairman, quickly sprang upon the platform, and shouted 'Citizens of Massachusetts, do you believe, from the specimen that has just left the platform, that the adult *coloured* population are able to take care of themselves?' 'Yes,' 'yes,' resounded from every part of the audience, followed by loud and prolonged applause."[43]

CHAPTER 4

Throwing Down the Shovel
(CIRCA 1840–1850)

Born to no inheritance but poverty and contempt, the children who this day appear before you owe all that they are to the liberality of a generous public. But for that liberality, we, like thousands of our brethren, might have continued to be the degraded descendants of despised parents. If our lot had been cast in a more Southern section of this land of liberty, our country and our home, we might have been the victims of that policy, which excludes the light of knowledge from the minds of those of our colour; it would have been against the law for us to learn to read and write.
—An Address Delivered at a Public Examination, NYAFS, by
    James Fields, Written by H. Ketchem, Esq., circa 1821

THE message of James Fields's address[1] is clear: the Black child needed to break from his history. As the New York African Free Schools taught their students through a variety of means, good students needed to divest themselves of the weighty inheritance bestowed on them by their parents. Only by finding new benefactors in a new land—amidst the munificence of New York, far from the "Southern section" of "our country and our home"—would they be able to transcend the living death of ignorance and slavery. The past was dead, or if it wasn't, it needed to be killed off and left behind.

Twenty years after young James Fields gave his speech advocating dislocation, his schoolmate Henry Highland Garnet would find himself haunted by the generations of "despised parents" whose demands for recognition and for justice would not die easily. For James McCune Smith, the autopsies of dead Black children represented a set of facts to be set straight. For Garnet, the dead demanded a different sort of reckoning. The haunting gothic poetry that he had so favored in his youth now found its way into a political imagination that sought to make sense of a world in which the past overwrote both the present and the future. As he moved into his career as a leader and minister, Garnet drew upon a deep sense of history to wrestle with life in a country in which time kept seeming to turn back on itself.

As he emerged from a youth marked by continual disruption, Garnet found the 1840s a relatively stable time in his life. In 1841, longtime friend and mentor Amos Beman presided over the wedding of Henry and Julia Williams, whom Garnet had admired since their days attending the ill-fated Noyes Academy. Theodore Wright, who was part of the generation that had attended the New York African Free School before Garnet and James McCune Smith had, provided the benediction.[2] The wedding day ushered in a life-long partnership. An activist and organizer in her own right, Julia would become a vital partner in Garnet's efforts both at home and in the field. Garnet was quite aware of his good fortune in gaining Julia's hand, and as his friend Alexander Crummell related, remained as enraptured by his beloved after the marriage as he had been while courting her.[3]

Shortly after his wedding, Garnet was installed as first pastor of the Presbyterian Church in Troy, New York. It was a parish plagued by poverty. Many people filling the pews were fugitives from slavery, having arrived in town with little more than the clothes on their backs. Surrounded by reminders of their own repeated upheavals, Henry and Julia got to work trying to create a haven for those hoping to put slavery behind them. Their success was remarkable. Garnet's charismatic speaking style served him well both in the pulpit and in the classroom, and both the parish and the Sunday school were soon full. Having been a student for so long, Garnet now emerged as an accomplished teacher.

He treated children with both affection and respect, and by all accounts they returned the sentiment. "They all loved him," Alexander Crummell attested. "[E]verywhere they flocked around him; everywhere he was the object of their idolatry; so great was the playful element in his nature, so long did he carry the feelings of childhood into the maturity of age, that children forgot his seniority and thought themselves for the time romping and sporting with a playfellow."[4] Garnet's refusal to create clear dividing lines between adults and children was reflected both in the classroom—where he taught adults and children together—and in his speaking career, where he embraced young people—both male and female—as cospeakers and as valued audience members.

When Garnet taught in Geneva, New York, at a school that—in his words—had been "colonized by the injustice of our fellow citizens" and left without "adequate support," his lessons were so popular that the classes often spilled out into the surrounding yard, as the small schoolhouse could not accommodate the student body, which included both genders and all ages. Much as Charles Andrews had done at the New York African Free Schools, Henry Highland Garnet now presided over public displays of the students' achievements. At one such event, an observer noted with pleasure that "the elocution class was composed both of adults and juveniles" and that the "younger aspirants exhibited those powers, which by good cultivation, are destined to make their fathers and mothers proud."[5] Garnet, who had written a good deal of original poetry as a student, clearly encouraged his students to cultivate their own creativity.

Both adults and children stood up and read from original compositions, many of them, according to one observer, "giving unmistakable evidences of genius." Never one to blend into the background, Garnet was not above providing some inspiration of his own. One of the themes presented on by students shared the name of a poem he had published a year earlier: "Things I Love."[6] Undoubtedly, students were inspired by their teacher's history as well as by his eloquence. Like so many of them, Garnet was a fugitive, a man who had to break with his birthplace and who knew well the rapidity with which slavery could emerge from a seemingly discarded past to claim whatever future one hoped to access.

While Garnet's post upstate kept him apart from the bustle of New York City, he worked in tandem with New Yorkers like James McCune Smith to advance the personal and political well-being of Black families. When wealthy abolitionist Gerrit Smith decided he would give away thousands of acres of land to African American families, he trusted both Henry Highland Garnet and James McCune Smith with the charge of finding worthy recipients. Because New York had a property requirement for voting rights, the opportunity to own plots of land carried with it the hope of both economic and political power. The schoolboy friends were both scrupulous about selecting only the most worthy recipients of such an opportunity. Even so, the process gave both Garnet and Smith ample opportunities to view the challenges Black men faced throughout the state. In one 1846 letter, Garnet returned the deeds that he had asked Gerrit Smith to bestow on a man named Mose, because the man "turns out to be a drunkard and lately has had the delirium tremens."[7] James McCune Smith lamented the lack of literacy among the community. He noted sadly that only one recipient out of seventeen could sign his name, "and he a runaway slave!"[8] That incident, among others, was a stark reminder that learning was just as important as land for empowering the race. And promoting education, especially among the young, was a cause to which both men were dedicated.

Henry Highland Garnet, like James McCune Smith, spent much of his career striving to enable and empower children, often alongside women who were making such work possible. Besides his teaching, Garnet often sought out young people to mentor them, creating spaces in which their voices could be heard. He often brought fugitive youth with him on stage during speaking engagements, as he did in 1848 with three formerly enslaved sisters, ranging in age from fifteen to twenty.[9] When the question of allowing a recently self-emancipated young man to function as a convention delegate was raised, Garnet was among the first to support the notion.[10] In this work, he had an able partner in Julia, who often worked alongside him in his teaching and ministerial duties. She also served as a careful reader and advisor on his speeches.[11] When Garnet was away on a speaking engagement, the ministry at home continued under her able supervision. She was an active member of the

Female Benevolent Society of Troy, an organization that would serve as the first audience for Garnet's ambitious manifesto, *The Past and the Present Condition, and the Destiny, of the Colored Race*. As with so many Black women working to support both local and national causes, much of Julia's work was unrecorded. "Her devotion to the anti-slavery cause," read her obituary, "and her sacrifices for the fleeing fugitives, may not be recorded by human pen, but the recording angel has written them."[12]

Garnet centered children in his ministerial and advocacy work, seeking to give them an agency that the law so often denied. In the political speeches that would soon make Garnet famous, however, he bemoaned the lack of choices those children had to shape their own destiny. He increasingly rejected any hope of a future that could be reached through conventional notions of progress, whether it be individual, national, or racial.[13] As the decade progressed, his public speeches grew only more strident, depicting a world in which the past made demands of the present in ways that haunted both white and Black futures. In an 1839 speech, Garnet's vision shared more with the gothic novel than with the uplift ideology espoused by most of his contemporaries.[14] Imagining how the future world would view his present time, Garnet depicted the excavation of a house of horrors. The "light [of] the present epoch of English history . . . shall reflect over all the dark places of the earth—the dungeons of cruelty—the prison houses of despair, and the tombs of buried rights."[15] History, for Garnet, functions with the detachment of a student performing a postmortem. One can look upon the crimes that were perpetrated, he suggested, to illuminate the dark, diseased places, but the horrors themselves will remain static, frozen in time before the resurrectionist's shaky light. When in 1842, Garnet created a call for a Colored Convention to take place, his prose crackled with frustration at the lack of progress. Although "time has made another annual round since we last made preparations to meet in Convention," little had happened. "During that short period the past world has been in motion, either making progress towards truth and justice, or retrograding from those great principles." Although it was painful to admit, the call read, the fact that time was still operating in retrograde was "too evident to be denied."[16]

Rather than a comforting narrative of development, Garnet's call for political action paints a picture of oppressive stasis that flattened the difference among birth, death, and reproduction. In the moribund timescape Garnet depicts, children were not harbingers of the future, but instead jetsam borne aloft on a current that would loop back to return them precisely where their parents had been. "If in chains we were born, and if in them we shall die," he told prospective convention delegates, "in the name of God who loves and pities the humble struggling poor, let no one think of transmitting his chains to posterity." Even as he imagined a future in which his contemporaries died in chains, he urged his audience to fight with all they had. They might not be able to stem the current, but perhaps they could leave some jutting debris that would at least memorialize the passing of time. "If we shall have nothing else to leave our children but battered shields and broken swords, that will have borne us through many a mortal battle, together with unsullied names, they will shed tears of gratitude over the war-worn bequests and give our poor names a place in their memories."[17]

And Garnet did indeed head into the conventions of that year ready for "mortal battle." He climbed the podium at the 1843 Convention of Colored Citizens in Buffalo, New York, with a speech in hand that would revolutionize the abolitionist movement. His "Address to the Slaves of the United States of America" sent shock waves through the international abolitionist community. Notably, he crafted the speech in collaboration with his wife, Julia. When accused of being influenced by white agitators, Garnet would insist that he had written the speech without any input from white collaborators. He shared his planned remarks with two people, he declared, one of whom was a "colored brother, who did not give me a single word of counsel." The other person was his wife, Julia. He suggested that they often operated as a creative team, even if her name did not appear as a coauthor. If "she did counsel me," Garnet insisted, "it is no matter, for 'we twain are one flesh.'"[18]

In the convention minutes, Garnet's "Address" functions like a rhetorical black hole—we cannot see it, but all events in its horizon are shaped by its cataclysmic gravity. At the meeting, everyone talked about Garnet's words, but the words themselves were too dangerous to repeat verbatim in the convention records. We do know that Garnet spoke for an hour and a half without a pause, calling for a radical departure from pacifist moral suasion and instead urging enslaved people to rebellion and resistance. "It was a masterly effort," the minutes relate. "The whole Convention, full as it was, was literally infused with tears." When the speech concluded, there was "great applause."[19] "I have never listened to eloquence," wrote one onlooker, "until I heard Henry Highland Garnet."[20] Amos Beman said that it was "an address one of the most powerful and eloquent that ever fell from human lips. Stern men were moved by it, and shaked as the wild storm sways the oaks of the forest, every soul was thrilled, every heart melted, every eye suffused with tears, as in language as vivid as lightning, he portrayed the wrongs and sufferings of the slaves, the tyranny and wickedness of the Slaveowners."[21] "None but those who heard that speech," abolitionist William Wells Brown would later write, "have the slightest idea of the tremendous influence which he exercised over the assembly."[22]

After they had recovered from their collective shock at Garnet's masterful performance, delegates began to panic. The South still lived in terror of a slave rebellion. Such an open call for resistance—from a fugitive slave, no less—could bring a fierce response, both by southern firebrands and by the northern politicians who sought to appease them. Charles B. Ray, the coeditor of the *Colored American*, stood aghast in the crowded room. He immediately set upon damage control. Like many editors then and now, Ray suggested that some careful pruning would have to be done before the speech was ready for public consumption. Garnet bristled. His response to this call for collective editing seems to have been a second speech in itself. Garnet, "fearing the fate of the address, if the motion prevailed, proceeded to give his reasons why the motion should not prevail, and why the address should be adopted by the Convention, and sent out with its sanction." In so doing, Garnet "went into the whole merits of the case. He reviewed the abominable system of slavery, showed its mighty workings, its deeds of darkness and of death—how it robbed parents of children, and children of parents, husbands of wives; how it prostituted the daughters of the slaves; how it murdered the colored man."[23]

As a student at the New York African Free School, the proud and ambitious Garnet "suffered no rivalry." "He always stood first," recalled Alexander Crummell, "and no one could surpass him."[24] But in that hall in Buffalo, there was another man who refused to take a back seat to anyone. Frederick Douglass was astonished by Garnet's rhetorical doubling down. Garnet stood as perhaps the most commanding and electrifying force in the abolitionist world of 1843, but Frederick Douglass had both the personal and the intellectual charisma that made him a rising star.[25] Two years before he wrote his famous slave narrative, Douglass had already impressed men like William Lloyd Garrison, who had found him "in physical proportion and stature commanding and exact—in intellect richly endowed," and "in natural eloquence a prodigy."[26] Now this prodigy stood in a convention hall, trying to make sense of what was probably the most powerful speech he had ever heard. And what he had witnessed scared him. This was "too much physical force," Douglass declared, "both in the address and the remarks of the speaker." He was for "trying the moral means a little longer." Douglass felt that these words, if distributed, would leave the convention delegates with blood on their hands. There would be violent uprisings that "he wished in no way to have any agency in bringing about." Rather, such violence was precisely "what we were called on to avoid."[27]

It would take Douglass nearly a decade to embrace the sentiments in Garnet's speech. To be fair, as James McCune Smith noted, Douglass had had fewer years as a free man to think through the issues than Garnet had. One could trace in Douglass's writing, Smith noted, a series of developments that followed in the footsteps of Garnet and other trailblazers. "I have read his [news] paper very carefully," Smith noted in 1848, "and find phase after phase develops itself as regularly as in one newly born among us. The Church question, the school question, separate institutions, are questions that he enters upon and argues about as our weary but active young men thought about and argued about years ago when we had Literary societies!"[28] Garnet, of course, had been a leading voice in those very literary societies. While Douglass was rarely willing to explicitly admit the inspiration Garnet might have provided, there are more than a few traces of his influence in Douglass's work.

Douglass's 1852 novella, *The Heroic Slave*, centers on the story of Madison Washington, one of the heroes Garnet evokes in the "Address." Notably, the epigraph from Douglass's work echoes the very same quotation from Byron's *Childe Harolde* that Garnet had been fond of since the early 1840s. Garnet had used it again to open the 1843 speech that Douglass had so strenuously objected to.[29]

> Hereditary bondsmen, know ye not,
> Who would be free, themselves must strike the blow!

It was not until 1848 that the speech that had so galvanized Douglass, and many others, could be found outside of the memories of those who had attended the convention. In that year, the address would be published, bound with David Walker's incendiary 1829 *Appeal to the Coloured Citizens of the World*. According to James McCune Smith, John Brown, the strident abolitionist who admired both Garnet and Walker, had put up the money to pay for the binding and publishing, although historians have doubted whether the perpetually cash-strapped Brown would have been able to raise the funds. Whether or not he had helped to financially support Garnet's address, Brown had found its arguments thrilling, and would later seek out Garnet's' counsel as he plotted his own path to revolution.

David Walker's twenty-year-old essay had created a deep panic throughout the South upon its first publication, as copies of the *Appeal* turned up in Virginia and Georgia weeks after its initial publication in Boston. The circulation of Walker's words in 1829 amplified the South's fears of a rebellious contagion that Nat Turner's bloody 1830 rebellion seemed to verify. Walker's *Appeal* was branded "seditious" and would precipitate a legal prohibition against circulating abolitionist literature in the South. Authorities in Savannah, Georgia, instituted a ban on the disembarkation of Black seamen, because they worried that the sailors would bring copies of the *Appeal* with them and distribute them through illicit networks.[30] As for Walker, he would be dead within a year of the initial publication of the *Appeal*. Although the current consensus is that Walker died from tuberculosis, many in the Black community believed he had been poisoned, a belief that Garnet mentioned, though he did not affirm that he himself believed it.[31]

Garnet's admiration for Walker's life and work connects the two speeches published nearly twenty years apart. Walker's *Appeal* had been published within a year of the slave catchers' raid on the Garnets' family home in New York City. Surely Walker's description of slavery as world-destroying would have appealed to a young Garnet whose home had just been ravaged by those seeking to drag his family back to enslavement. "I say if these things do not occur in their proper time," Walker tells us in one of the *Appeal*'s most surreal moments, "it is because the world in which we live does not exist, and we are deceived with regard to its existence."[32] Garnet, who had seen first-hand how quickly the comforting story of movement across state lines to freedom could dissolve into the hellish unmarked time of slavery, must have felt acutely that the world in which he thought he lived did not really exist. Or, at the very least, his existence within it was so tenuous that the world itself seemed illusory.

The compact book that includes the words of both David Walker and Henry Highland Garnet is, in many ways, a ghostly engagement, as Garnet pairs his own (rejected) call for rebellion at an 1843 convention with Walker's 1829 militant response to slaveowners and would-be colonizers. It is unclear how much of Garnet's original speech has been preserved in this later publication, or how much Garnet might have amended it to better participate in conversation with Walker's *Appeal*. Many have considered this posthumous collaboration as Garnet picking up Walker's rebellious torch, as both men called for violent resistance. And indeed both works are unapologetic calls for freedom, and both men do not shy away from the possibility that violence will attend such freedom. Yet, rather than passing the generational torch from Walker to Garnet, these two appeals collectively mourn time's refusal to progress at all. The torch simply remains burning in the same place. In this context, the time between Walker's first printing of the *Appeal* and its 1848 republication serves both as a rebuke and a lament. Garnet's "Address" reiterates Walker's words, and thus cannot help but testify to the need for them to be repeated—the answering call remains delayed, postponed, while American slaves continue to move from "time to eternity," without any significant change in their story.

Both Walker and Garnet were obsessed with the concept of children being denied access to the future, and both authors were tortured by the concept of a heredity that chains a child, not just to slavery itself but to the immobility that slavery manifests. Children, parents, grandparents—all were caught on a hellish wheel that turns in place, but never advances towards any new possibility. "Forever" is a word that haunts Walker's *Appeal*, applying both to Black people—doomed to be "SLAVES to the American people and their children forever!"—and to whites, who are deluded into believing that somehow "the blacks are not men, but were made to be an inheritance to us and our children forever!!!!!!"[33] Eternity, for both Walker and Garnet, stretched before them as a cruelly endless cycle, in which the lives of parent and child were interchangeable. Both men viewed optimistic American narratives of growth and progress as damning evidence of how deeply mired Black Americans remained in the muck of slavery and prejudice.

During the decade when Walker first published the *Appeal*, Garnet and his schoolmates were being taught that they needed to self-orphan in order to move up in the world. Garnet's "Address" twenty years later echoes Walker's rage at how the United States sought to cut off African Americans from their personal and national histories. In 1829, Walker took deadly aim at the Colonization Society, which he saw as a particularly pernicious attempt to convince Black people to orphan themselves from America itself. His anger is palpable when he cites a speech in which pro-colonizationist Henry Clay paints himself as "an orphan boy, penniless, a stranger to you all," who has somehow found a happy home in Kentucky. "Hearken to this statesman indeed," Walker declared with biting sarcasm, "whom God sent into Kentucky, an orphan boy, penniless and friendless, where he not only gave him plenty of friends and the comforts of life, but raised him almost to the very highest honour in the nation." Clay's tale of physical mobility translating into social mobility was, like so many of Walker's cited sources, a white-authored fiction. (As the son of a well-to-do slaveowner with a step-father pulling strings on his behalf, Clay hardly met the criteria of an outcast orphan.) Yet the affecting story of an orphan's *bildungsroman* was particularly appealing to Clay's Kentucky friends and particularly galling to Walker because of the way it echoed the justifications for Clay's pet project, African colonization, a movement that sought to orphan African Americans from their national birthright. Of course, as both Walker and Garnet knew all too well, the world of kind mentors that had enabled Clay's rise would never emerge to help Black orphans. No, for Garnet's teachers, and for Henry Clay himself, the only hope for Black children was to leave their actual parents, and instead somehow embrace the metaphorical parentage of Africa as an ancestral homeland. Like the Israelites of old, the colonizationist legend promised, Black people would be free only when they left the site of bondage and headed to the promised land.

Like the narrative of the wandering but ultimately triumphant orphan, the Exodus story was a staple among colonizationist arguments. Like the ancient Israelites, the argument ran, slaves needed to leave the land of oppression and strike out on their own. For Henry Highland Garnet, this story was just another bait and switch, and his address rejects the biblical story as an enabling narrative. For African Americans, Garnet insisted, movement did not provide progress to a promised land, but rather evoked the often-overlooked part of the Exodus story: the years of fruitless wandering in the desert. There was, quite simply, nowhere to go. "It is impossible," Garnet insisted, to act "like the children of Israel" and "make a grand Exodus from the land of bondage. THE PHARAOHS ARE ON BOTH SIDES OF THE BLOOD-RED WATERS! You cannot remove en masse, to the dominions of the British Queen—nor can you pass through Florida, and overrun Texas, and at last find peace in Mexico."[34] For Garnet, there was no promised land, certainly not one in Africa, that could offer a different future.

If the progressive narrative of growth through movement could not offer redemption, what could? In spite of what many—including the southerners who so feared these men—have seen in both Walker's and Garnet's texts, the counternarrative they provide is not solely, or even primarily, of violent rebellion. Garnet's response to history's stagnation was not to try to escape it, but to reside within it. Anticipating the powerful role civil disobedience would play in African American resistance, Garnet responded to the failure of progress not by forcing things forward but by advocating stillness. He did indeed cite past rebels—heaping praise upon Denmark Vesey, Nathaniel Turner, and the *Amistad*'s Joseph Cinque—but after cataloging their bravery, he brought the comparison to an end. Although these brave men acted violently, Garnet told his audience, he "would not advise you to attempt a revolution with the sword, because it would be INEXPEDIENT. Your numbers are too small, and the rising spirit of the age, and the spirit of the gospel are opposed to war and bloodshed."[35] The answer, instead, was to refuse to move, to simply stop, and thus gum up the gears of slavery's cyclical time. Do not raise your hand in violence, Garnet tells the enslaved people who are the object of his "Address," "but from this moment cease to labor for tyrants who will not remunerate you."[36] "Brethren, arise, arise!" Garnet exhorted the enslaved millions. "Strike for your lives and liberties. Now is the day and hour. Let every slave in the land do this, and the days of slavery are numbered."

In Garnet's rereading of Walker's words, and in his own published "Address," freedom comes from resisting the siren call of progress and mobility. Garnet ends his sketch of Walker's life with Walker's decision not to move, even though his life was in grave danger. Although friends begged Walker to move to Canada until the furor subsided, Garnet reported that "Walker said he had nothing to fear from such a pack of coward blood-hounds. Said he, 'I will stand my ground. Somebody must die in this cause.' . . . He [Walker] did not leave the country, but was soon laid in the grave." For Garnet, to resist meant refusing the promise of progress, to stand one's ground even as the slave power threatened to rip it from beneath your feet.

Garnet had been taught since his days as a schoolboy that white people owned time—that his "graduation" could only mean removal to an ahistorical Africa. Garnet's response in the "Address" is to render that time unproductive. Karl Marx, who would write of the general strike in *Capital*, volume 1, a generation after Garnet's "Address" and two generations after Walker's *Appeal*, hoped that such a work stoppage would create a profound power shift. As Gyatri Spivak has written, Marx hoped that by stopping work, laborers "would know that they were, together, 'the agent of production,' and that if they stopped, then production stopped."[37] Garnet, in 1848, also looked for a change in class consciousness. If enslavement placed the enslaved outside the rules of time, he insisted, then slaves must refuse to honor the ways in which time is organized. Rather than hoping to progress to a freedom that was white people's to give, they must instead stand in place, refusing a story that had been written to keep them walking in circles.

As the years progressed, Garnet's political vision would grow still more haunted by the specters of time out of joint. In a speech given to the Female Benevolent Society of Troy in 1848, Garnet looked at an audience of women, his wife among them, and sought to provide a vision of a future that they and their children could share. "Let us ascend that sublime eminence," Garnet exhorted the audience, "that we may view the vast empire of ruin that is scarcely discernible through the mists of former ages." But for Garnet, standing at the mountaintop only allowed him to better view the ghosts that truly claimed the landscape:

> The silence that reigns in the region where the pale nations of the earth slumber, is solemn, and awful. But what think ye, when you are told that every rood of land in this Union is the grave of a murdered man, and their epitaphs are written upon the monuments of the nation's wealth. Ye destroyers of my people draw near, and read the mournful inscription: aye, read it, until it is daguerreotyped on your souls. "You have slain us all the day long—you have had no mercy." Legions of haggard ghosts stalk through the land. Behold! See, they come: Oh what myriads! Hark! Hear their broken bones as they clatter together! With deep unearthly voices they cry, "We come, we come! For vengeance we come! Tremble, guilty nation, for the God of Justice lives and reigns."[38]

As in his writerly conversation with the great David Walker, Garnet found the lines between past, present, and future dissolving into one sustained cry of grief. This grief, like the ghosts that invoke it, defied linear notions of time.[39]

By insisting on the haunted, circuitous routes time was taking in Black history, Garnet was deviating from the uplift discourse favored by much of the Black community, including his friend James McCune Smith, who argued that investing in education and community building would provide gradual progress. That progress, Smith and others insisted, would defy the colonizationist argument that Black people were doomed to perpetual stasis as long as they remained on American soil.[40] While the events of the 1840s had rendered James McCune Smith less sanguine about the power of specimens of Black excellence, he remained steadfast in his belief that Black people, like Walker, must stand their ground on American soil.

So James McCune Smith, along with many of Garnet's old schoolmates, would be deeply shocked to learn that Garnet, who wrote so admiringly of Walker's refusal to move, suddenly seemed willing to embrace the siren song of colonization. In January 1849, not quite a year after Garnet published his revolutionary "Address" alongside Walker's anticolonizationist manifesto, Garnet unleashed an entirely different firestorm in the Black abolitionist community. "I hesitate not to say," Garnet wrote in a letter addressed to "Friend Douglass" and published in Frederick Douglass's *North Star*, "that my mind, of late, has greatly changed in regard to the American Colonization scheme [the plans put forth by the American Colonization Society]. So far as it benefits the land of my fathers, I bid it God-speed; but so far as it denies the possibility of our elevation here, I oppose it. I would rather see a man free in Liberia, than a slave in the United States."[41] This was an equivocal declaration, at best, but it was enough to shock Garnet's contemporaries. Although he states that he opposes colonization as "it denies the possibility of our elevation" in the United States, Garnet refers to Africa, not America, as the "land of [his] fathers," a stark deviation from the Black community's insistence that their ancestral claims to the United States were just as valid as any white man's. It was a profoundly disruptive statement coming from such a pillar of resistance to all sorts of white paternalism. Samuel Ringgold Ward, Garnet's cousin, was among the first to ask for an explanation for such a dramatic reversal. Ward, like Garnet, had escaped from slavery to make his way to New York City and had, in fact, lived at the Garnets' family home on Leonard Street upon first arrival. Ward too had attended the New York African Free School on Mulberry Street. Since then, he—like his cousin—had established himself as a minister and as a force in Black abolition. Both cousins had joined the Liberty Party, over the objections of abolitionists loyal to William Lloyd Garrison.[42]

Yet this long history together had not prepared Ward for Garnet's announcement. Ward wrote a public letter that asked, with exaggerated politeness, if he had heard Garnet correctly about his tentative support for the work of organizations like the American Colonization Society, and their scheme to send freedpeople to Liberia. Surely, he suggested, he must have misunderstood Garnet's meaning. He had hoped, he wrote, that Garnet would enlighten his readers "in regard to what phases of 'the American Colonization scheme' had presented themselves to you in such attractive forms as to 'change your mind greatly of late,' and to engage your complacency." Ward, like so many others, was at a loss as to what had caused such a drastic change in his friend's thinking. He wanted answers. "I . . . still expect to hear the reasons for the 'change,'" he wrote. The community demanded an explanation that would be as "full and explicit as one would naturally expect from Henry Highland Garnet."[43] Garnet's shift did seem inexplicable. In 1843, Garnet had angrily rejected the colonizationist argument that freed slaves could embark on a new exodus, and he had published that argument in 1848. Now, in 1849, Garnet seemed to think that the promised land was a real possibility. "Other people," he wrote in response to his cousin's inquiry, "become great and powerful by colonization. Our cousins, the children of Shem and Japhet, spread over the world by voluntary emigration; but we wait till we are 'forced from home and all its pleasure,' and then refuse to remove from our prison-house. In a word, we ought to go anywhere, where we can better our condition."[44] Garnet now saw Noah's wandering sons as useful role models for former slaves. Like Shem and Japhet, Garnet seemed to suggest, African Americans needed to embrace the idea of wandering—not to find a particular resting place, but to "spread all over the world." To move was not just to grow, but to conquer.

In truth, Garnet never would give an explanation that seemed satisfactory to those who found his shift in thinking a betrayal. He did suggest, rather obliquely, that new "developments have been made in relation to the descendants of once glorious but now fallen Africa, and these have changed my mind."[45] What precisely the new developments were remained unsaid, at least in the newspaper. It is likely that Garnet was heartened by the fact that Liberia had recently been established as a free-standing republic. But Liberia's independence was not the only change in the world that might have shifted Garnet's perspective.

In 1848, a revolutionary spirit had pervaded Europe, encouraging Garnet, among others, to imagine resistance in global terms. Like the fantasy of Lancasterian education that had shaped the New York African Free School, Garnet and many of his contemporaries imagined revolution as reproducible across national boundaries. He had seen the possible alliances between slave uprisings and other forms of resistance as early as 1843, when his "Address," coming hard on the heels of the 1842 Chartist crisis and general strike in the United Kingdom, urged enslaved people to throw down their tools and refuse to work.[46] Now, in 1848, both white and Black Americans found common cause in the worker uprisings that were sweeping Europe. Writing from Italy, the transcendentalist writer Margaret Fuller noted the similarities between antirevolutionary and pro-slavery arguments. "I listen to the same arguments against the emancipation of Italy, that are used against the emancipation of our Blacks. . . . I find the cause of tyranny and wrong everywhere the same—and lo! my country the darkest offender."[47] No longer was the United States the only young nation, writing its own coming-of-age story. Now the possibility of youth seemed to extend to ancient nations as well. "All eyes continue fixed upon France and her infant republic," Frederick Douglass wrote, "the offspring of her recent revolution."[48] The movement against slavery could now be linked to a global uprising against other forms of political and financial tyranny. The "despots of Europe—the Tories of England, and the slaveholders of America," Frederick Douglass wrote, all share the state of being "astonished, confused, and terrified" by the "humble poor, the toil-worn laborer, the oppressed and plundered, the world." The "fall and crash of royalty in France" Douglass noted, was happening "simultaneously" as a "terrible noise rung out from the galling chains of fettered millions in our own land." In short, in light of the events in Europe, "a ray of hope penetrated the lowest confines of American *slave* prisons, imparting firmness of faith to the whip-scarred *slave*, and fear and trembling to the guilty slaveholder."[49]

Henry Highland Garnet saw revolutionary resistance as a force that could travel across races and nations, ultimately toppling a host of systems all over the world. In 1849, he attributed a mass escape of enslaved people to precisely this sort of revolutionary contagion. In a Troy newspaper, he reported that the "result of the grand sympathy meeting, got up in Washington, to glory in the success of Republicanism in France . . . in favor of the rights of man, appears to have been, to lead a number of slaves, who were probably listeners, to think that they too were to share in the glorious boon of freedom."[50] The possibilities were exciting, especially for someone like Garnet, who had suffered so many traumatic reminders that his nation could not imagine him as a citizen. Now, the events of 1848 suggested, African American struggles were not an isolated battle for belonging but rather part of a global uprising that centered fugitive slaves like himself as citizens of the world.

Garnet's choice to include African colonization in his new global vision would cost him friendships and respect. It has almost certainly deprived him of his full due in the history of abolitionism. Before he declared himself open to African colonization, he was, in the eyes of many, a powerful leader within the Black abolitionist movement, certainly on a par with Frederick Douglass. In an 1848 letter to Douglass, a group of admirers wrote to say that they had lithographs of Douglass, Garnet, and other leaders "struck off, to be hung up in our parlors and the parlors of all men who are true to the bondman . . . to point them out to our children as the reformers who have marched in the forefront, battling for our rights as men and as Americans." Although there were several lithographs made, the admirers only sent the two most important with the letter: "We forward you on the portraits of yourself and Mr. *Garnet*, which you will please accept from us, and as we get out the rest, we will forward you one of each." Neither Douglass nor Garnet, it seemed, was content to share the limelight, and as the competition between them intensified, Garnet's openness to colonization became a particularly sore point, especially as Garnet had been quick to call out Douglass for any perceived alliance with colonizationist principles. For example, Garnet publicly excoriated Douglass in August of 1849 for using the phrase "we have no country" in an editorial about the state of African American rights. He went so far as to compare Douglass with the pro-slavery John C. Calhoun, who, along with other colonizationists, insisted that Black people could never be Americans. The attack, for Douglass, was unforgivable. From that moment onward, he wrote, he would never "be deceived into the belief that Mr. Garnet is a man of veracity and honor." And in truth, many doubted Garnet's "veracity and honor" when he, just a few months after calling out Douglass for a phrase that could be vaguely linked to colonization principles, openly and publicly declared himself friendly to the notion of African colonization.

As the debate over the global dimensions of the struggle raged in the newspapers, Garnet's parish in upstate New York continued to reverberate with the very American trauma felt by the fugitive slaves who sought sanctuary there. In 1850, one particular fugitive would come into the community who would change the Garnet family forever. Stella Weims,[51] a teenaged runaway, had settled in Geneva in the hopes of finding a safe haven. Young and beautiful, she was particularly valuable, which might account for a local doctor plotting with slave catchers to have Stella recaptured. Luckily, the plot was discovered, and Stella was delivered in the middle of the night to Garnet's home, where he was able to protect her from the slave catchers' grasp.[52] At the time of this daring rescue, Stella was the age of Garnet's own sister when she had been swept up by authorities seeking to return the family to slavery. Faced with an echo of his own family's struggle, Garnet and Julia opened their hearts and homes to the young girl. The family hid her, and according to census records, adopted her as one of their own family in 1850.[53]

While Garnet and Julia did much to minister to those who had made the perilous journey from slavery, there were reminders everywhere that any public space was a dangerous one for a Black person to occupy. In 1848, Garnet himself was on a train traveling from Douglass's town of

Rochester to Canada when a conductor insisted that he move his seat because of his race. Garnet, always a fierce guardian of his own dignity, told the conductor he was not "accustomed to yield up my rights without making a semblance of lawful resistance."[54] He walked back to his original spot. At that point, the conductor and an accomplice beat Garnet savagely, without any regard for the fact that his status as an amputee made it an even more unfair fight than it might have otherwise been. During the scuffle, he was dangerously close to being thrown beneath the wheels of the train, which would have surely killed him. In spite of the odds against him, Garnet fought back, and survived to tell the tale. It would prove a life-changing event.

The outrage was widely reported upon, and was even featured in the English newspaper *Monthly Illustrations of Slavery in Newcastle-upon-Tyne*, edited by Anna H. Richardson and her husband Henry, British abolitionists who had long sought to aid African Americans, and particularly those formerly enslaved. Having read of Garnet's plight, the Richardsons invited Garnet to leave the United States and work with them in England in favor of the Free Produce movement.[55] Garnet, who had never been abroad (indeed, the train attack kept him from crossing the national border into Canada), was intrigued. Surely his ambition—and his competitive nature—urged him to take the opportunity of traveling to Europe, a journey that had proved so profitable to both James McCune Smith and Frederick Douglass. In addition to the allure of travel, Garnet found the invitation to work on behalf of the Free Produce movement enticing. He "deeply sympathize[d]" with the principles of the movement, which argued that the best way to fight slavery was by cutting off the demand for slave-grown products.[56] If no one bought sugar or cotton from slave states, the argument ran, then buying and owning slaves would no longer be lucrative. The force of the market, Free Produce advocates contended, could add considerable weight to the work of moral suasion.

Anna Richardson, the woman who extended the invitation to Garnet, was no stranger to the American abolitionist cause. In the 1840s, Anna and her sister-in-law Ellen Richardson had been instrumental in raising the funds that ultimately bought Frederick Douglass his freedom. In spite of their shared history, or perhaps because of it, Frederick Douglass launched a particularly bitter attack on Garnet once he heard about the proffered hospitality of the Richardsons in the United Kingdom. Garnet, he insisted, had never cared a whit for the work advocated by the Free Produce movement. Taking particular issue with Garnet's turn away from William Lloyd Garrison's exclusive reliance on moral suasion, Douglass painted Garnet as a dangerous firebrand who would make for a bad ambassador. He "has made many speeches in favor of insurrection among the slaves," he warned, "and these sentiments have never to our knowledge been recalled nor repented of. Now for such a man to appeal to the moral sense of England, and ask the moral aid of England for the abolition of slavery, is the veriest hypocrisy and hollowness." In addition to being a firebrand, Douglass asserted, Garnet was a mercenary, willing to speak on behalf of any cause that could pay his way: "The party who has invited him to England, hires him to advocate a given movement; and Mr. *Garnet* like a practical man, prepares himself for his office."[57]

Garnet, for his part, immediately sought to wound his opponent on what he saw as a weak spot: Douglass's obvious and insatiable ambition. Garnet had been electrifying audiences when Douglass was nothing but an unknown fugitive, and he was not going to let Douglass forget it. In response to the accusation that Garnet was seeking fame by attacking him, Garnet slipped in the rhetorical knife and turned. "Permit me, my dear sir," he wrote to Douglass, "to say, that if I were even as ambitious of fame as yourself, I could pursue my course without adverting to you, or without having the honor of your acquaintance, either personally or by reputation."[58] Douglass was, in a word, jealous. "Ah sir," Garnet prodded, "the green-eyed monster has made you mad."[59] As satisfying as he might have found this editorial sparring, Garnet's natural tendency to step up to any conflict and swing for the rafters had created deep rifts, not just between himself and the man who would become the most influential Black abolitionist in the United States but with many of his other friends and schoolmates. Before this particular spat was over, Douglass was openly calling him an enemy.[60]

Faced with bitter political divisions in print, Garnet faced another painful set of separations once he made the decision to take the

Richardsons up on their offer to sail for England. He could not afford to bring his family—Julia, his children, James and Mary, and his adopted daughter, Stella—with him. Besides, Julia was pregnant, which made an overseas journey especially risky. As a man who had repeatedly been torn from his homes, he could not have found it easy to make the decision to leave Geneva, New York, and his beloved family. Hoping for the best, he boarded a ship bound for Liverpool, much as his friend James McCune Smith had done nearly twenty years earlier. And as it had for his old schoolmate, the opportunity to live outside the United States would forever change Garnet's approach to the problem slavery posed to his home country. The Free Produce movement offered a wealth of opportunities to think through how capital and commerce formed the foundation for the slave trade. His attendance at international gatherings would further advance his tendency to see American slavery as a problem that needed global solutions. His experience—and his political philosophy—would also be shaped by the trials of his newly adopted daughter. She, along with the rest of the family, would eventually join Garnet in his travels across Europe and the Caribbean in the frantic hope that wandering would somehow allow her the ability, if not to move forward, at least to escape slavery's insistent gravity, a force that sought to bring them all down.

CHAPTER 5

Pumping Out a Sinking Ship
(CIRCA 1850–1855)

WILLIAM: Good Morning James. Where are you going so early?

JAMES: I am going to school William.

WILLIAM: To school! Why do you go so soon as this? I am not going yet this long while—

JAMES: That may be your pleasure William. This is mine.

WILLIAM: Not altogether my pleasure either James, for I have been teasing my Mother for my breakfast for some time, and she says, "no hurry child, no hurry" and sends me to play a little longer.

JAMES: Well I love to be obedient to my parents and know it to be my duty, but I really think that if I could not get my breakfast in time for early school, I should run off without it, for half an hour's study over my sum or over any part of my other exercises at school, is of more consequence to me than even my breakfast—

WILLIAM: I have tried that James, but find that if I adopt that plan I may go without not only my breakfast, but my dinner also, for although my parents are perhaps as kind and indulgent as any parents can be in other respects, yet in this they seem to take but little concern. I have often thought it a great pity that they have not to pay 3 or 4 dollars a quarter for my schooling as our neighbor George's parents have to pay for his. I think then they would reckon every half hour and every minute that I were absent from school, a loss of money at least. They don't think as Doctor Franklin did—that "time is money" and especially, that my time to me is more precious than money itself—

JAMES: Why William, you both please and distress me. I am pleased to find that the later hours at which you are noted for going to school is

not your fault and am at the same time greatly distressed to hear that
your parents, being so much older and who ought to—

WILLIAM: Stop James! I can't hear a word against my dear parents. I
can excuse them, because they have but little learning themselves, and
don't know the value of it, nor do they know how much time it takes
to make one a good scholar.

—A Dialogue Spoken by James M. Smith and William Hill at a
public exam in 1822.

Written for the occasion by C. C. A., Teacher.[1]

I N 1822, a nine-year-old James McCune Smith acted his part in a skit,
telling a fellow NYAFS student to shift his allegiance away from his
lackadaisical mother and towards the rigor celebrated by white schoolmasters. It was one of the first examples we have of a pattern that would
shape Smith's life and career. From his earliest days, he was asked to play
a part that advocated abandoning sentiment, either towards family or
towards the past such family embodied, in order to move ahead in life.
If, like the anonymous parent in his skit, a student's own mother was so
warped by slavery's cruel chronologies that she could not keep up with a
schoolmaster's timetable, then the proper response, the skit insists, was
to leave her behind.

As he continued to build his career in the 1850s, Smith had, in fact,
flourished by cultivating a certain clinical detachment from sentiment.
That careful objectivity, paired with an adherence to the rules, and his
powerful intellect, had allowed him to attain professional credentials that
had been denied to so many of his peers. The need for control had not
dissipated once his academic career came to a close. His work as a physician and pharmacist, both in his private practice in New York City and
at the Colored Orphan Asylum, required that he maintain a certain distance from the suffering that consistently claimed his attention. When,

in 1849, he wrote so dispassionately of the orphan Omo's autopsied body, it spoke of a self-possession that he had cultivated from his teenage years.

In truth, keeping his distance seemed to come easily to Smith, who had a naturally cautious, fastidious nature. As a young man in his twenties, Dr. Smith's impressions upon his return to New York would not have been out of place coming from an easily scandalized elder. He wrote disapprovingly of the seductions to be found on Gotham's streets, lamenting the presence of "policy gambling, [and] porter houses, with their billiards and cards," which created "a gang of lazaroni of both sexes, women hastening through the streets, with their bonnets untied: men shirtless and shoeless, hanging round the corners."[2] His objections to the slovenly dress of his neighbors echoes the chiding character he played as a nine-year-old: he knew what it took to get ahead, and he was not afraid to tell the Black community that they needed to change to move forward. He urged, instead, that Black people look to men like Frederick Douglass or Henry Highland Garnet as exemplars of what Black excellence could achieve. The racism that occupied the hearts of so many white people seemed impermeable by appeals to sympathy, so Smith had long ago learned to eschew emotion in favor of the cold, hard, irrefutable world of facts.

In a New York City street corner in 1852, this same reserved, highly educated physician would dissolve into wracking sobs during a conversation with a disabled, impoverished news vendor. The encounter had begun as a bemused meditation on how the sight of this poor man had the capacity to move jaded New Yorkers to a sympathy that appeared almost involuntary. As Smith looked on from a distance, he watched with some amusement as a host of undesirables showed humanity to the news vendor, seemingly in spite of themselves: "Many a 'b'hoy,'[3] half covered from last night's debauch," he noted, "staggers a square out of the way, to deal with [the news vendor], and many a child, with half tearful eye-lid, runs across the way, passing a dozen vociferous newsboys, to buy a paper from the poor legless man." A dandy, who usually considers, Smith relates, "the negro almost a dog," nonetheless "snatches up a paper, and with half-averted face, throws down four times its worth, and rushes away from the human sympathy that has stolen away into his heart." Always the clinical observer, Smith smiled approvingly at the sight of so many people unable to keep their emotions from getting the better of them.

Yet in a moment, Smith slipped from his accustomed role of analyst and found himself just another man on the street, no different from the degraded "b'hoys" and dandies moved profoundly by a sympathy he had not planned on feeling. The transformation happened immediately and accidentally. Smith, in his self-appointed role as clinician-journalist, asked the news vendor when he had lost his legs. The man replied that it had happened on board the ship *Tuscarora*, which had wrecked on its travels from Liverpool to New York and cast several sailors, including the news vendor, upon the shore in the dead of winter. The vendor barely survived the ordeal, suffering frostbite so severe that his legs had to be amputated below the knees. Still searching for more data, Smith asked when the tragic event occurred. When the man replied that it had happened "Christmas Eve, two years ago," Smith was floored. "'*Christmas Eve, two years ago!* 1849!'" he cried out. Once the date was uttered, everything changed. This singular point in the calendar, an arbitrary arrangement of numbers, united the destinies of these two men, who until those fateful words were spoken, stood on the other side of a vast chasm of class, education, and sympathy. No more. "The tears," Smith wrote, "rushed from my eyes: for on that very night, when the poor sailor struggled with the cold and storm, and met his terrible misfortune, there came into my household a messenger for my first born: sweet, patient little sufferer, after a year of hopes and fears, and deep agony." On that same Christmas Eve, his beloved daughter Amy had breathed her last. The child had been ill for a year, but had on that holiday evening been "gladdened with tomorrow's Christmas tree and the expected adornings from a mother's loving hand."[4] She did not live through the night to participate in the Christmas morning festivities.

The 1850s were a time of tremendous change for the United States, and they proved no less transformative—and painful—for James McCune Smith. His early investment in tracing the logic of cause and effect, his belief in the transcendent, timeless power of facts and figures to overcome the falsehoods of prejudice and the slave power those lies supported would, in an extended literary conversation with Frederick Douglass, give way to investment in a new sort of sympathy, one invested in the Black home and workplace. While Smith would never wholly abandon the work of holding up specimens of excellence to convince whites of Black equality, he would augment that strategy with a deep faith in what he considered "the noiseless work" carried out by African American people, not just in the working world but in the sacred, besieged space of the Black family. This shift in philosophy was undoubtedly shaped by the seismic political shifts in the nation, and by the evolution within abolitionist thought in which Black people became more insistent on speaking for themselves. But for James McCune Smith, the sharpest turn in his thinking would be framed by the death of his children. All his carefully accrued knowledge could not prevent the loss of three more children to illness in the years following the loss of his beloved Amy.

Smith's remarkable achievements had allowed him—perhaps more so than any of his schoolmates—to believe in time's progressive power to effect positive change. After the death of his children, Smith wrote of how time itself warped around the grief, circumventing the linear progression of cause and effect that had marked so much of his political and scientific thought to date. "Oh," he wrote to friend Garret Smith in 1855, shortly after the loss of three children in quick succession, "it is sad to have no children playing around the hearthstone. I seem suddenly to have leaped over a long period of life." At forty-two, Smith felt himself an old man, his heart metaphorically broken. In truth, it was already beginning to physically weaken. He confessed that he longed for "that meeting hereafter" when he would be reunited with his little ones.[5] He would not have long to wait. He would be dead of heart trouble within ten years.

The grief he shared with the poor news vendor heralded a shift not just in the doctor's relationship with a particular street merchant but also in his relationship with the Black population of New York City itself. As Smith tells it, the shared grief the date held for both men united them not only in emotional sympathy but in financial and—eventually— political solidarity. "News Vender!" Smith declared, tears still in his eyes, "you must have your shop! Your story must be printed and sold. A little place must be hired. And your first stock in trade shall be purchased from the sum left behind by the little girl who found rest in heaven, while you manfully met and battled with your severest ill on earth."[6]

A bit more than a year after Smith published his account of commiserating with the news vendor, he would implement this moment of emotional and financial sympathy on a much wider scale. At an 1853 convention held in Frederick Douglass's home base of Rochester, New York, Smith laid out an audacious plan for economic and educational unity among African Americans. His proposed National Council of Colored People was designed to help Black communities make their own success, rather than rely on changes in white sympathies to allow for it. Although part of Smith's plan did include a publishing committee dedicated to printing "replies to any assaults, worthy of note, upon the character or condition of the Colored People," the bulk of Smith's agenda did not focus on changing the minds of white detractors. Rather, his blueprint for a national council emphasized creating networks of mutual support that would allow Black labor and Black capital to grow and flourish. Among his proposals was a "protective union" and a committee of "business relations" that would create a registry of "Black mechanics, artisans and business men," as well as a separate registry of "colored men and youth" seeking "employment and instruction." There were also plans to create a Manual Labor School, with a farm attached—a decidedly different model of education than the one Smith had experienced, but one he felt would be best suited to serve many impoverished children in the community. Perhaps he had been influenced by the great success of his friends Henry Highland Garnet and Alexander Crummell, who had acquired a postsecondary education at the Oneida Institute, which required all of its students to engage in hours of "muscular labor" every day.[7] For those who already had skills, the council would help them find work, issuing regular reports "on any avenues of business that they deem inviting to colored capital, skill and labor." These mutual aid reports, rather than the responses to the "assaults" on Black capacity, would be circulated and placed in "advertisements in papers of the widest circulation."[8] Those advertisements—as well as the reports—would often feature in *Frederick*

Douglass' Paper, as collaboration on the council and the manual school plans would be one of the many partnerships the two men would share over the decade.

Even as Smith forged ahead with a political plan designed to empower and educate the Black working class, he continued his literary exploration of the community so far removed from the sort of lives that he had been taught to revere and promote. Between 1853 and 1855, he wrote a series of creative essays, sketching the lives of everyday Black New Yorkers. The series was cumulatively titled "Heads of the Colored People"—a sly nod to the phrenological attention to skulls that Smith had been seeking to refute from the moment he had returned from medical school. "Heads" is a remarkable series of essays that examined the work Black people did, ranging from the ghastly deals made by gravediggers to the tireless labor of a single mother who took in ironing. Just a few years earlier, Smith had written disdainfully about the three "Rum Palaces" that had opened "for the run of colored men alone." He had been so vociferous in his criticism of the bars, and the crowds that they attracted, that he was threatened with a lawsuit. For Smith, such deleterious street life threatened the very future of the race. "My hopes of the children are faint," he wrote to friend Gerrit Smith, "if they are to remain under city influence."[9] In light of Smith's prior disdain for the underclass, Frederick Douglass was perplexed by his decision to write about city life and the working-class Black New Yorkers who lived it— the very people he had held up as exemplars of decay and decline. Why, Douglass wondered, would Dr. James McCune Smith want to fill the columns of *Frederick Douglass' Paper* with portraits of people "too often seen either in rags and idleness, or dressed up in the gaudy trappings of waiters and flunkeys"? He worried that these humble portraits of poor African Americans would provide evidence for "the popular verdict respecting them . . . that they are a shallow, frivolous, and servile race, to be pitied perhaps, but wholly destitute of those qualities which command respect." Why not, Douglass asked, in an editorial that dropped the names of Black ministers, businessmen, and store owners, write of these more worthy "specimens of what might be presented"? "Will not my able New York correspondent," Douglass implored, "bring some of the real 'heads of the colored people' before our readers?"[10] Smith wrote on, undeterred, about the lives of washerwomen and gravediggers.

There is a note of unrelenting grief sounding through these essays. In *The Inventor*, published in September 1853, Smith attributed both the piece's delayed publication and its composition to the spirt of his lost child. These "sketches," he explained, "were sadly interrupted by the long and painful illness of one whose little chair is vacant by my hearthstone, whose little grave is filled on the hillside." Yet if the child's chair is vacant, his influence is wrenchingly immediate: "Again and again, as I sit by my easel, brush in hand, spirit fingers weave his golden hair upon the canvas and those sad eyes light upon me, and spirit voices break the stillness of the night, in cadences now light and airy, now sobbing in keen agony."[11] Smith, the man of science, the staunch believer in inexorable progress, now found himself in a position to better understand the work of his friend Henry Highland Garnet, who wrote so movingly about being stranded in time, beset by ghosts of what had been forever lost. In much of his writing throughout the 1850s, memories of Smith's lost children shaped his prose, their "spirit fingers" leaving their marks as clearly as Smith's own pen.

Even as the deaths of his children put him in a better position to understand the mournful strain in Garnet's philosophy, Smith did not share his old friend's inclination to leave the country. Rather, his grief led him to focus on the future of Black children in the United States—"to look into other little glad eyes, and listen to other little glad voices" while trying "to reason myself out of the selfishness that they are not mine."[12] In that effort, he spent much of the 1850s in a series of collaborations with Frederick Douglass, a man equally committed to thinking through the future of art and work for African Americans on their native soil. At the same time that Smith published the "Heads" sketches, Douglass began thinking about his second autobiography, a narrative that would expand on his first life story. This time around, Douglass would distance himself from William Lloyd Garrison, whose influence had helped get the *Narrative* published, and whose introduction evinces surprise at Douglass's eloquence. Noting that Douglass had chosen to write the *Narrative* himself, Garrison wrote that, if one considers "how long and dark was the career he had to run as a slave" and "how few have been his opportunities to improve his mind," Douglass's literary masterpiece was, in Garrison's judgment, "highly creditable to his head and heart."[13] Douglass was not interested in earning another round of patronizing praise for being an admirable specimen.

As he prepared to publish a second version of his life story, Douglass wanted a different sort of validation. He turned to James McCune Smith, whom he considered without rival in terms of talent and learning. Smith, who had declared years earlier that he "loved" Douglass for "his whole souled *outness*," accepted the honor gladly.[14] In addition to his admiration for Douglass, Smith was particularly interested in the opportunity the project offered to think through the process of growing up in a slave nation. Much of his political and literary work in the first half of the 1850s was aimed at reclaiming and rethinking his own childhood and education. Even as he seemed unable to resist peppering his "Heads of Colored People" sketches with erudite references in Latin, he found much of his own early life reflected in the hardships and humble abodes of the lower class. In one notable example, his 1852 sketch "The Washerwoman" provides tantalizing glimpses into Smith's own life story, and reflects an investment in Black motherhood that would resonate throughout his introduction to Douglass's second autobiography.[15]

Like Smith's own mother, the washerwoman in the "Heads" sketch is "self-emancipated." Her physiognomy shows not a timeless type but rather a body rendered strong by hardship: her "delicately formed hand and wrist" had been transformed by "knotted muscles and bursting veins" created by her "seemingly unending toil with the smoothing iron." The washerwoman's house is full of unironed clothes, but also full of books. Portraits of local community members adorn the walls, including one of "Sammy Cornish," whose work for the New York African Free School would probably have made him a feature in Smith's own childhood home. It does not take much imagination to catch a glimpse of a young James McCune Smith in the book-loving son of the washerwoman, a "good-for-nothing looking quarter grown bushy headed boy, a shade or two lighter than his mother, so intent on 'Aladdin; or the Wonderful Lamp' that he had to be called three or four times before he sprang to put fresh wood on the fire."[16]

This modest sketch of an unwed mother and her illegitimate offspring—"there was no evidence around the room that he had ever called any one father"—was precisely the sort of story that Frederick Douglass might consider a portrait of "contented degradation."[17] But while the abode Smith depicted might have been humble, the washerwoman was anything but: her act of self-emancipation resonates with the famous showdown between the young Douglass and the slavebreaker Covey. In perhaps the most famous moment in Douglass's 1845 autobiography, Douglass decides he will no longer submit to the brutal Covey's punishments. He stands his ground, and after a prolonged battle, fights his tormentor to a draw. It was, to Douglass's mind, a singular moment of self-creation, the act with which a "slave was made a man."[18]

James McCune Smith, surely familiar with this celebrated scene in Douglass's life, portrays a similar showdown between the enslaved washerwoman and her master. While much of the background is left in the shadows, the confrontation is set into stark relief in a "scene [that] was short and decisive." She had borne her enslavement patiently, Smith tells us, "until one day, when she had reached woman's years." On that fateful day, "her so-called master, . . . with whip in hand, had called her up stairs for punishment." The "tall, stout man had raised his arm to strike," only to be stopped in his tracks. She openly defies him: "'see here'—fiercely exclaimed the frail being before him, 'if you dare touch me with that last, I will tear you to pieces!'" The effect is powerful. The "whipper, whipped, dropt his uplifted arm" and quietly slunk downstairs.[19]

In his 1845 *Narrative*, Douglass tells us he had to fight for two hours to "whip his whipper." The washerwoman does it with a single sentence. Somehow, something about her demeanor stopped the white man cold. Maybe it was her physical strength that cowed him: Smith's depiction of the woman as a "frail being" was certainly ironic, especially after he had carefully described how her "delicately formed hand and wrist" was swollen with "knotted muscles and bursting veins." Smith's mother, Lavina, did compare favorably with the fictionalized washerwoman's physical strength: the 1860 census indicates that she was still going strong at seventy-five, living with her successful son and his family.[20]

Frederick Douglass alluded to a woman who shared much with Smith's washerwoman in *My Bondage and My Freedom,* in which he elaborated on his famous fight with the slavebreaker Covey. In the 1855 rendition of his momentous battle, Douglass wrote that he owed his victory in no small part to the sacrifice of an enslaved woman, Caroline. She was, Douglass wrote, "a powerful woman" who "could have mastered me very easily." Covey called on her to do precisely that, ordering her to help him subdue Douglass as the two men tussled on the ground. She refused to do so, and her act of principled disobedience is what enabled Douglass's triumph. It also resulted in her own brutal punishment. Caroline did not appear at all in the original *Narrative,* and her inclusion in Douglass's second telling of his life story reflects a new attention to— and admiration for—women that both Smith and Garnet were reading in one another's work.

In a later "Heads" essay, we meet yet another woman whose courage and sacrifice enables the survival of others. Anna Downer stands as the hero of the incongruously titled "The School Master," a sketch that features neither school nor master. Historian John Stauffer suggests that the disconnect between title and content was born of grief. Smith, Stauffer suggests, fresh from the loss of three children in the space of two months, could not bear to write about a schoolroom filled with young, eager students.[21] Instead, the sketch moves from a discussion of the Crimean War's carnage to the lives claimed by the merciless ocean waters as the transatlantic ship the *Arctic* sank with four hundred passengers on board. The details of the *Arctic's* loss reads like an early version of the story of the doomed *Titanic,* including the fascination that the wreck held for the larger public. Articles telling the story of the wreck, printed and reprinted in several newspapers, provided a cinematic series of glimpses into the tragedy as it unfolded. Much of that coverage featured Captain Luce, a white man who was celebrated as a hero for his intention to go down with the ship. Accounts featured heartrending scenes, including a macabre reverse-receiving line, where passengers stood patiently behind one another to take turns bidding the captain farewell as the ship inexorably sunk into the sea.[22] There were also moments of high adventure and heroism, featuring scenes of the captain threatening desperate men to leave room in the lifeboat for women and children. If he had actually made such threats, they did little good. Not one woman or child escaped death at sea. Even Captain Luce's small son did not survive the wreck, a tragedy the captain held up as evidence of his own selflessness. As Luce related it, when asked if they should place his small son in the lifeboat, giving him a chance of survival, he stoically replied, "I should not allow it until other people were provided for."[23] In short, a father's adherence to his own code cost his son his life. For James McCune Smith, a man dedicated to holding fast in a nation whose racial politics seemed poised to drown all hopes of a meaningful future for Black children, the image of a child doomed by his father's decision would probably have had painful resonances.

In "The School Master," Smith displaces Captain Luce's largely self-serving narrative of manly valor to feature a woman who places service to her community over personal survival. Anna Downer, a Black woman who had worked her way up to stewardess on board the ship, was sometimes mentioned in published accounts of the *Arctic*'s loss, although never by name. In Smith's essay, his personal memory of Downer is inextricably woven—by "the spirit fingers" of grief—with the loss of his own children. "The last time I saw her, was at my door," he related, "when I gave her a sad, sad message to take to a mutual friend in Liverpool. The next day, she sailed to return no more; and others too have since gone from that door, to return no more." And in Smith's recounting, it is Anna Downer's noble death, rather than Captain Luce's hapless survival, that provides the true moral of the *Arctic*'s tragic story. As the ship continued to take on water, amidst the widespread panic that had male crew members shoving women aside as the men clambered into half-full lifeboats, Anna bravely stayed below decks. There she remained, working fiercely at the water pumps long after there was any hope that her work would meet with success. As Smith relates, "The Captain stepped below and found her alone at the pump. With resolute and aforethought purpose there she labored, and when told to desist, exclaimed, 'Captain, I am willing to pump as long as I can work my arms!'"

Smith, who had been impressed by Melville's *Moby-Dick*, offers Anna Downer's courage as a sharp counterpoint to the sort of megalomania manifested by Captain Ahab.[24] Melville's novel spent hundreds of pages tracing Ahab's single-minded quest to avenge his own loss. In his obsessive mission to repay blood for blood, Ahab criminally neglects the pain his pursuit causes all around him. In contrast, Anna Downer's resolve, equally determined—and equally doomed—sublimated her own needs to focus on saving the hundreds that relied on the ship staying afloat. Clearly, Smith saw a national lesson in Downer's sacrifice, one that he himself would seek to follow. "Brethren," Smith told his readers, "this great ship of state in which we [live], is no fairer to look at, nor of better material, nor statelier mould, then the ill starred *Arctic*: she sails too, at fullest speed without signal, through sunshine and fog. Do not her sides already gape, and the wild tide of damning oppression rush in?" The life rafts of political parties and of emigration were not going to offer any real escape, Smith felt sure, even as the prospects for the national ship looked ever bleaker. And "yet," he insisted, "it is our duty to work—work as dying Anna Downer did, *as long as we can move our arms!* We may not save the ship, but like that noble woman, we may leave a deathless name."[25] Smith, perhaps no longer sure that he could predict victory with scientific precision, now offered a model that honored the work of struggle, regardless of the results. The doctor who, a few years earlier, had believed that faith "in the stability of things," like the relationship between cause and effect, was all that kept life from being made "dismal" by "uncertain anticipation," now told himself—and his readers—that they all needed to work hard, even though no one could know if, or when, the reward might come.[26]

Even as he found himself coming closer to Henry Highland Garnet's pessimism about the possibility of forward progress, Smith found himself buoyed by Frederick Douglass's steady rise to fame. In their extended conversation—both in the pages of newspapers and in the text of Douglass's *My Bondage and My Freedom*, both men sought to reconcile the role of the individual with obligations to the larger community. In this, they were participants in one of the fundamental debates of American literature about the relationship of the individual to the larger collectives of state and community. In his 1836 essay "Nature," Ralph Waldo Emerson exhorted his readers to demand an "original relation to the universe," devoid of obligations to the past. "Cast the bantling on the rocks," Emerson wrote in "Self-Reliance," an 1841 essay that gleefully declared, "I shun father and mother and wife and brother, when my genius calls me." It was vital to remember that "we are men," Emerson told his readers, "not minors and invalids."[27] What one should do or think if one happened to be a minor or an invalid was apparently beneath comment. In 1851, Herman Melville's Ahab emerged as both a celebration and a lament for the singular pursuit of personal satisfaction at the expense of social obligations.[28] Henry David Thoreau's 1854 *Walden* spoke with sorrow of men "whose misfortune it is to have inherited farms, houses, barns, cattle and farming tools." Better for them, he suggested, "if they had been born in the open pasture and suckled by a wolf, that they might have seen with clearer eyes what field they were called to labor in."[29] The proper place for American men to stand, these works seemed to suggest, was in a field devoid of any contact with, or obligation to, the history that preceded them. In stark opposition to this radically self-contained philosophy, Harriet Beecher Stowe's 1852 novel *Uncle Tom's Cabin* (which would outsell the works of Melville, Emerson, and Thoreau several times over) insisted on the obligation of every American to "feel right" about the suffering of others. Her antislavery depiction of lost children and grieving mothers celebrated a vision of political action deeply embedded in a familial sense of connection. In Stowe's world, shared loss created the foundation for shared action, often led by women.

In many ways, Frederick Douglass straddled these two competing visions of an American ideal. He embodied a particular vision of Byronic individualism worthy of applause by Ahab himself—his famous fight with Covey was a powerful depiction of a passionate rebel rising against the numbing demands of conformity. But in the literary collaborations he had with his friend James McCune Smith, including his work on *My Bondage and My Freedom*, he attended more carefully to the networks of largely unknown family, friends, and allies that had participated in creating such a specimen of Black excellence. For his part, Smith, who had eagerly embraced the explanatory power of the individual specimen as a young man, had begun to see the work of resistance as diffuse rather than concentrated, to see the battle lines strung across generations rather than contained within the actions of any one individual. Transferring both knowledge and resistance to future generations was central to a transformation that, he admitted, was embedded in a future so distant that the progress towards it was imperceptible.

The renewed commitment of both Smith and Douglass to doing the work of community building heightened their distress at how emigration and colonization had captured geniuses like Henry Highland Garnet and Alexander Crummell. Although Douglass had great respect for the education of his friend James McCune Smith, he worried that Black children receiving lessons from white schoolmasters would be unable to work among their own people. At the same convention where James McCune Smith had unveiled his plan for a National Council of Colored People to support working-class Black interests, Douglass presented a letter in which he lamented "that education and emigration go together with us." Looking to the New York African Free School as one example, Douglass argued that "as soon as a man rises amongst us, capable by his genius and learning, to do us great service; just so soon he finds he can serve himself better by going elsewhere. In proof of this, I might instance the Russwurms—the Crummells and others—all men of superior ability and attainments, and capable of removing mountains of prejudice against their race, by their simple presence in the country; but these gentlemen . . . have sought more congenial climes where they can live more peaceable and quiet lives."[30] Unlike Anna Downer, Douglass suggests, these educated men had been taught to prioritize "how he can serve himself better," rather than how he might best serve his community. Henry Highland Garnet is not explicitly mentioned in Douglass's lament, but it is safe to assume that he was included in the overall rebuke. Garnet, who had recently left England only to head for Jamaica, was certainly among the "others" that Douglass reproached for their inability to withstand the difficulties of the United States. In a later refrain, published in *Frederick Douglass' Paper*, James McCune Smith mourned the "absence of Garnet, and Ward and Crummell from among us." For him, "the secret" to their emigration was the lack of appreciation they received from Black people, who had so internalized self-hatred that they could not truly admire anyone of their own race.[31]

Smith's own relationship to white role models had undergone a substantial change since his schoolboy years. His decision to write stories about and for the Black community instead of finding proper specimens to impress white intellectuals emerged in tandem with Douglass's own increasing distance from the role that Garrison and other white abolitionists wanted him to play. In *My Bondage and My Freedom*, Douglass describes his increasing impatience with mentor William Lloyd Garrison's insistence that he simply "tell your story," again and again, with little change. Although Douglass had not attended the New York African Free School (or any school, for that matter), his position would have struck both James McCune Smith and Henry Highland Garnet as familiar. Like a New York African Free School student, Douglass was the pupil of a teacher who fawned over his talents, even as the instructor fretted about how to keep those talents tethered to a child's capacity. Feeling uncomfortably like a schoolboy performing a script for a carefully selected audience, Douglass found he "could not always obey" Garrison's stage whispers to repeat his story without emendation, "for" he wrote, "I was now reading and thinking. New views of the subject were presented to my mind. It did not entirely satisfy me to narrate wrongs; I felt like denouncing them. . . . Besides, I was growing, and needed room."[32]

But there had been little room in Garrisonian circles for Douglass to move beyond being the remarkable adolescent who found his way to freedom. There was only one story everyone wanted to hear, reanimated nightly by Douglass's stage presence. As his learning advanced beyond that of a precocious teenager, Douglass threatened to inject a sense of progress into a narrative that depended on reiterating a childlike need for help—on a perpetual, unchanging need, demanding white rescue. Douglass was told not only to keep to the story but to make sure to tell it as if he were still living it, down to the slave dialect whites imagined he would speak. "People won't believe you ever was a slave, Frederick, if you keep on this way," one white tutor warned. "Better have a little of the plantation manner of speech than not; 'tis not best that you seem too learned."[33] If the first *Narrative* was a heroic story of Douglass's refusal to remain under the thrall of slaveholders, *My Bondage and My Freedom* was another coming-of-age story, one in which Douglass threw off the tutelage of white abolitionists in favor of Dr. Smith, the man he found "foremost" among the "intelligent men of color all over the United States who gave me their cordial sympathy and support."[34]

For his part, Smith, in his introduction to *My Bondage*, diverts from the standard logic of the novel of education, in which adults impart lessons to children. Rather, the star student of the New York African Free School viewed Douglass's evolution of character as something that emerged in opposition to, rather than in accordance with, the lessons imparted by institutions and the white men who run them. Even as Black children continued to exceed expectations in dozens of schools across the North, the argument still persisted in the 1850s that the habits of an enslaved childhood would forever blight the capacity for freedom and self-governance. In response to this persistent story of perpetual childhood stasis, Smith's introduction places Douglass in a succession of children whose childhood hardships enabled powerful resistance in later life. Unable to wholly keep himself from acting the part of the scientist holding up specimens, Smith cites the "rapidly accumulating . . . evidence [of] equality" that became manifest in the remarkable Black men "scarce one remove from barbarism—if slavery can be honored with such a distinction." Deprived and enslaved children, Smith points out, nonetheless "vault into the high places of the most advanced and painfully acquired civilization."[35] Douglass was, of course, one of those men. So was, in James McCune Smith's estimation, his former schoolmate Henry Highland Garnet and his cousin Samuel Ringgold Ward. "Ward and Garnett [*sic*], Wells Brown and Pennington, Loguen and Douglass," Smith declared, "are banners on the outer wall, under which abolition is fighting its most successful battles, because they are living exemplars of the practicability of the most radical abolitionism; for, they were all of them born to the doom of slavery, some of them remained slaves until adult age, yet they all have not only won equality to their white fellow citizens, in civil, religious, political and social rank, but they have also illustrated and adorned our common country by their genius, learning and eloquence."[36]

Smith did not only see the growth of those born "to the doom of slavery" as an indicator of equality in adulthood; he found greatness within

Black childhood itself. He, like Douglass, attributed nuanced political and philosophical yearnings to a young boy in the direst of circumstances. In Smith's estimation, Douglass the child deserved easily as much attention as the undoubtedly impressive Douglass the man. Always a keen analyst, Smith hypothesized that Frederick Douglass must have been "a shy old fashioned child," who was capable of discerning injustice and of discovering his own self-worth. He imagined the young Douglass "occasionally oppressed by what he could not well account for, peering and poking about among the layers of right and wrong, of tyrant and thrall, and the wonderfulness of that hopeless tide of things which brought power to one race, and unrequited toil to another, until, finally, he stumbled upon his 'first-found Ammonite,' hidden away down in the depths of his own nature, and which revealed to him the fact that liberty and right, for all men, were anterior to slavery and wrong."[37] In the 1840s, Smith had frustrating arguments with phrenologists who looked to ancient fossils to "prove" that the African race was destined to remain at the bottom of the social ladder for all time. Now, in 1855, Smith saw Douglass's hidden "Ammonite" as evidence of inner treasure, forged not only in spite of, but in response to, white lessons in subordination and suffering.

Douglass, too, locates a yearning for freedom, a rage at injustice, and undaunted courage in the heart of a young enslaved boy.[38] In the story he relates about his own youth, the slave child gains strength not by following the instructions of white masters but by absorbing the intended lessons in oppression and subverting them. Perhaps one of the most frequently quoted scenes in his first autobiography depicted Douglass as an eight- or nine-year-old child learning an important lesson by reading *against* the grain of his master's explicit instructions about the dangers of literacy. Listening to his master insist that reading was dangerous for slaves, Douglass learned precisely how powerful the written word could be. In *My Bondage and My Freedom*, Douglass insists that it was precisely his youth that allowed him to come to this realization. "Wise as Mr. Auld was, he evidently underrated my comprehension, and had little idea of the use to which I was capable of putting the impressive lesson he was giving to his wife. *He* wanted me to be a *slave*; I had already voted against that on the home plantation of Col. Lloyd."[39] It was Auld's arrogant belief that children could not form their own ideas, or resist adult structures, that tricked him into giving the life-altering lecture in front of the young Douglass. Like James McCune Smith's news vendor, who becomes permanently free from slavery's clutches because of his disability, Douglass's eventual freedom becomes possible precisely because of his alleged insufficiency—it is only because he is thought to be too young to think, and too small to work, that he finds the space to imagine revolution.

It was, Douglass related in 1855, the supposed insufficiency of childhood that created a ripe field for political awareness. He recalled how when he was "eight or nine years old"—the very age when Smith was learning lessons about the inefficacy of Black mothers—he wished "I had never been born. I used to contrast my condition with the blackbirds, in whose wild and sweet songs I fancied them so happy! Their apparent joy only deepened the shades of my sorrow."[40] Douglass rejected the idea of a blank slate that would, through the careful adult lessons impressed upon him, turn into what they desired. Instead, he was acquiring a political awareness that developed both apart from and in opposition to what the adults in charge were proclaiming. "There are thoughtful days," Douglass asserted, "in the lives of children—at least there were in mine—when they grapple with all the great, primary subjects of knowledge, and reach, in a moment, conclusions which no subsequent experience can shake. I was just as well aware of the unjust, unnatural and murderous character of slavery, when nine years old, as I am now."[41]

James McCune Smith found Douglass's depiction of childhood's "thoughtful days" so compelling that he quoted it at length in his introduction, where he, like Douglass, took pains to highlight the power an enslaved child possessed—and the strength that the child drew from his mother. One of the earliest lessons James McCune Smith learned at the New York African Free School was embedded in a script insisting that Black boys should turn away from their mothers in order to move into a higher level of society. If Douglass had tacitly embraced that lesson in his 1845 *Narrative*, he, in conversation with James McCune Smith, revised the story considerably in 1855. In his second autobiography, Douglass related to the reader the "life-long, standing grief" that he knew "so little of my mother, and that I was so early separated from her. . . . The side view of her face is imaged on my memory, and I take few steps in life, without feeling her presence; but the image is mute, and I have no striking words of hers treasured up."[42] Bringing Douglass's mother to life as a person and as an influence on the man who would come to embody Black abolitionism was one of Douglass's and James McCune Smith's most important additions to Douglass's life story.

While we have no physical description of Douglass's mother in the first autobiography, *My Bondage* provides a vivid portrait, declaring that an image in Prichard's *History of Man* so closely resembles his mother that he looks upon it with feelings "others experience when looking upon the pictures of dear departed ones."[43] James McCune Smith, who had spent the past decade engaged in scientific battles with authors of such purportedly learned "histories" as the one Douglass cites, could not resist pointing out the irony of Douglass "finding" his mother in a text often cited to illustrate the eternal supremacy of the white race.[44] "The head [Douglass] alluded to is copied from the statue of Ramses the Great," Smith explains, "an Egyptian king of the nineteenth dynasty."[45] The authors of the *Types of Mankind* had reproduced that image to approvingly point out the "superbly European!" features of the ancient king. Douglass's claiming that same image as a remembrance of his enslaved mother offers a radically different genealogy. "The Egyptians," Smith exhorts his reader, "like the Americans, were a mixed race, with some negro blood circling around the throne, as well as in the mud hovels."[46] Douglass and Smith both could find ancestral ties in ancient history as easily as any striving Caucasian.

Further, Smith argued, it was clear which part of this "mixed" ancestry had been instrumental in bringing Douglass's genius forth in the world. For "his energy, perseverance, eloquence, invective, sagacity, and wide sympathy," Smith wrote, Douglass was "indebted to his Negro blood. The very marvel of his style would seem to be a development of that other marvel,—how his mother learned to read."[47] For James McCune Smith, painting Douglass's enslaved mother with the brush strokes reserved for Egyptian kings offers a new vision of Black progress.

Rather than learning at the knees (or whiphandles) of white men, in *My Bondage* both Smith and Douglass hold up the generational legacies handed down by Black women. It was to his mother that Douglass owes the "strong self-hood" that allowed him to throw off the instructions of white pedagogues, "to measure strength with Mr. Covey, and to wrench himself from the embrace of the Garrisonians."[48]

The respect Frederick Douglass and James McCune Smith felt for one another, and their increased commitment to Black-led education and action, manifested in the political as well as the literary realms. As they prepared *My Bondage and My Freedom* for publication, Smith and Douglass engaged in another collaborative project—the inaugural convention of the Radical Abolitionist Party, in which both Smith and Douglass took leading roles. Smith was actually invited to chair the proceedings, and he did so with "ability, urbanity, and impartiality."[49] Henry Highland Garnet was not mentioned in the convention minutes—he was in Jamaica at the time. But his influence was everywhere felt, if not explicitly acknowledged. The Radical Abolition Party that now brought Frederick Douglass, James McCune Smith, Gerrit Smith, and John Brown together to plan political and physical revolution had grown out of the Liberty Party Garnet had championed over a decade earlier.[50] The Liberty Party's insistence on explicit political action to further the antislavery cause was in direct opposition to William Lloyd Garrison's investment in moral persuasion. At the time, Garnet's investment in the political cause put him at odds with contemporaries like Douglass who had still been aligned with Garrison's ideology. Garnet had tried to introduce measures supporting the Liberty Party—and its political agenda—at the 1843 convention where he had given his famous speech, offering resolutions that insisted that "it is the duty of every lover of liberty to vote the Liberty ticket."[51] But at every turn, he had been opposed by Douglass, William Wells Brown, and others who reminded Garnet that Garrison and other "friends in Massachusetts" did not believe in party politics.

James McCune Smith had taken the Liberty Party to task repeatedly, ultimately leading to a bitter rebuke from Garnet in 1844. In a blistering editorial, Garnet decried how his old schoolmate "rushed with Quixotic fury upon the Liberty Party." He bemoaned what he saw as the propensity to attack "the faithful friends of freedom, whose names are enrolled far beyond the short-sight of James McCune Smith, M.D." Never able to leave a fight without dispatching a killing blow, Garnet cast Smith as a servile teacher's pet, willing to do the bidding of any white man who could offer him a reward. James McCune Smith and his party felt most at home, Garnet wrote in an editorial, "when they are fawning around the feet of their oppressors." When "their masters desire them to do a piece of dirty work," Garnet taunted, "they give them a small loaf of *sweet cake*, and, spaniel like, they hunt down their own race to disgrace them."[52] If in the 1840s Garnet had sneered at Smith's prolonged tendency to play the role of eager student, by 1855 Smith had come to embrace a very different set of lessons than the ones they had both been taught as boys. James McCune Smith, like Douglass and others, fervently supported the Radical Abolition Party platform, which echoed the Liberty Party's insistence that "the ballot box" could push the country out of slavery's grip. Meanwhile, across the ocean, Garnet seemed unwilling to return to the United Sates at all, much less fight to vote in its elections.

At the 1855 convention, James McCune Smith, an avid reader of white-authored documents throughout his youth, now read from a different script, one inspired by Henry Highland Garnet in his radical speech of 1843. As a result, the Radical Abolition Party platform offered powerful reinterpretations of the American creed. Collectively, they disputed the assertion that "our fathers" had "intended to protect slavery, while their words, in the Constitution, required its suppression." Smith and Douglass—one the son of a self-emancipated Black woman and one a self-emancipated slave—now claimed the authority to author not only their own stories but the nation's. The platform they helped craft insisted that both the Black and the white members of the party "hold ourselves at liberty and under obligations to use the Constitution according to its *righteous language*, and against their *unrighteous intentions*." If the founders were dishonest in formulating the language of American governance in the eighteenth century, in 1855 Douglass and Smith, along with John Brown, Gerrit Smith, and others, took it upon themselves as a duty "to defeat such dishonest purposes and intentions if they can, by interpreting the language according to its natural and just meaning."[53] No longer the students, these men were prepared to correct the faulty lessons of those who had claimed the mantle of author and teacher. Those corrections, they now knew, could prove violent. As historian John Stauffer has argued, this meeting was one of the catalysts for John Brown's bloody raid on slaveholders at Harper's Ferry.[54]

Although James McCune Smith had come to reckon with the prospect of violence, he still felt that the path forward was one where hate could be replaced by love—between and for African Americans. The true revolution, Smith had become convinced, would come when African Americans came to rely on one another by shedding hatred for themselves and their history—perhaps the most deeply embedded lesson they had been taught. It was this division among themselves, Smith was sure, that presented the greatest obstacle to achieving freedom. Even as he viewed distrust and division within the community as a "heart problem," his diagnosis was steeped in the language of science. He urged leaders to "take a clear view of the nature of our dividedness," in the hopes of coming up with a cure that would allow African Americans to "substitute mutual attraction for mutual repulsion, love for hate." It would not be an easy task: the lessons of white supremacy had become embedded at the cellular level. "There is so much to overcome," Smith lamented, "myriad molecular affinities for myriad molecular repulsions."[55] Even Smith would not be able to fully follow his own prescription. In the decade to come, his hatred of African colonization schemes would push him into open conflict with his old friend Henry Highland Garnet, who felt that the best way to escape the crushing burden of prejudice would be to invest new energies in Black nations far from the schoolhouse where he and Smith had learned their early lessons in racial self-deprecation. Together, both men would bring their prodigious talents to bear on the question of whether they could ever claim a place in the American nation, as the nation itself would succumb to bitter divisions about what that future could look like.

Napoleon Francois Charles Joseph. Ink drawing, 1825, by James McCune Smith. New-York
Historical Society & Museum, New-York African Free-School Records, vol. 4.

CHAPTER 6

Follow the Money, Find the Revolution
(CIRCA 1850–1855)

A MONG his formidable talents, the young James McCune Smith had been an adept visual artist. At least two of his childhood drawings survive in the records of the New York African Free Schools. The lesson behind one of those drawings—a rendition of Benjamin Franklin, replete with coonskin cap—is not hard to deduce. Franklin was celebrated throughout the early republic, held up as a model for young people to follow. The reason why a twelve-year-old Black student spent a significant part of his day drawing the likeness of Napoleon Francois Charles Joseph is harder to discern. Napoleon Francois Charles Joseph (more popularly known as Napoleon II) was the son of Napoleon Bonaparte. At the age of three, he was named the heir apparent to all his father's wealth and power. Shortly after, however, the tables turned. The defeated Napoleon Bonaparte was forced to abdicate all claims to power for himself and for his progeny. We do not know if young James McCune Smith, or the classmates who probably admired his handiwork, took heart from this story of the defeat of hereditary power. If Napoleon II's fate was not secured by his father's high status, perhaps their own fates were not doomed by their fathers' lack of it.

At the time when James McCune Smith was sketching his portrait of a royal exile, Henry Highland Garnet was in the midst of his own frantic exodus, running with his family away from the Maryland plantation where he had been born into slavery. Now, as an established minister, husband, and father headed for England, Garnet found himself once again far from home, stepping into a new world that promised freedom from afar, but that got decidedly more complicated up close. As he stepped off the ship after crossing the Atlantic in August of 1850, there was another relative of Bonaparte ruling France, having risen to the throne after the June massacre of 1849 that crushed the dreams of a global alliance that the revolutions of 1848 had raised. Although the little Bonaparte that Smith had sketched back in New York had died in 1832 without leaving an heir, his cousin had recently come to power. That cousin dubbed himself Napoleon III, reaffirming the brief, largely symbolic reign of the young boy whose likeness Smith had drawn with such pathos.[1] And France was not the only site where the hopes of the 1848 uprisings had been dashed. Throughout Europe, one after another, the gains of revolution were being lost. Revolutionary thinkers such as Karl Marx and Friedrich Engels had fled to England to escape persecution. The famed Hungarian rebel Kossuth had been imprisoned.[2]

Still, as Garnet set foot on the other side of the Atlantic, he found himself as far from slavery's grasp as he had ever been. He followed in the wake of many of his friends and colleagues. James McCune Smith, who had come to Scotland to get an education, had declared that it had been the only place he had ever been able to feel fully free.[3] That sentiment—that the British Isles were a bastion of freedom standing in stark contrast to the slave-ridden United States—was a refrain echoed by many abolitionists, including Frederick Douglass and William Wells Brown. Indeed, Brown's missives from Britain cast it as a place where both slavery and prejudice were nowhere to be found. "*No person of my complexion,*" he wrote in July of 1849, "can visit this country without being struck with the marked difference between the English and the Americans. The prejudice which I have experienced on all and every occasion in the United States, and to some extent on board the *Canada*, vanished as soon as I set foot on the soil of Britain."[4] In Brown's telling, the British were so innocent of slavery's cruelties that the very sight of a slave shackle shocked them into silence. He had brought such a shackle with him in his luggage, and the customs inspector who discovered it was awestruck. All other activity stopped while "this democratic instrument of torture became the centre of attraction; so much so, that instead of going on with the examination, all hands stopped to look at the 'Negro Collar.'" The collar, so alien to freedom-loving Englishmen, seemed a portent of evil to the customs officials, and they rushed through the rest of the inspection as "if afraid that they would find something more hideous."[5]

When Frederick Douglass had visited England four years before Garnet, he too had insisted on drawing sharp, bright lines between his own slave nation and the free British Isles. He dismissed the notion that the enslaved in America and the factory worker in England had much in common. Speaking in Moorsfield, England, Douglass decried the logic by which reformists sought to define "every bad thing by the name of slavery," thereby diluting slavery's horror through trite analogy. There was no comparison between America and England on this matter, as far as he was concerned. No waged working conditions, no matter how bleak, could be equated with the "granting of that power by which one man exercises and enforces a right of property in the body and soul of another."[6]

Such statements were certainly music to the ears of those in England and Scotland who took great pride in their role as leaders in a global abolitionist movement. They relished the satisfying perch on the moral high ground looming over the allegedly freedom-loving slaver colonies that continued to engage in the most tyrannical of practices.[7] That dividing line between slave and free also allowed the moneyed classes in England to divert criticism from the low wages of the working class. As long as they were receiving any wages at all, the argument ran, they suffered little in comparison with the enslaved in the United States. Slavery was often cast as a unique moral scourge, the result of cruelty, largely unrelated to the other abuses of capitalism that had caused such unrest throughout Europe.

Garnet had a decidedly different understanding of the relationship between the United States and England. Everything Garnet had experienced up until this point had taught him about slavery's terrifying ability to overrun any boundaries that land or law seemed to place around it. So even after crossing the ocean, and stepping foot in a slave-free country for the first time, he saw slavery's insidious influence in the seemingly innocent activities of everyday British life. In one of his first public appearances, he stood before a rapt audience in Gateshead and held up the cruel instruments of the slave master back home. He first produced a whip, and then a set of chains "imposed upon the necks and limbs of the slaves," encouraging the audience to gasp at a horror so far removed from their own experience. Like the customs officials who were aghast at their brief contact with the "Negro collar" Williams Wells Brown had brought from America, the crowd in Gateshead was eager to establish its moral distance from slavery's violence.

Garnet paused, looked out at the crowd gasping at the proffered instruments of torture, and told them that they were as guilty as the bloodthirsty overseer that wielded them. As the *Anti-Slavery Reporter* related, Garnet told the audience that for these instruments "he was indebted, not to America, but to England! Yes, Birmingham was the place in which the shackles were forged [and] which the manstealer placed upon his prey." He jokingly warned that the crowd should worry about being arrested, since "Lord Brougham had obtained a law in 1840 that made it a felony to aid and abet the slave trade." And aiding it they were, he insisted, as long as their purchases put profit in the pockets of slaveholders. For Garnet, the chains around the necks of slaves were the moral property of everyone who benefited from this global system of oppression: "While Americans built the fastest ships," Garnet said, "to waft the poor negro from slavery, Portugal and Spain supplied the crews, and England wove the fabrics that were given in exchange for the captive African and forged his chains."[8] Slavery was a global system of profit, he contended, and it would take a global realignment of trade and wealth to truly bring it down.

In a move that both evoked and amended the work of earlier Black abolitionists, Garnet then launched into "a rude song said to be the composition of a slave." He stood above a spellbound crowd with a slave collar and sang of chained slaves heading to sorrow and destruction.[9]

See these poor souls from Africa,

Transported to America:

We are stolen, and sold to Georgia, will you go along with me?

We are stolen and sold to Georgia, go sound the jubilee.

See wives and husbands sold apart,

The children's screams!—it breaks my heart.

Such songs had long been popular in Great Britain. William Wells Brown had collected this very tune—"The Song of the Coffle Gang"— and published it in *The Anti-Slavery Harp* in 1848. When the great Black Shakespearean—and New York African Free School alumnus—Ira Aldridge performed across Europe, he was often interrupted by requests for such "negro songs."[10] For many European audiences these heartbreaking compositions offered entertaining glimpses of an exotic culture far removed from their own lives.[11] Garnet, however, allowed no such comforting distance. He connected the awful collar—and the laments of those tortured by it—to the everyday actions of the well-meaning people standing in front of him.

It is no surprise that the song Garnet chose contained the familiar images of distraught mothers separated from children, and wives crying for their lost husbands. Like many other abolitionists, Garnet drew attention to slavery's devastation of the family, and its particular victimization of women. He would also, in speech after speech, insist that women were central to the fight ahead. As a man who had watched Black mothers transform the New York African Free School through boycott, a man whose wife was dedicated to the protection and education of fugitives, and whose visit on British soil was facilitated by British activist Anna Richardson, he eagerly embraced the Free Produce movement's argument that women's roles as homemakers had significant economic and political power. "Let the ladies take it into their hands," he told the crowd. "Let them reject all articles that were the produce of slave-labour; let them keep on asking for free-labour goods, and they might depend upon it the shop-keepers would supply them, some from motives of humanity, others from motives of interest, and others as the only means of getting rid of an annoyance." Slavery, he insisted, could not be stopped without major changes in the circulation of wealth—changes that could be wrought by women, who made the bulk of the household purchases. "Why was it that the African slave-trade had increased instead of diminished, after all the exertions made to put it down?" he asked. "Because there had been a constant and increased demand for slave-grown productions in the British market. Let there be a demand for free-labour produce, and the cause would cease; let the public move first, and all the great firms who supplied the country must follow as a matter of course." Once the ladies made that demand clear in their daily routines, Garnet felt sure the nation would follow.[12]

Garnet's work on behalf of the Free Produce movement was part of a larger conversation connecting the slave laborer to the British worker and consumer. This conversation was joined by, among others, Karl Marx. "Direct slavery is as much the pivot upon which our present day industrialism turns as are machinery, [and] credit," Marx insisted as early as 1847. "Without slavery there would be no cotton, without cotton, there would be no modern industry. It is slavery which has given value to the colonies which have created world trade and world trade is the necessary condition to large-scale machine industry."[13] Historians have increasingly made the case that slavery was indispensable to modern capitalism as we know it.[14] Garnet was among those who saw these connections clearly in the mid-nineteenth century. Working on behalf of the Free Produce cause, which sought to undermine slavery by cutting off demand for its products through consumer boycotts, Garnet also came to see the nodes of commercial exchange as parts of a network that connected purportedly free markets to the relentless slave labor of the American South.

As a student at the New York African Free School, Garnet had been taught to admire the colonial ambitions of the Lancasterian system of education, a model that prided itself on its ability to crank out well-trained students who could adapt to different locales, laws, languages, and labor practices. Garnet and his classmates were held up as evidence that a standardized system would reliably yield a similar product: an educated workforce free from the "biases" of their instructor and, arguably, devoid of any strong attachment to place or politics. Garnet, it was becoming increasingly clear, had absorbed this lesson in metropolitanism. However, both his life experience and his work with the Free Produce movement had rendered him skeptical of Lancaster's original mission—to use metropolitan students to strengthen a growing vision of global capitalism that would require a docile, mobile labor force.

As he traveled across Britain and other locales in Europe, Garnet began to envision a different kind of mobility. By pointing out the hidden suffering in slave-produced consumables, and by exposing slavery as the force underlying "free markets," Garnet sought to reclaim the power of circulation. His sense of commercial mobility did not arise as explicit support of the industrialists who sought—as Lancaster had at the New York African Free Schools—to present their work as free from any political import. Instead, he imagined commerce as a collective means of redistributing power. Shortly before leaving for England, Garnet had become convinced that the problems of American slavery would persist well beyond any hopeful legal changes. No matter what the laws might say, he argued, the still-growing walls of capital would keep Black people in perpetual subjection. The well-established and ever-strengthening power of the moneyed classes would simply make it impossible for Black people to flourish within existing structures. "Those who dwell in the Eastern and Middle States will be crushed to death by old aristocratic arrangements, and by the ponderous wheels of wealth and the various forms of monopoly," he wrote in a letter to "Friend Douglass" in 1849. He had begun to think that the answer was the same for the free man as it had been for his fugitive parents: to get as far away from slave power as possible, even if it meant emigrating to Africa, "the land of my fathers."[15]

Garnet's view that colonization could benefit "the land of his fathers" had provoked horror among his colleagues and schoolmates in New York. The idea, however, had gained some credibility abroad, and not just with wealthy moguls looking for new markets or with slaveholders worried about freedpeople in their states. Early socialist thinkers had also toyed with the idea that the colonies could serve as a means of redistributing wealth and labor. In the heady days of 1848, the *New York*

Daily Tribune reprinted a piece from a Yorkshire newspaper that suggested that France needed to rethink the funds wasted on keeping the poor in workhouses. Better to spend the money, the columnist argued, to resettle the marginalized in the colonies. This was the route "most rational and likely to be most beneficial to all classes in the long run. If the colonies [were] thus formed," he suggested, and "the laborers were properly organized, we have little doubt but they would be completely successful and convert the unemployed artisans and laborers of France into a source of strength for the Republic."[16] The colonies, in this view, could function as sites where nations could invest in their most vulnerable citizens.

The British, too, Garnet felt, needed to deploy their colonies as a form of reparations for those who had been harmed by slavery. Soon after his arrival in England, Garnet fired off a letter addressed to his cousin Samuel Ringgold Ward, declaring that he was "annoyed to see anyone who, like you and I, has tasted the bitter cup of slavery, withholding his influence and talents" from the Free Produce movement's call to radically alter the flow of money supporting slavery. Ward went one better, declaring that the national leadership of England needed to prioritize investments in the products sold by emancipated slaves in free colonies: "The English who have, at the expense of $100,000,000 freed the negroes of the West Indies, were recreant to their own principles, if unwilling to give a preference to the proceeds of their till, over that of the stolen products of American man-stealers and women-whippers."[17] For Garnet, legal emancipation was only the first step. Former enslavers were now obligated to provide financial support to enable those they had harmed in order to enact true freedom.

Whatever dreams Garnet might entertain of freedom through movement in Europe and Africa, back in the United States, the passage of the Fugitive Slave Act effectively rendered the entire country one vast, inescapable slave pen. When Garnet had left for England, Congress had been in heated debate over slavery's spread. His own anxiety about the fate of friends and family back home was only heightened by the barrage of questions that met him in Europe. "I had scarcely reached the shores of England," he wrote to his friend Gerrit Smith back in

Petersboro, "when it was asked—'How comes on the slavery question in America? Will that nefarious compromise pass?'"[18] Before long, the question would be answered, and the news would be shattering.

Emerging out of a series of compromises, the Fugitive Slave Act allowed federal agents to issue warrants for the capture of enslaved fugitives. Further, the law compelled all American citizens to assist with their apprehension, on pain of imprisonment. While Garnet's childhood experience with slave catchers had taught him well that there was no fully free soil in the United States, the passage of this act was a crushing blow. In the 1820s, every Black child knew that slave catchers could come at any minute. In 1850, every American citizen was rendered a slave catcher. When Garnet's sister had been captured two decades earlier, she had been brought before Richard Riker. In his court, with the help of others within the community, she was able to successfully plead her case. Under the Fugitive Slave Act, many of those captured would not be afforded even that feeble protection. And when a hearing was given, there were few incentives to do justice by the captive. "The law appointed Commissioners to try cases of this kind," Garnet explained to an English crowd. The "Commissioners received five dollars as their fee, even if the person claimed is not actually reduced to slavery again. . . . If they condemned him, however, these worthies got ten dollars!"[19] Instead of progressing toward freedom, the entire nation had effectively slipped back into a slave territory.

Garnet was devastated by the news. "When the first intelligence reached us," he wrote to Gerrit Smith, "my soul was filled with grief and alarm, and the surrounding darkness was impenetrable to my feeble vision."[20] He grieved to see a "great nation bending all its energies to make more secure the bondage of a race they have brutalized and bound. With the perseverance of devils, they have toiled and maneuvered until they have made every inch of their soil the hunting-ground for human blood-hounds."[21] Back in Geneva, New York, Garnet's own family, along with his vulnerable congregation, was squarely in the sights of those bloodhounds. While Julia had lived as a free woman for decades, her own sister had not. Having one family member enslaved would make it still more likely that Julia would be deemed a fugitive as well.

And of course, Garnet himself had openly proclaimed his fugitive status from his earliest days as an orator. His wife and children were in very real danger. Stella Weims, the teenaged fugitive they had taken into their home as an adopted daughter, had already had one narrow escape from a slave catcher in New York, even before the act had passed. There were dozens of fugitives in the congregation Garnet had left behind. If they were not themselves in jeopardy from this cruel new law, they would almost certainly have a close friend or family member who was at risk. Everyone was terrified. As Garnet told a crowd in London, seventeen of his flock had packed up and left the country within months of the act's passage.[22]

Back in upstate New York, Julia was at her wit's end. In addition to the worries created by the Fugitive Slave Act, the cares of tending to a frightened and confused congregation, and the work of being the sole parent to a young family, Julia found herself in dire financial straits as the winter dragged on. She had given birth to a little boy in October 1850, and named him Henry, after his absent father.[23] By February of 1851, both the baby and their older boy were sick, and she had no money to care for them and keep the household running. In desperation, she wrote to family friend Gerrit Smith to tell him that she had not received the money Garnet had sent home; she felt it was likely that it had been lost at sea. At any rate, she had not heard from her husband at all since December.[24] She was out of money, alone with the worry of two sick children, one of whom seemed to worsen by the day. Seven-year-old James was "considered very sick," though she hoped he was not "dangerously ill." In addition to the mislaid money from England, there had been difficulties with other promised payments gone awry. She had no choice but to ask Gerrit Smith for money. The letter is brief, but one can sense deep turmoil beneath Julia's businesslike request. She had "much more to say," she wrote, "but this must do at present."[25]

On March 1, Julia's bad situation turned still worse. Henry and Julia's beloved son, James Crummell Garnet—his middle name an homage to his father's childhood neighbor and NYAFS schoolmate Alexander Crummell, and his first name a possible nod to his friend James McCune Smith—died from his long illness.[26] With Gerrit Smith's help, Julia made arrangements for herself and the remaining children to join Henry in England. Dealing with her grief, she managed to put their affairs in order, pack a lifetime's worth of belongings, and board a transatlantic steamer as a single Black woman with children, a status that almost certainly would have drawn the scorn of several passengers. There seemed to be several delays, and Henry Highland Garnet spent the summer of 1851 anxiously awaiting the arrival of his little ones. Finally, late in the summer, Julia and Henry were reunited. Henry was able to meet his infant son, Henry, for the first time, and grieve with his wife over the son they had lost.

The gloom of the austere and lonely months Julia had passed the previous winter in Geneva was at least partially dissipated by the warm reception she received in England. By the time she and the children had arrived, her gregarious and charming husband had built a large community of friends and allies. After their arrival, the family was treated to several gatherings of well-wishers welcoming them to Europe, and extending the hope that they would stay. At one event, several ministers spoke to the assembled crowd of between three and four hundred people. By all accounts, the gathering reverberated with "an excellent feeling" towards the fugitives, who finally, perhaps, felt welcomed to a home they could claim for themselves.[27] For the first time in his life, Garnet and his family were truly safe. He was in no hurry to place them in danger again. Now surrounded by his loved ones, Garnet continued to gather momentum for the Free Produce cause, and for the investment in the West Indian colonies that the cause supported.

By 1852, Garnet was spending considerable time in Scotland, the land where his old schoolmate James McCune Smith had found encouragement and opportunity. And as the year drew to a close, Garnet seemed destined to benefit from Scotland's generosity as well. As Frederick Douglass would report tersely in his newspaper back home, "Mr. Garnet, formerly of N.Y., has been designated as a missionary to Jamaica, from the United Presbyterian Church of Scotland. He is a colored man," he reminded his readers, perhaps expecting that they would have forgotten him during his long absence. In any case, this man of color "was the first ever sent out by that organization."[28] Garnet was thrilled by the offer. Here, at last, was the chance for him to put his nascent philosophy to work. He would labor alongside free people of color, helping them to prosper, and by prospering, to defeat slavery's pernicious legacy. The wheel of fortune and of history seemed to be moving at last. After his success in Europe, travel ushered in possibility as well as peril. Heading to a place free from slavery offered the perfect opportunity to imagine not just progress, but the form that progress would take.

Yet even as he made remarkable headway in his plans to relegate slavery's power to the past, that very past reached out—as it had all his life—to tear away his newly found security. As the Garnets got ready to head to Jamaica to begin their new lives, a letter arrived from Charles B. Ray, a man Garnet had known for years. Ray's personal charisma rivaled Garnet's: he had a presence that commanded respect, and a capacity to involve himself in twenty projects at once. Born in Massachusetts, Ray had long been active in New York abolitionist circles. Throughout the 1840s and '50s, he worked as a member of the New York Vigilance Committee, a group dedicated to assisting runaway slaves. He had aligned himself with James McCune Smith in his work on behalf of Smith's New York Society for the Promotion of Education among Colored Children. Garnet had run into him on numerous occasions, including the Buffalo convention where Garnet had given his revolutionary address in 1843. And at that convention, both Ray and Frederick Douglass spoke against publishing Garnet's words. At other times, Ray and Garnet had worked as allies in their work to support fugitives. On at least one occasion, Ray reported having collaborated with Garnet and his old friend Theodore Wright in an endeavor that successfully stewarded twenty-six fugitives to Canada.[29]

Now, Ray reached out to his old friend about a new set of runaways, and this time, Ray's tale of distress was far too close to home. He told Garnet that the family of Stella Weims, Garnet's adopted daughter, was about to be separated and sold into slavery. Ray had run into Stella's father, John Weims, in New York City in the spring of 1852, when John Weims had been in town trying to ascertain Stella's whereabouts. Weims had hoped, Ray reported, to enlist his daughter in raising funds to buy her mother and seven siblings out of slavery, now that their enslaver had died. At first, the father had hoped that he and his daughter could share the joyful work of reuniting the family without fear of sabotage. John had been promised by his family's enslaver "that he should have the privilege of purchasing them at a very low price" once he had died. Once Weims had determined that Stella had left for England, he continued to raise money and returned home to begin the process of buying his family out of enslavement. When he arrived, however, he found his wife and children in a slave pen, terrified and helpless. In a stunning betrayal, the heirs of the Weimses' deceased master had sold the entire family—mother and seven children—to slave traders. They would probably be separated and enslaved for the rest of their lives.

John Weims was frantic. He was also trapped. Even if he was able to raise the money to pay the exorbitant prices the traders were now demanding, he would have to leave the state to do so. Maryland's restrictive laws required that he, as a free person of color, receive the endorsement of several white men for the privilege of leaving the state and returning.[30] He spent precious time gathering the necessary signatures, and went on to do a remarkable job of fundraising. Still, he came up far short of the high price traders were demanding for his flesh and blood. Desperate, Weims met with Charles Ray again in September, in the hopes that Ray's extensive network might be enlisted in his cause. Ray offered to write to Garnet, both to alert him to what had happened and to see if he might be able to leverage his considerable popularity to fundraise on behalf the Weims family. In that letter, Ray wrote of a father's despair—"we can judge his feelings, but cannot describe them"—and of Weims's efforts to save his family from the auction block. Apparently the traders had offered to sell the man his own wife and youngest child for nine hundred dollars. So far he had been able to raise six hundred, and they needed to somehow make up the balance. The rest of the family—"five boys and a beautiful girl of sixteen," Ray noted laconically, "will have to go." Their only hope was to have friends keep track of whose hands they fell into, and then, with luck, their father could track them down and try to purchase them when further funds had been raised. Things were indeed desperate. Ray's request was straightforward, but it was anything but simple.

"Will you," he asked Garnet, "lay the case before British abolitionists, and solicit a little assistance?"[31]

Delivered just as the family was preparing to leave for a new life, Ray's letter was a twofold shock to the whole household. Stella was "overwhelmed with grief" at the news that her mother and siblings were likely to be lost forever.[32] Garnet reported that her "distress is so great that I fear she will lose her reason."[33] She was not alone. "[A]ll of us are smitten as if by death," Garnet wrote. In fact, it was "worse than death; in the grave, the weary are at rest, the wicked cease from troubling, and the slave is free from his master. . . . O what a world it is! What cruelty, what inhumanity does man show towards his fellows!"[34] The entire family mourned slavery's cruel capacity to once again dismantle the hopes of a peaceful future, even across the ocean.

Worse still, the solution seemed nearly as painful as the problem. Garnet had spent the past two years tirelessly campaigning for a change in the slave economy. Again and again, he had told the English people that it was immoral to spend even the pittance required for sugar in one's tea, because that money would support the cruel slaveowners who produced those goods. Now, his old friend and collaborator Charles Ray wanted him to ask these very same people to pay slaveowners directly—to literally buy slaves from them. It was a conundrum. Garnet, usually so quick to leap into action, was, at least in his initial response to Ray, hesitant. He was planning to leave for Jamaica in two weeks, he told Ray, so "[w]hatever is done is to be done quickly." But whatever it was that should be done, Garnet was not ready to mention. He closed the letter with the noncommittal assertion that "no one will ever have cause to regret that he was instrumental, in the hands of our Heavenly Father, in restoring this unhappy family to each other's society."[35]

Yet Garnet did not remain passive for long. He did not leave for Jamaica on November 1 as he had planned. Unable to bear Stella's grief and distress, he drew upon the fame and goodwill he had built during his two years in Europe and launched a subscription drive to raise money to buy the Weims family away from the slave traders. As he had throughout his time abroad, he counted on the assistance of his friend and colleague Anna Richardson, who eagerly sprung to action. She wrote directly to

Charles Ray, assuring him that "we will not rest til the Weimses are free." Even she was surprised by the amount of interest the case had aroused. Perhaps, she mused, "the masses in this country did not know til *Uncle Tom's Cabin* was in every one's hand, what some of us knew—that these horrible things were of daily occurrence."[36] And indeed, the British public, whether driven by *Uncle Tom's Cabin*'s heartrending depictions of separated families or by the respect they had for Henry Highland Garnet or a combination of both, opened their pocketbooks in short order. By early November, Garnet reported that the fundraising efforts in Newcastle-upon-Tyne, Glasgow, and Edinburgh had raised three hundred pounds in three weeks.[37]

Garnet, of course, refrained from noting the contradiction inherent in leading a fundraising effort that would ultimately line the pockets of greedy slave traders. But there were plenty of others who pointed out that this short-term solution was counterproductive in the long run. "Buying slaves is not anti-slavery business," wrote one commentator in the *Anti-Slavery Advocate*, "for it does nothing to help on the redemption of the race, or the abolition of the system; but leads us away from our proper work."[38] No less than antislavery celebrity Harriet Beecher Stowe—the author of the very *Uncle Tom's Cabin* that had created such a fervor for reuniting families—agreed. Even though she had previously been involved in similar efforts, Stowe now argued that buying slaves from their master was of "doubtful utility." Though well intentioned, such vigorous fundraising ultimately hurt the cause. It was "more than probable," she suggested, "that many masters play upon the sympathies of Northern people to enhance the value of their slaves." And unfortunately, that seemed to be exactly what happened. Even though over one thousand pounds were raised, the seemingly limitless generosity of the British just encouraged those holding Stella's family to raise their prices to still higher levels. The negotiations would drag on for years, with the enslavers walking away with thousands of dollars in their pockets, and at least of two of the children lost to the confusing maze of the domestic slave trade.[39]

As the year came to a close, and Garnet once again prepared to bid farewell to England, he did so overshadowed by his adopted daughter's grief, and with the admonitions of many allies ringing in his ears. Some went so far as to say that Garnet's work on behalf of purchasing the Weims family was a pro-slavery act. "Buying slaves from their masters is continually represented as the true anti-slavery plan," one commenter sniped, "by the most rampant American pro-slavery papers." Advice came in from all sides, all of them taking Garnet to task for his choices. One part of the editorial suggested that the fundraising on behalf of the Weimses actively supported slavery. The second part suggested that Garnet's tireless work on behalf of Free Produce was not only undermined by his fundraising to ransom slaves but was in and of itself a waste of time. There was as big a danger "of our suffering from a plague of larks by the sky falling," the commenter mused, "as there is of slavery being starved out by the common consent of mankind to consume no more slave produce."[40]

Still, the fundraising continued. Finally, in January of 1853, months after his proposed date of departure, Garnet and his family finally boarded a ship bound for Jamaica. This trip, like every other journey Garnet had ever taken, would not be easy. Shortly after their departure, they encountered a fearsome storm. Garnet told friends how a "mighty wave struck our ship on her bows, and carried away her figure-head and breakwater." The ship had been disabled and was probably taking on water. For several hours the passengers "expected to go down every moment."[41] They somehow made it into a safe port in Madeira, Portugal. After some repairs, they took off once again and made it to Jamaica safely.

Once there, Garnet was delighted by what he found. He felt, he told friends, that after "a long life of wandering up and down," he and his family were "at last at home." In what must have been a remarkable sight for someone who had literally had the ground torn away from beneath his feet in former homes, he now could look out on stately grounds allotted to him—three lush acres hedged in by cacti and beautiful trees swaying in the island breezes.[42] For the first time, Henry Highland Garnet looked about him and saw free Black people everywhere. Although Garnet had certainly lived in Black neighborhoods before, he had never lived in a Black community where all were free from the dread of the slave catcher's midnight knock upon the door. He was charmed by his accommodations, his family "greatly and agreeably surprised" with his new parish, which he found to resemble an English country parsonage. There was a white freestone church that he found "large and comfortable." The schoolhouse, too, was in good shape. As inviting as the tropical scenery might have been, Henry and Julia took no time to luxuriate in it. They immediately set to work, and with remarkable results. According to biographer Joel Schor, in their first year in Jamaica, the Garnets revived the day school, doubled attendance at services, and opened a Female Industrial School.[43]

But even in the midst of such activity, among people hungry for his leadership, the ambitious and charismatic Garnet felt like an outsider. As a man who had long enjoyed a playful back and forth with peers, Garnet seemed a bit uncomfortable with the reverence the Jamaicans displayed towards him. He found them "painfully polite," showing a deference that testified to a stark difference in status that Garnet had not anticipated. Because "I am the only Black man in this vicinity in the position of a minister," Garnet realized, "they look upon me as a prodigy." His education placed him in a different caste, even among those who shared his complexion. "Strange to say," he related, the Jamaicans "call me 'buckra' (white) which is certainly a singular title to give *me*."[44] If they found Garnet a bit alien, his first impressions of them returned the favor. It "must be admitted," he wrote, "that this beautiful and fruitful country is in ruins, morally and commercially. God is now settling a long account which he has against the people. Licentiousness prevails to a horrid extent. So you see the missionary has a strong tide to stem."[45] And at least one way he found to stem the tide was to turn his eyes back to the United States.

In August of 1853, eight months after his arrival, Garnet was once again the subject of discussion in New York City papers. He placed an advertisement hoping to recruit "70 colored laborers" to work in Jamaica. In response to those who might wonder why they would want Americans to work in a country already full of laborers, Garnet pointed out that the "Creole is naturally indolent" and seemed to be "destitute of sufficient physical energy to impel them to hard labor." They might easily do "three times the amount of work which they now accomplish," Garnet noted, which would still come up short of "an able bodied American" who "would do four times the amount." In the face of the Jamaican laborer's seeming lethargy, "the planters are anxious to see the example of our people's industry and 'go-ahead' enterprise."[46] Whether it was an internalized sense of national pride or merely homesickness, Garnet felt that the answer to Jamaica's problems could be found in an American work ethic.

His colleagues at home, however, wished that Garnet would focus on America's own problems. Frederick Douglass, commenting on Garnet's advertisement—which he had dutifully republished in his paper before critiquing it—was exasperated by Garnet's call for hard-working people to leave the country. "The kind of colored men Mr. Garnet wants in Jamaica, are like himself, a part of the life-blood of colored America; and we are opposed to its being drained off either to Canada, Jamaica or Liberia." Instead, Douglass insisted, "Mr. Garnet had better come home. He, and men like him, can do more good here than anywhere else in the world."[47] Another commenter in Douglass's paper, the Reverend William H. Bishop, lamented that a "few years ago we could point with complacency to Samuel R. Ward, Henry Highland Garnet, Alexander Crummell, Hosea Easton and others, but death and colonization have removed those great men from amongst us, and we are left to struggle on without their immediate help." It was a combination of "Death, Liberia, and Jamaica that have made sad havoc amongst us in this respect."[48]

By 1855, Douglass was placing the call for Garnet's return at the center of editorials. "We want such men as Ward, and *Garnet*, and Crummell, *at home*. They must come and help us." Those working for the cause needed their "mighty energies to bear upon the redemption of our race, and our whole race, from every species of oppression, irrespective of the form it may assume, or the source whence it may emanate."[49] The situation at home was indeed dire. The Fugitive Slave Act robbed fugitives and abolitionists alike of their peace of mind. In that sorrow, the Garnets had a full share, even as they kept their distance from the United States. As the news trickled in about the ongoing attempts to purchase Stella's family, it became increasingly likely that at least some members of her family would be lost forever. Still worse, as a fugitive herself, Stella would not be able to reunite with her family in the United States at any time in the foreseeable future. She pined for home, even as she knew the pain it would hold for her.

But there would be pain enough for all in Jamaica. In the winter of 1855, a fever took hold of the entire Garnet family. Stella, already worn down from grief, grew more ill by the day. When it became clear that she was near death, Garnet came to her bedside. Sick with the fever himself, he sought to prepare his adopted daughter for her final journey. He came to her bedside and told Stella that "her race had nearly run." After hearing this dire news, Stella paused, drew a breath, and told Garnet, "There is only one thing I wish for in this world—I want to see my mother." Garnet, long separated from those he had known and loved since childhood, felt a deep sympathy with her longing. There was no person present, Garnet declared, "who so well knew, the deep meaning of that expression" as he did. Rather than having found liberty by crossing borders, Garnet shared Stella's sense of grievous loss in exile. He looked upon the dying young woman and saw "on the bed of death, a helpless innocent, a beloved young woman, who by the inhumanity and wickedness" of slaveowners had "been driven from her mother and father." She was, without a "crime or even accusation, exiled from her native land" and lay "dying among strangers," straining to see through the "gathering mists of death" to "far away across the ocean, the loved scenes of her childhood."[50] She died with hope of heaven, Garnet reported, and he thanked those who had raised money to help her family. "May God bless those kind friends in Britain who so nobly contributed toward emancipating that poor slave 'mother' for whose sake her dying daughter only wished to live."[51] Stella died on December 12, 1855. As someone who had experienced violent separation from his own family when New York slave catchers came calling, Garnet was shattered by the tragedy of burying Stella far from a mother she would never see again.

Julia, terrified of losing another child to the fever that had settled in among the family, took their daughter, Mary, and little Henry and returned to the United States, where she would suffer from protracted illness but eventually recover. They would not, it was clear, be returning to Jamaica any time soon. Garnet, alone and ill, turned his sights back to the country he had said he would be happy never to see again. Jamaica might well have been out of reach of the slave traders, but Garnet had come to see himself as an exile, far from childhood friends, far from the fight, and, thus, too far from freedom. Having buried his adopted daughter in Jamaica, far from the grave of his oldest son buried back in New York State, he had painful reason to doubt the colonial promise that one place can be just as good as another. Still suffering from illness himself, Garnet was perhaps worried that he too would die "among strangers" on an island across the ocean from the beloved landmarks of his own New York City childhood. The past had come to claim him once again.

He made plans to return home and did so in March of 1856. It was, he told friend Gerrit Smith, profoundly "cheering" to see the "old faces" and "families" in the "dear native land" he had left behind six years ago. Frederick Douglass gave him a warm welcome, which Garnet found "gratifying in the extreme." In response to Douglass's warmth, Garnet declared, "I give my heart and hand in the good cause."[52] Yet Garnet's heart—like that of the nation he had just returned to—was deeply divided. Even as he basked in the warmth of familiar faces, he still had tentative plans to return to Jamaica. He was not ready to abandon the hope that colonial enterprises might give Black Americans the leverage that would allow them to truly rip up slavery at its roots.

Garnet's sympathy for colonization was not as unpopular among African Americans as it had been when he had left in 1850. By 1854, up to 25 percent of the Black population in Ohio favored emigration, a trend echoed by increasing support in Pennsylvania, Maryland, Washington, DC, and Vermont.[53] Yet among his close friends and colleagues James McCune Smith and Frederick Douglass, the prospects of emigration and colonization were still firmly beneath contempt. As the country drew ever closer to war, and with it the almost unthinkable possibility that the United States would become a truly free nation, Douglass, Smith, and others saw the suggestion that Black people pack up and leave as nothing short of the basest betrayal. Garnet, who, like the fictional hero in Harriet Beecher Stowe's *Uncle Tom's Cabin*, felt drawn to the promise of an African "republic of picked men,"[54] would find himself an exile on the very streets where he had pledged—alongside his dear friends at the New York African Free School—to wage a lifelong battle for freedom.

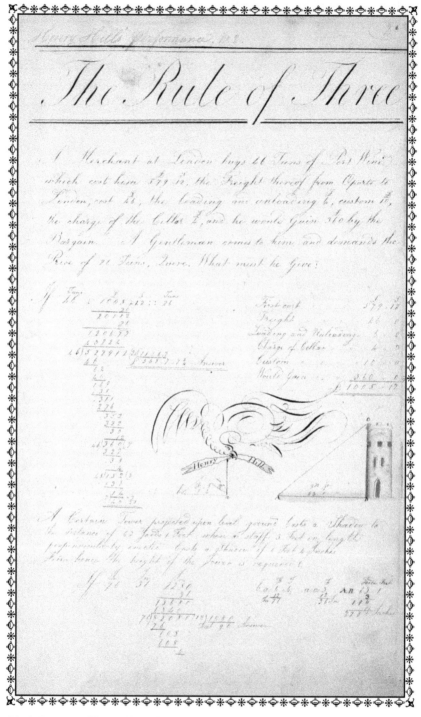

Math Examples, Henry Hill. New-York Historical Society & Museum, New-York African Free-School Records, vol. 4.

CHAPTER 7

Bitter Battles, African Civilization, and John Brown's Body
(CIRCA 1856–1862)

A s part of the curriculum at the New York African Free School in the 1820s and '30s, students were given math problems that invited them to see themselves as merchants trading stocks. These lessons were among the most explicit means of conveying the hope that the children—many of whom, like Henry Highland Garnet and James McCune Smith, were legally the property of others—could enter a world where they not only could own property but also could profit from the exchange of it.

In 1860, Smith, exasperated with Garnet's pessimism, insisted that the future conjured by their schoolboy math problems had come to pass. "Do you ever go to Wall Street?" he asked his old friend and schoolmate. "Have you noticed quite a number of colored youths, neatly dressed, hurrying from bank to bank with vast sums of money in their hands? Do you not know as well as I that it only requires dash and pluck for these young men to rise higher and higher?" Smith's appraisal rendered Black children and Black bank accounts equally ripe for growth in the new decade. He hoped his appeal would bring the wayward Garnet back to a proper alignment with his own youthful dreams, which he urged his friend to remember. "More than a quarter of a century ago," Smith chided, "you and others, among whom I was the humblest, pledged yourselves to devote life and energies to the elevation . . . of the free colored people on this, the soil which gave them birth." As boys, they had promised to keep working at this goal until one of two things happened: the freedom of Black Americans had been achieved, or the world had proved that such a feat would remain forever impossible. "You know," he insisted, "that neither of these things have happened."[1]

James McCune Smith, struggling with increasingly poor health, was desperate for his childhood friend to see that the seeds they had planted so long ago were bearing fruit. For his part, he felt he had stayed true to their youthful pact. Since his return from Glasgow over twenty years previously, the physician had stayed put, dedicating himself to furthering the cause of "colored people, on this, the soil, which gave them birth." As an editor, a counselor, a physician, and a tireless advocate for the Colored Orphan Asylum, Dr. Smith had stayed the course, his feet planted solidly on New York streets, determined that careful, methodical work would, with time, create the results both he and Garnet had pledged as their life's work. As schoolboys, they had been told that colonization held their only future. Their own schoolmaster had been convinced that his students could never truly be Americans. For Smith, the progress of the "colored youths" on Wall Street was powerful evidence that their cause was in fact moving forward. He could not believe that his old friend could not see its progress. For his part, Garnet had seen nothing upon his return to the United States after his extended stay in the United Kingdom and Jamaica that convinced him that any meaningful progress could be made, or that the fight for true freedom could ever be won within the nation's boundaries.

By the time Smith wrote the letter to his friend in 1860, two events had shifted the ground upon which both men had stood. In 1859, their mutual acquaintance John Brown had initiated a failed revolution at Harpers Ferry. In 1858, Henry Highland Garnet had created the African Civilization Society—an organization that shared personnel, lodgings, and—many would argue—goals with the hated American Colonization Society. Even as Garnet rejected the pleas of Smith, he was, in many ways, enacting the lessons of their alma mater even more powerfully than his friend the star student had. Garnet's choice to create the African Civilization Society was deeply influenced by the dual lessons the New York African Free School had provided. At that school both Garnet and

Smith had been trained in the Lancasterian belief that a system—and the pupils trained in that system—could be endlessly reproduced and exported across the globe. From there, it was a small jump to endorsing a colonialist model in which well-trained African Americans could move seamlessly to Africa and reproduce the "civilization" they had acquired in the United States.

Not that Garnet would have called his organization colonizationist—or allowed anyone else to call it that with him in the room. "It has been said that I am a Colonizationist," he cried in front of a rambunctious crowd in Boston. "I am *not* a Colonizationist. Any man that says I am behind my back is an assassin and a coward; any man that says it to my face is a liar, and I stamp the infamous charge upon his forehead! I have hated the sentiments of the American Colonization Society since my childhood."[2] But many in the Black activist community, including James McCune Smith and Frederick Douglass, were largely unconvinced by Garnet's protestations. They found what seemed a full-throated embrace of one of the most pernicious anti-Black forces of the century to be a profound betrayal. Frederick Douglass dismissed Garnet's insistence that he was independent from the American Colonization Society, calling the white colonizationist Benjamin Coates "the real, but not the ostensible head of [Garnet's] African Civilization movement."[3] There was some truth in the accusation. Not only was Coates—a Quaker merchant who had been a longtime proponent of the American Colonization Society—a member of Garnet's African Civilization Society, but the African Civilization Society shared a building (as well as an acronym) with the New York branch of the American Colonization Society.[4] Coates himself would have been inclined to agree with Douglass's assessment that there was little daylight between the aims of the two organizations. "Many consider the African Civilization Society only African colonization under another name," Coates wrote in a letter to R. R. Gurley, "which it really is."[5]

Garnet was able to angrily refuse the title of African colonizationist, even as he literally advocated for setting up an African colony in Yoruba, because he insisted that the difference between emigration and colonization lay, not in the intentions of the settlers themselves but in who was heading the effort. If Black people were in control, he argued, the settlement project could not be called colonizationist. The key distinction, as historian Ousmane Power-Greene has suggested, was "Black agency."[6] Perhaps. The insights of postcolonial scholarship have made it more difficult to overlook the imperial ambitions that undergirded the ACS's belief that Christianity and Americanness were inherently civilizing forces that should be imposed on sovereign people and nations, no matter who led the charge.

Certainly there were distinctions between emigration and colonization. There were key differences between plans made to emigrate to Haiti, or even Canada, in which free Black people would seek to assimilate into the existing cultural and legal structures, and plans, like Garnet's, to "civilize" Africa. The constitution drawn up at the African Civilization Society's inception explicitly set up the organization's object as "the destruction of the African Slave-trade, by the introduction of lawful commerce and trade into Africa." Alongside this work of liberation through commerce, the society sought to bring about "the civilization and Christianization of Africa, and of the descendants of African ancestors in any portion of the earth, wherever dispersed." Yet even as there was an undeniably colonialist echo to the society's call to "civilize" Africa, the constitution also privileged Blackness itself as the basis for the new, powerful nations that Garnet felt sure would rise from this movement. In the end, the organization would promote "Self-Reliance and Self-Government on the principle of an African Nationality," with "the African race being the ruling element of the nation, controlling and directing their own affairs."[7]

For James McCune Smith, the only true hope of self-reliance was to stand rooted to his native soil and invest in the future of African American children. While Garnet had been building a reputation in Europe and Jamaica, Smith had spent his days investing in the health and education of the next generation of African American children, whose accomplishments, he believed, would further demolish the white prejudice that colonization advocates insisted would never dissipate in the United States. And in truth, the progress that the Colored Orphan Asylum had made since its humble beginnings in the 1830s was little short of miraculous. A sturdy four-story brick building on a pleasant parcel of land on Fifth Avenue between Forty-Second and Forty-Fourth Streets, the asylum included spacious play rooms, productive gardens, a bathing room, and at least three classrooms.[8] There was hot and cold running water throughout, and a separate hospital wing. The building was adjacent to the Croton reservoir, supplying ample fresh water, and the grounds supported a robust garden of fruits and vegetables. All these improvements showed Dr. Smith's influence. He had recommended the most hygienic facilities possible, and had worked assiduously to raise funds for their addition to the asylum. The hospital had been a project particularly dear to the physician's heart, created shortly after the cholera epidemic of 1849 that took the lives of many children at the asylum, including Omo, or Henry the Little Bushman, and that had cast its shadow over the city the same year that Smith's own first-born child had become ill.

Thomas Henry Barnes, a young boy who entered the institution in the summer of 1860, recalled that James McCune Smith was considered a resource for Black families in need throughout the city.[9] When Barnes's aunt was desperate to find an education for him and his brother, she went to Dr. Smith, who convinced her to enroll the boys at the asylum because of the excellent educational opportunities it afforded. On the day he arrived, Barnes, who was six years old at the time, did not encounter the asylum as a study in Dickensian gloom but rather recalled fondly how he was "graciously and cordially received, all formalities necessary arranged." During their introductory tour, the brothers would have noted that both Black and white women were responsible for supervising the children, and that the curriculum included a healthy dose of the arts. The asylum's choir—featuring both boys and girls—was often invited to perform at local schools and churches. Barnes's recollections reveal that the children felt empowered to create their own curriculum, and that they sometimes resisted the assignments imposed by some teachers. They formed secret societies and engaged in "funny, thrilling episodes to escape detection."[10]

James McCune Smith's time with the asylum children probably reminded him of his own school days on many accounts, but never more vividly than on performance days. If anything, such performances were more popular in the 1860s than they had been when Smith stood in front of NYAFS gatherings in the 1820s. Crowds for the Colored Orphan Asylum productions filled spaces as large and grand as the Great Hall in the Cooper Institute, which could seat well over a thousand people, and had hosted luminaries including Abraham Lincoln. While we know very little about how Smith and his classmates felt about performance days in the 1820s, Thomas Barnes's memoir relates that he found asylum events a heady mix of excitement and terror. Barnes recalled one performance at the Cooper Institute in which a group of boys were set to perform a complicated skit involving four different speaking parts. The first boy stood on stage, beginning a speech that the second student was supposed to interrupt. However, that second student, John Doran, took one look at the "great throng of expectant faces, took violent stage fright and would not go." The teachers were aghast. While the first boy stood, forlorn, on stage, repeating his single line, the adults pleaded with Doran to head on to the stage and read his part. It did no good. Finally, in a panic, the teachers "resorted to force, but Doran being a stout young lad, concluded that it would be a fight to the finish" and gave as good as he got. The audience, a bit confused by the sight of one child repeating the same line over and over while hearing a huge commotion behind the curtain, seemed to decide that it "was all in the play" and applauded heartily.[11]

Before and after such galas, James McCune Smith was a constant presence in the lives of these children, and did not hesitate to push them to what he felt was their furthest potential. He took particular interest in their educations as well as their health. One young student was heartily enjoying the relaxing curriculum afforded to him in the hospital (apparently a nice young teacher would read stories to the invalids). Understandably, the boy resisted Dr. Smith's medical opinion that he was ready to return to regular classes, insisting that he still did not feel well. The doctor found the perfect remedy. "Give Thomas a dose of cod liver oil every night and morning," he told the attendants. "Perhaps he will prefer that to school." The youth was back in class after the second dose.

Having spent so many of his days tending to the growth and development of New York City's Black youth, Dr. Smith—always a believer in the power of evidence to shape the arc of history—could not understand why his friend Garnet did not share his optimism. Garnet's insistence that the best future available for Black children lay outside the borders of the United States stood as a sharp rebuke to the work Smith had been doing for the past three decades. It was also, in Smith's opinion, a rebuke to Garnet's own youthful promises, a rejection of Garnet's own inspirational words of 1843, in which he had urged his fellow African Americans to "arise, arise!" to "strike for your lives and liberties."

Smith was not alone in wondering how, at the very moment when many of his former rivals were finally ready to act on the bold vision articulated in the "Address," Garnet himself seemed ready to abandon the fight. By the mid-1850s, Garnet's early calls for rebellion—once shunned as too incendiary—were increasingly accepted as the only way forward. By 1856, even the reserved James McCune Smith had called for physical—as well as political—resistance to slave power. "Our freedom must be won," he insisted, "and the sooner we wake up to the fact, the better." It was better, Smith now acknowledged, to follow in the footsteps of Nat Turner and Denmark Vesey than to hope to win over the hearts and minds of oppressors through logic or empathy. "They will never recognize our manhood," Smith realized, "until we knock them down a time or two; then they will hug us as men and as brethren." Tired of the endless debating around the alleged superiority found in cranial specimens, Smith had finally embraced a different approach to white skulls. "That holy love of human brotherhood which fills our hearts and fires our imagination," he lamented, "cannot get through the—in this respect—thick skulls of the Caucasian, unless beaten into them."[12]

John Brown, who had been inspired by Garnet's early philosophy, initiated a history-making plan to rain violence down upon slaveholders' "thick skulls."[13] Having read Garnet's fiery 1843 "Address to the Slaves of the United States," Brown felt sure that slaves all over the nation would rise up, if only given the proper opportunity.[14] Brown had met Garnet earlier, and the two men had clearly been impressed with each other. It was Garnet, along with his friend J. W. Loguen, who had introduced Frederick Douglass to Brown.[15] "In speaking of [Brown] their voices would drop to a whisper," Douglass recalled, "and what they said of him made me very eager to see and to know him."[16] As historian John Stauffer has chronicled, Douglass, along with James McCune Smith and Garnet's longtime friend Gerrit Smith, all did get to know John Brown. All four men were invested—to varying degrees—in Brown's growing determination to throw a spark into the tinderbox of slavery and consume the nation in cleansing violence.[17] In fact, it was during a two-week stay with Frederick Douglass at his home in Rochester that Brown wrote his "Provisional Constitution," a document Douglass would keep in his possession until the end of his days.[18]

Brown had long felt that Garnet was a natural ally, and earnestly lobbied him to enlist in the uprising he had hoped to initiate.[19] In a momentous meeting, Brown laid out his plan for nothing short of a nationwide revolution to the man who had, in 1843, urged his enslaved brethren to "awake" and heed that "millions of voices are calling" them to "arise from the dust."[20] After laying out his plans for violent rebellion, Brown turned to his visitor. "Mr. Garnet," he asked, "what do you think of it?" Garnet paused and looked at John Brown. "Sir," he replied, "the time has not come yet for the success of such a movement." Garnet worried that the spark Brown hoped to create simply would not ignite a rebellion among the enslaved. Without reliable forms of communication, there was no way to create the necessary organization. But it was not just the lack of information in the South that was the problem. Garnet insisted that "our people in the North are not prepared to assist in such a movement, in consequence of the prejudice that shuts them out from both the means and the intelligence necessary."[21] In other words, he did not believe that either his northern allies or his enslaved compatriots could spontaneously rise to create the sort of widespread change Brown hoped for. Frederick Douglass also declined to actively participate in the raid.

Undeterred, Brown engaged in his rash plan. On October 16, 1859, he led a small but heavily armed band to attack the US military arsenal at Harpers Ferry, Virginia. He had hoped that the raid would prove only the first stage in a viral rebellion that would create a stronghold of self-emancipated slaves in the mountains of Maryland and Virginia. As Garnet predicted, many local people did not know of the coming rebellion. The flame that Brown had hoped would engulf the South sputtered out: there was no mass uprising. After a series of mishaps led to Brown's capture on October 18, he faced trial on the charges of treason against the Commonwealth of Virginia, multiple first-degree murders, and inciting an insurrection. The Virginian jury, after deliberating for only forty-five minutes, came back with a guilty verdict on all counts. Brown was sentenced to death.

It is difficult to overstate the effect Brown's raid on Harpers Ferry had on the nation.[22] The attack was the leading story in papers throughout both the North and the South. In the eyes of both nineteenth-century contemporaries and twenty-first-century historians, Brown's actions were a tipping point, speeding the momentum with which the nation would dissolve into bloody conflict. For slavers, the prospect of armed abolitionists invading the South to set enslaved people free was terrifying. The South, always already fearful of slave rebellions, now cast Brown's actions as part of a broad conspiracy supported by the highest realms of power in the North.[23] For their part, many in the North were anxious to maintain peace at any cost, and were more than willing to help root out the rebellion that Brown had fomented among his fellow abolitionists. No one suspected of collaborating with Brown was safe, no matter where they lived. Reporters descended on Gerrit Smith's town of Petersboro, where Henry Highland Garnet had spent many pleasant evenings with his good friend. Authorities were determined to find the evidence that would conclusively prove the collaboration between John Brown and Gerrit Smith that everyone was sure had taken place. The whole town was on edge, with neighbors creating a makeshift watch to protect against "a Southern mob" that might carry Gerrit Smith off in the night.[24] And he was not the only one in danger. Governor Wise of Virginia, armed with no more evidence than a written dinner invitation Frederick Douglass had extended to John Brown, charged Douglass with "murder, robbery, and inciting civil insurrection in the state of Virginia."[25] Douglass beat a hasty retreat to Canada, for he almost certainly would have been arrested if he had remained in Rochester.

Henry Highland Garnet's association with John Brown and his well-earned reputation as a firebrand put him at considerable risk. He knew all too well how quickly the fears of white people could erupt into life-threatening violence. As he had done so often in his career, Garnet turned to the women around him for strength to wade into the fight. At a time when many of his compatriots were lying low, Julia helped Henry to organize supporters, and made public assertions of their loyalty to Brown and his cause. She gathered Black women at the Garnet house in the weeks leading up to Brown's execution day to commiserate and to strategize. Julia almost certainly helped to craft a collective letter from the women of Shiloh Church that called John Brown "our honored and dearly-loved brother." While the letter was framed as one group of wives and mothers extending sympathy to John Brown's soon-to-be widow Mary, there was steely resolve underlying the condolences. Although these Black women were well aware of their status as "poor and despised people," they were determined to exert political pressure on the status quo. "We intend by God's help," they told Mary Brown, "to organize in every Free State, and in every colored church, a band of sisters" that would further the cause for which Brown had given his life.[26]

On the tense day of John Brown's execution in Virginia, over a thousand soldiers stood, stony-faced, determined to ensure that no one interfered with the execution. For days, authorities had been monitoring incoming train travel, denying passage to anyone considered suspicious. As Brown was led to the scaffold, soldiers held onlookers off at the end of a bayonet. Governor Wise was not about to let any show of unrest spoil his demonstration of state power.[27] On that same day in New York City, Henry Highland Garnet planned to gather his congregation at Shiloh Church to mourn John Brown, and to praise his radical action. Before the public eulogy planned at the church at midnight, Henry and Julia held a gathering at their house at 4:00 p.m., "attended chiefly by ladies," where everyone prayed for John Brown and the cause they shared with him.[28] As midnight approached, and with it the long-dreaded hour, Garnet climbed the pulpit and looked out at his congregation. He saw their grief, and shared their anxiety about the storm everyone could feel gathering about them. Once he began speaking, however, it became clear that Garnet was not there to try to calm the blowing winds of unrest, but to fan them further. He made no conciliatory gestures, but instead held John Brown up as an unequivocal hero.

In the middle of the night, before a congregation of hundreds, Henry Highland Garnet was once again the fiery orator who urged uprising, consequences be damned. He told the emotional crowd that it was because of "the ungodly conduct of the slaveholder" that "there was any necessity for shedding blood at all, and therefore, upon the heads of these men must rest every drop of blood that has been shed." Even as Brown was being executed for rebellion and murder, Garnet insisted that neither accusation was true. Brown, far from a murderer, was a patriot: "If John Brown was wrong in trying to secure liberty to the oppressed," he declared, "then George Washington was wrong in giving liberty to this continent." After likening the man who had sought to spark a national conflagration over slavery to the father of the country, Garnet went on to say that Black people should not distance themselves from Brown's actions, but rather applaud them. John Brown's actions were, in short, a "blessing to the slaves." Their "only regret should be that the movement had failed."[29] He urged the congregation to emulate Brown, and to "prefer liberty to death" in the continued pursuit of freedom for all Black people.[30]

Howls of protest at Garnet's bold words reverberated in pro-slavery newspapers across the nation. Much as James McCune Smith and Douglass had done at the Radical Abolitionist Party convention, Garnet had taken it upon himself to recast the nation's founding as a lesson in abolitionist bravery. A commentator in Houston sputtered at the audacity of associating "the name of George Washington . . . in a Christian pulpit with a cut throat traitor" like Brown. Garnet's sermon was cited as yet another reason the nation was doomed to split apart. For southerners, preachers like Garnet "filling the pulpits of New England and New York with rant about [Brown], may make the union of these States an annoyance and a vexation too great for endurance."[31] Garnet's defiant eloquence had, once again, placed him in the crosshairs of white anger.

James McCune Smith, always more wary of the spotlight, took a quieter approach to the furor that followed Brown's execution. Although he had been an associate of Brown's, there were no official accusations hurled his way. While his own public response to Brown was muted, he might well have had some hand in the inclusion of the uncharacteristically feisty entry of a teenage admirer of Brown's raid, whose words were published in the Colored Orphan Asylum's twenty-third annual report. Anna Marie Piner, a thirteen-year-old girl who had been recently indentured in Philadelphia, wrote a letter to "her dear young friends" with her opinion of John Brown's raid. The Colored Orphan Asylum reports were usually scrupulously devoid of political material, for a variety of reasons. To begin with, the female managers of the asylum were already assuming a more public role than was generally permissible for respectable women. If they shifted their message from childcare to political agitation, they jeopardized both funding for the asylum and their reputations. Further, many of the asylum's male benefactors were sympathetic to colonization, so the institution had to thread a very narrow needle.[32] The asylum might have had no official opinion about the slavery debate, but as Anna Marie Piner's letter home indicates, the children who lived there certainly did. Taking on the "exciting topic of the day," Anna Marie asked her compatriots, "Do you think it was wise for him to lay down his life for these slaves?" Her only critique of Brown was that he did not go far enough. "Why did not he do what he intended and been done with it?" she wanted to know. Speaking of John Brown's botched escape plan, Anna Marie declared that "he ought not to let the train [go] on." Then "he could have done what he wanted and fled to the mountains."[33]

Even as he kept a relatively low profile, James McCune Smith, who had always admired Garnet's defiant courage, was probably thrilled to read his old friend's rebellious praise for John Brown. But if he had thought that Garnet's bold speech meant that he had declared himself ready to dig in and fight on American soil, he would soon be newly disappointed. John Brown notwithstanding, Garnet showed no sign of abandoning the African Civilization Society that he had created and continued to promote as the decade drew to a close. The city's abolitionist community was up in arms—for many, including James McCune Smith, the African Civilization Society was a travesty and a betrayal to the cause. On an April night in 1860, the city's Black population gathered to debate Garnet's intentions. To be exact, the event announcement asked "the colored people of New York and the vicinity" to "pass judgment" upon the African Civilization Society, founded and still championed by

Henry Highland Garnet. A group of notable community members were there, including Ransom F. Wake, who had taught at the African Free School and had been among the dignitaries gathered to welcome the young James McCune Smith back to the United States. Charles B. Ray, who had worked so closely with Garnet to free the Weims family, was also in attendance. Both men, along with many others, signed a statement decrying the African Civilization Society as "a co-worker in the ranks of our enemies."[34] One of the loudest voices of opposition was George Downing. In 1841, as a young man, Downing had stood in the Philomethan Hall alongside Henry Highland Garnet, as they practiced poetry and dialogues together as members of the Phoenix Society in New York.[35] Now, Downing drew on his carefully honed oratorical skills to call Garnet a traitor for his alleged embrace of the colonizationist cause.

According to the *New-York Daily Tribune*, the public meeting was packed to the rafters, with up to twelve hundred people in attendance, divided fairly equally between detractors and supporters of Garnet's African Civilization Society. Downing began the meeting by reading condemnations of Garnet's endeavor. It must have been particularly painful for the proud Garnet to stand and listen to a letter from his old friend Gerrit Smith—with whom Garnet and his family had lived in Petersboro for weeks at a time—read as evidence against him. In front of over a thousand people in his home town, Garnet was subjected to hearing someone read Gerrit Smith's declaration that he was "most decidedly opposed to the Society" that Garnet had founded. Finally, at the end of his patience, Garnet demanded that another letter be read that would answer these criticisms. Many women in the audience—almost certainly joined by Julia Garnet—"were unanimous" in their support of Garnet, chanting, "The letter! The letter!" Downing sought to shut down the response, simply stating that the letter was unavailable, and then moved to proceed with the public pillorying of Garnet and the ACS. Garnet, not about to be so easily dismissed, sought to take the floor by force, initiating a raucous struggle. "The excitement rose to such a height that [Garnet] was surrounded by those opposed to him, whereupon his friends also came up and some violent demonstrations were made." The crowd was quick to respond to the heated exchange, egging the two men on, shouting, "Go in Garnet!" or "Downing!" Peace was eventually restored, but not for long. Once the hall was quiet enough for speakers to be heard once again, Downing called the African Civilization Society "an auxiliary to the Negro Hating Colonization Society" and called Garnet "a convicted liar." Garnet lunged at Downing, the lights were turned off, and the entire gathering was ushered outside, where "threats of violence" accompanied the crowd's slow dispersal.[36]

James McCune Smith had not attended that particular meeting, it seems, but he was more than willing to add his voice to the chorus condemning Garnet for his unrepentant championing of the African Civilization Society and, later, for his work as an agent advocating Haitian immigration.[37] Dr. Smith alternately tried flattery and accusation to sway his old school friend from a path he considered widely dangerous and personally hurtful. How, he lamented, could "our Henry Highland Garnet, an acknowledged leader among us, long known, well tried through many a gallant fight, in this our present hour . . . accept an agency to drive us out—for you will not lead—from our chosen field of battle!" Smith felt betrayed by Garnet's decision to use his eloquence to give "aid and comfort" to the "devilishness" of telling Black people to leave "the white man's country." He decried the abuse of Garnet's electrifying charisma to trick his community into believing that they must "desert our homes, our duties, our destinies!" Moving in for the kill, Smith declared that Garnet made his choices solely in pursuit of either money or fame. Garnet's sudden embrace of Haiti as a new site of emigration was motivated, Smith declared, by salary rather than philosophy. It was "filthy lucre" rather than "reasoning" that had brought about Garnet's "call" to promote this new venue for emigration.[38]

Garnet was deeply hurt by his schoolmate's accusation that his life's work had all somehow been one long pursuit of money, and he hit back hard. Stung by the implicit accusation that he was cravenly submitting himself to the colonizationist agenda, Garnet reminded his friend that he, along with Smith, had had to fight "from [the] Mulberry street school-house to the City Hall Park, sprinkling our hot young blood along the streets of New-York" just to get to school. How then, could Smith, of all people, accuse him of cowardice? "You know," he told Smith, "that I have never from that day to this . . . quailed before an oppressor of my people." It was his old friend the doctor, he insisted, who had forgotten where he had come from, and who greedily hung onto wealth, refusing to return it to the communities he was supposedly protecting from Garnet's siren song of desertion. Garnet recounted a story in which "an Irishman pointed out a beautiful mansion currently under construction" on Sixth Avenue. The mansion in question was James McCune Smith's. "I looked upon it," Garnet wrote, and "felt proud of the success of my early friend." But that pride soon turned to shame as he "looked in vain to discover a dark face at work." According to Garnet, James McCune Smith had refused to hire Black workers. It was the rich doctor, Garnet suggested, not the hard-working minister, who was the real mercenary. "And you anti-emigrationists, Dr. Smith," he sneered, "are no better than their hard-hearted white brethren. You likewise 'do not employ niggers.'"[39] Perhaps, Garnet implied, Smith thought his money would render him white, and therefore safe from the trials that Black people had to face on American soil. In Garnet's eyes, it was Smith who had betrayed their schoolboy pact to fight for equality. "Your conduct in this matter," he wrote to his old schoolmate, "is perfectly consistent with Dr. Smith, the autocrat of the West Broadway drug shop of 1861—but it is very unlike James M'Cune Smith thirty-five years ago."[40]

The strife that tore apart these two schoolboy friends was emblematic of an ever-widening division over the future of Black Americans. These widening fault lines would soon tear the nation itself in two. As the United States moved closer to war, everyone would be asked to choose between two different visions of a national future. In one, America could grow—perhaps slowly—into a promised maturity that would leave slavery behind. Or, as the South insisted, time could be brought to a standstill, or at least be made to wander around the same spot without perceptible change. On April 12, 1861, the months of threats and counterthreats finally came to a head when Confederate guns fired on Fort Sumter, an act that historians have come to designate the first salvo of the Civil War.

The war offered a new hope for the emancipation he had been fighting all his life to achieve, but Henry Highland Garnet still felt that the future lay across the Atlantic. He set plans into motion to return to Britain once again to raise funds for his African Civilization Society's plan to settle in Africa.[41] Ironically, even as he seemed to be turning his back on the fight for Black people to inhabit the role of full American citizens, on the way out he struck a blow for African American citizenship by insisting he be identified as a US citizen on his passport. Although Black people had received passports in the past, the documents would usually identify the person as "dark" in complexion, thus sidestepping the question of the person's race or, more importantly, whether someone of that race could carry a government-issued document that declared him or her a citizen of the United States. The question had only become more fraught since the 1857 Dred Scott decision, in which Judge Taney had read the opinion famously declaring that the "free negro of the African race, whose ancestors were brought to this country and sold as slaves," could never be a citizen "within the meaning of the Constitution of the United States." Because of this permanent, irrevocable noncitizen status, the Court declared, an African American had "no rights which the white man was bound to respect."[42] So when Garnet demanded, in 1860, to have his name affixed to a passport, he wanted to make a statement. He insisted that the passport list him *both* as Black and as a citizen. "That point had to be tested," Garnet said, so he might as well "do it at once and let color assume its rightful place." Some time later, US Secretary of State Seward signed the paperwork asserting that a Black man, Henry Highland Garnet, was a United States citizen. It was a stunning public rebuke of the Supreme Court decision. "What will become of Judge Taney," jeered one newspaper correspondent, "when he hears this?"[43]

Henry once again took leave of Julia, whose leadership in the community was largely acknowledged as one reason why Garnet could be an effective emissary abroad.[44] Still, there were painful echoes of his earlier trip. Once again, he was leaving with the excoriations of friends and fellow abolitionists ringing in his ears. Thoughts of what had befallen his family—the loss of his young son—on his first transatlantic journey also seemed to fill his thoughts. Now, writing home ten years later, Garnet seemed transfixed by the plight of another child, dying on an ocean voyage with his heartbroken father. The child, about two years of age, had just lost his mother, and his father with an "aching heart, was on his way back to his native England with his motherless babes." Tragically, the toddler died during the passage home. Garnet reported that the grief-stricken father begged the crew not to cast the child into the sea in a winding sheet, as was the custom, but to instead fashion a coffin for him. They did so, and the entire ship—crew and passengers—gathered for the burial at sea. Garnet stood among them, praying along with the "solemn burial services of the church of England." When the service was over, the board bearing the tiny coffin was tilted towards the sea. "A little splash was heard, and the last remains of the young voyager disappeared in a moment." "Just then," he told Julia, "the sea sent up one of his awful and terrible wails which no mortal can describe, and the foam of his billows seemed to spread a white pall over the tombless grave." Always the minister, Garnet took comfort in the vision of a place and time beyond earthly cruelties. "But the sea shall give up its dead, and they that are in their graves shall hear the voice of God, and come forth." Perhaps thinking of his own lost little one, he found himself imagining "how sweet . . . that heaven [would be] to each!"[45]

Yet, even as Garnet carried the weight of past griefs with him, much was different about this journey. On his initial trip over, Garnet had been confined to his cabin to eat a lonely dinner each night, so that his presence would not offend racist American passengers in the dining room. "How changed now," he remarked to Julia in a letter. After checking into a spacious first-class room, he took his place in the dining room, each evening, where he was seated between "two young American gentlemen." The dinners passed pleasantly. He half-jokingly reported to his wife that he "did not receive a look, or hear a word during the whole voyage, that grated upon my very sensitive feelings."[46]

While Garnet's explicit goal was to raise money for the controversial—and some would say counterproductive—African Civilization Society, his charisma and eloquence were still great assets in the American antislavery cause. Frederick Douglass, who had openly called Garnet an "enemy" for deserting American soil back in 1850, had, in 1861, sent his longtime rival off with "warmest regards and full confidence" in his powers of persuasion. Although Douglass lamented that Garnet was leaving the United States "at a critical period," he knew well that the famous

orator "can do much for us in Great Britain." Now that war had broken
out, the support of the British could well make the difference between
success or failure. "The influence of that country," Douglass acknowledged, was "of vast importance to the regular American Government
and to the slaveholding rebels." Douglass felt sure that Garnet's "color,
as well as his high character, will give him influence . . . and enable him
to battle successfully" with those who sought to "create sympathy with
Southern slaveholders."[47]

The pull of sympathy with southern slaveholders was not simply an
aesthetic or political choice for the working-class people of Liverpool,
Manchester, and Birmingham, who were already suffering the effects
of what would come to be called the cotton famine. The South had initially withheld commercial trade with England in the hopes of forcing
England to recognize the Confederacy as a sovereign nation. By the
time the Confederacy rethought that strategy, the northern blockade of
the South's ports was well in place. The effects were devastating. When
Garnet visited Birmingham in the fall of 1861, the working people there
were suffering mightily from the blow the sudden lack of cotton had
dealt to their livelihoods. He saw both the danger and the possibility
in the calamity that had befallen British textile workers—here was a
chance for another cotton market to arise from the ashes. He attended a
meeting called "for the purpose of considering the effects of the cotton
famine on Manchester and Birmingham industries, the best mode of
procuring a supply of cotton, and the opportunity the crisis affords of an-
nihilating the slave-trade by establishing the cotton industry in Africa."[48]
As the world economy shifted on its axis, Garnet sought to place Africa
in a position to ride the changing tide.

Cotton had caused untold suffering, God knew, but now, Garnet
hoped, it would provide a form of both financial and cultural redemption
for those who had been the victims of centuries of theft. Rather than
the erasure of history that many thought colonization would promise,
Garnet had come to believe that colonial investment both would make
the past visible and would make amends for the wrongs that past contained. He knew that he "would be pardoned in saying that England
owes a great debt to Africa," Garnet told the crowd in Birmingham. He

was "glad that she had begun to think about paying it."[49] There was some justice in the accusations that Garnet's African Civilization Society had too much in common with the white-run American Colonization Society, but Garnet had a vision of colonization that differed sharply on one key point: where much of the white energy around African colonization sought to erase the cruelties of enslavement by removing the evidence, so to speak, Garnet saw the move to African nations and colonies as a form of reparations. By making them centers of industry, and by placing the means of production in the hands of Black people, Garnet sought to put needed resources—and the power that inevitably accompanied them—in the hands of the descendants of slaves. He reminded the Birmingham audience that "every pound of cotton that came from America was fanned by the sights, wet with the tears, and stained with the blood of slaves." Black people had "enriched the commerce, enlivened the trade, contributed to the comforts, and administered to the luxury of England." In the past, the "soil of Africa . . . had been the theatre upon which many of Britain's sons had enacted the worst of crimes." Now, surely, "a great Christian people should hasten to make compensation." The audience cried out their agreement.[50]

In the desperate early days of the Civil War, the advocacy of Garnet and other abolitionists had a powerful effect. Although there was a small but vocal minority who argued that Britain's future depended on the success of the Confederacy, the nation held fast in support of the Union, even at the cost of considerable hardship to its own citizens. That support would be instrumental in the North's eventual victory, and the emancipation that victory would bring about. After the war ended, part of Garnet's global vision would be realized: there would be a profound shift in the loci of cotton production, and vast new markets would be opened. Tragically, that shift would not provide a form of reparations towards those populations that had been ravaged by the Atlantic slave trade, but would instead result in a different version of theft. Imperial control over Africa would intensify over the next century, to the great detriment of African peoples.[51]

Garnet returned to New York City once again at the end of 1861, amidst disheartening war news, massive uncertainty, and lingering hostility from many of his colleagues. He also faced considerable financial difficulty, as he had been temporarily stripped of his pastoral duties. Shortly before his departure for Britain, Garnet had been informed by the board of his beloved Shiloh Church that his services would no longer be needed. Earlier that year, James McCune Smith had accused Garnet of seeing his work at Shiloh as a means to personally "shine," by garnering the accolades of reporters from the "*New York Herald*, and *Tribune*, and *Times*." It was true that Garnet had embraced the fame that his prominent post had brought him. Some of the top journalists in the city had come to hear Garnet speak at Shiloh and marvel at the "electric current" his eloquence could generate.[52] Yet, even as the press thrilled to Garnet's eloquence, the American Missionary Association had grown exasperated with Garnet's ambition, and the travel schedule that accompanied it. They had begun to pull back their support of Garnet's position at Shiloh in the fall of 1859.[53] Now, in the winter of 1861–1862, Garnet was back in New York after an overseas trip that had been successful in some respects but had certainly fallen short of the goal of fully funding the African Civilization Society's next steps. In January, shortly after Garnet's return, the board of trustees had held a meeting seeking to drastically reduce his salary.[54] Unsure of how long he could hold on to his position as pastor, Garnet felt cast adrift once again, with no concrete plans about what to do next.

At about 10:00 one bitter cold night in February 1862, Garnet heard a commotion outside of his home on 174 West Thirtieth Street. Surely, he had experienced too many traumatic invasions not to feel some trepidation at the sound of a crowd jostling outside his door. Perhaps the group outside were slave catchers bent on retrieving "property," or rioters enraged by the fact that Black people lived among them. Upon approaching the entrance, Garnet was surprised to hear a boisterous rendition of "John Brown's Body." Someone was ringing his doorbell in tune with the song. He opened the door, to be nearly knocked over by a "joyful crowd." They quickly filled every room in the house. The ladies in the group, looking for Julia and not seeing her, took it upon themselves to retrieve her "by genteel force" from her bed to join the festivities.

And indeed, the crowd had come to be festive. Once the couple gathered themselves, the group—who had apparently been organizing this surprise visit for some time—began to unburden themselves of the baskets and bundles they had brought with them as gifts. There was an abundance of food—mutton, ham, as well as a variety of sweets, tea, and coffee. People also brought cash donations to help the Garnets through this time of financial difficulty. They also, it soon became clear, brought an intention to pay homage to the finest orator many of them had ever heard. Several people gave speeches, including at least one woman, all praising the couple for their strength and leadership. The gathering had apparently drawn congregants from churches all over New York City, but it had been organized by members of the Shiloh congregation. In spite of the board's previous complaints that Garnet had been too restless—too prone to travel—to fulfill his duties as pastor, the crowd uniformly insisted that Garnet was the only man they wanted to lead them.[55] One and all, they "pledged themselves to stand by their pastor, and hold up his hands." Henry Highland Garnet, they affirmed, had come home. They would fight to the end to keep him there.[56]

Eagle/Hail Columbia, unknown artist. New-York Historical Society & Museum, New-York African Free-School Records, vol. 4.

CHAPTER 8

The War's End and the Nation's Future
(CIRCA 1862–1865)

O N a May afternoon in 1862, Henry Highland Garnet looked out
from his platform at the thousands of people who had gathered at
the grand Cooper Institute and took a deep breath. He had barely slept
the night before and had been in front of hundreds of people since 5:00
that morning, leading an overflow crowd in prayer at Shiloh Church.
Now, in the afternoon, he stood in Cooper Institute's Great Hall—one of
the grandest structures in the city—as the building reverberated around
him with the low hum of hundreds upon hundreds of Black people who
had come to celebrate. As far as the eye could see, there were brown faces.
Many people had come from hundreds of miles away, all waving "snow-
white handkerchiefs." It was an unprecedented sight, one that, according
to newspaper reports, had an effect that "was electric upon those who
occupied the platform."[1]

Alongside Garnet on that energized platform were several men who
had known each other since their days as children at the New York
African Free School. The dais served as a veritable reunion of friends who,
in recent years, had strayed so far from their childhood intimacy. Patrick
Reason, a former NYAFS student and now a nationally renowned artist
and engraver, sat beside Garnet, enjoying the spectacular view. James
McCune Smith was there, eager to celebrate the day with his old friend,
even as they still sharply disagreed over Garnet's refusal to relinquish

his support for African colonization. And even George T. Downing, the former schoolmate who had nearly come to blows with Garnet at a bitter public debate over Garnet's support of the African Civilization Society, was there. On this day at least, there was no hint of the anger that had plagued their interactions for the past two years.

The occasion that had brought these disparate friends together was a hopeful one. Just a few weeks earlier, Abraham Lincoln had taken a step towards a goal few had hoped to see realized in their lifetimes. On April 14, 1862, Lincoln had signed the District of Columbia Emancipation Act, which had effectively freed all enslaved people in the nation's capital. It was far from an unambiguous success. The government paid the slaveowners for their "property," so the enslavers still profited from, rather than suffered for, their crimes. But still, the president had summarily ended slavery in the nation's capital, an act of profoundly hopeful symbolism. America, it now seemed, might not forever remain a slave nation. As George T. Downing declared, "The dark days of slavery were now vanished." African Americans now, at long last, "could rely on justice and law."[2]

Since he was nine years old, Garnet had spent every minute on US soil looking over his shoulder in fear of an approaching slave catcher, who would have the laws of the United States and the flag that symbolized those laws as validation of his cruel work. After this act of emancipation, Garnet felt he could finally see national symbols as signs of refuge. He directed the crowd to look up at the huge flag flying over the proceedings. America's shameful role as a slave society, Garnet told them, was now replaced by a "new beauty which the Stars and Stripes now assumed before all the nations of the earth." This nation was now *their* nation. Garnet urged his community to "be ready to answer the call of their country" and to work on behalf of "the establishment of Human Liberty." For him, at least at this moment, that work demanded keeping one's feet planted squarely on American soil. Even as he still held the title of the president of the African Civilization Society, Garnet stood at the podium and decried the "folly of entertaining the slightest thought of colonizing the emancipated slaves." Garnet looked out at the sea of faces in front of him and proposed three cheers for some of the very entities that had so long defined slavery as legal and Black people as less than human. He asked the crowd to cheer "the Union, the President, the Congress, and John Brown." The response was deafening, shaking the very walls.

James McCune Smith, who had always argued that progress was possible for Black people in the United States, was ready to see this first act of emancipation as the death knell of slavery itself. When he assumed the podium, he analyzed the day, as he often did, with a scientist's attention to the evidence before him. Examining the Emancipation Act, the physician performed a rhetorical autopsy on the very institution of slavery. They could now speak definitively, he suggested, of the "fallen plans and purposes of the slaveholder." Those plans had failed, and the institution was mortally wounded, if not already dead. Finally, it seemed the advancement he had long sought to document was now evident for all to see, and he urged the crowd to rejoice in "the rising hopes of the people who love good government."[3]

Even as everyone on stage saw this first emancipation document as a turning point so hopeful that thinking of colonization was mere "folly," even as thousands of Black people stood in the streets to cheer the American flag as the emblem of a home they could finally claim for themselves, that very document embraced colonization as the most viable future for African Americans. The DC Emancipation Act not only freed the enslaved people in Washington, DC, by paying out their former owners; it also appropriated one hundred thousand dollars for expelling those former slaves from the nation altogether.

When, a few months later, Lincoln signed a proclamation freeing all enslaved people in army custody, he designated even more money for a plan designed to expel them from the nation's borders. The sum of five hundred thousand dollars was set aside to aid in a colonization effort.[4] In the months leading up to the signing of the famous 1863 Emancipation Proclamation, Lincoln sought an audience with Black leaders in Washington, DC, to generate enthusiasm for a mass exportation plan. He brought these men to the White House, it seemed, not to gather their advice but to inform them of their fate. It is unclear why these particular individuals were chosen as the delegation, but judging by the meeting transcript, it seems that Lincoln had little conception of who they were, or even whether they were free or enslaved.[5] "You are here freemen, I suppose," he said to the assembled group, apparently not waiting for a reply. "Perhaps you have long been free, or all your lives." Their legal status mattered less to Lincoln than their racial status. His view on this count differed little from the view of the colonizationists that had shaped the curriculum at the New York African Free School: racial difference short-circuited any possibility for progress that time or education might otherwise enable. "You and we are different races," Lincoln said. "We have between us a broader difference than exists between almost any other two races. Whether it is right or wrong I need not discuss, but this physical difference is a great disadvantage to us both."

Apparently, Lincoln did not see the need to discuss much of anything with his visitors, as the meeting reads as a long soliloquy in which the president tells his silent guests that, as far as future citizenship may be concerned, there was no hope. Their current condition was as permanent, the perpetual suffering as evident and as nonnegotiable as the disease a physician might identify from examining a corpse. Even "when you cease to be slaves," he told them, "you are yet far removed from being placed on an equality with the white race. You are cut off from many of the advantages which the other race enjoy [*sic*]. The aspiration of men is to enjoy equality with the best when free, but on this broad continent, not a single man of your race is made the equal of a single man of ours. Go where you are treated the best, and the ban is still upon you. I do not propose to discuss this, but to present it as a fact with which we have to deal."[6]

This "fact" of immovable prejudice seemed to demand the same response for Lincoln in 1862 as it did for the New York African Free School administrators in 1832: colonization. Notably, Lincoln did not propose Africa in this meeting, but rather South America as the new Black Plymouth Rock. And like colonizationists before and after, the president sought to paint the act of Black removal and colonization as a chance to retell American history, and in the process rewrite the story of slavery's role in that history. In Lincoln's scenario, Black people could act the role of George Washington, and erase the blot that Washington's slaveowner status left in the history books. "In the American Revolutionary war sacrifices were made by men engaged in it; but they were cheered by the future," he told the men. "Gen. Washington himself endured greater physical hardships than if he had remained a British subject." Perhaps most important, the Black pilgrims Lincoln sought would be emissaries to a future in which their children could—like George Washington's imagined national children—benefit from their parents' dislocation from a history that would oppress them. Washington "was a happy man," Lincoln said, "because he was engaged in benefiting his race—[doing] something for the children of his neighbors, having none of his own."[7] So, Lincoln asked the men gathered before him, "Could I get a hundred tolerably intelligent men, with their wives and children, to 'cut their own fodder,' so to speak?" Perhaps sensing resistance, Lincoln lowered his estimate. "If I could find twenty-five able-bodied men," he mused, "with a mixture of women and children, good things in the family relation, I think I could make a successful commencement."[8]

The fissure that had been momentarily healed between factions that had James McCune Smith, Frederick Douglass, and George T. Downing on one side, and Henry Highland Garnet on the other, soon ruptured in the face of this new push towards colonization. For many, including those who were at the meeting itself, Lincoln's proposal was anathema. At least three of the five men to whom Lincoln had given his colonization lecture were active in the Social, Civil, and Statistical Association, an organization that shared James McCune Smith's dedication to fighting for rights on American soil. The organization even shared a name with a Philadelphia-based group dedicated to the same sort of local antisegregation advocacy that had been initiated by New York's Legal Rights Association, which had been cofounded by James McCune Smith and J. C. Pennington. The group urged Black people to start local legal rights associations, complete with female branches, and to advocate on the regional level.[9] Although there are gaps in the internal records of the DC Social, Civil, and Statistical Association, we do know that the organization followed in Smith's footsteps in one key regard: its insistence on providing factual data to refute the racist assertion that Black children could not grow into American citizens.[10] In 1862, members of the SCSA collected statistics about Black education and wealth—much as James McCune Smith had in the 1840s—to repudiate the claims that Black people would not be able to handle the burden of freedom.[11] Perhaps not surprisingly, the SCSA was violently opposed to the idea of mass emigration. When the organization heard that an emigrationist lobbyist named John D. Johnson had been going around saying that recent slaves were "mere children in capacity" and thus needed to be "sent out of the country whether they are willing to go or not," they collectively demanded that he leave town.[12]

Garnet, notwithstanding his Jubilee pronouncement that it was folly to entertain the idea of colonization, vacillated in the face of Lincoln's plan. "Let the government give [freed slaves] a territory, and arm and defend them until they can fully defend themselves," he wrote in an editorial in the fall of 1862.[13] In fact, Garnet would seek funding from Lincoln's allotment for his own colonization project in Africa. The war had loosened the convictions of many, as Black people found themselves careening between high hopes and repeated disillusionment as it became ever more clear that antislavery activists were not necessarily advocates of racial equality. Among the most poignant examples of the whiplash between hope and despair was the decision made by Lewis Douglass, Frederick's first-born son, to choose Garnet's path over his father's. The younger Douglass volunteered to participate in Lincoln's colonization plan, which was a devastating blow to his father. Although it had "been the hope and ambition of my manhood," Douglass wrote in the wake of his son's declaration, to see "my children usefully and happily settled in this land of their ancestors," he had not been able to convince his son that the dream was attainable. Events "stronger than any power I can oppose to them, have convinced my son that the chances here are all against him."[14] For Douglass, who had opposed the American Colonization Society throughout his career, his son's despair felt like a defeat. In this case, Douglass's loss would be a short-lived one, as his son was ultimately unable to take Lincoln up on his offer. The president's Central American scheme would never come to pass, despite hundreds of volunteers from the DC area alone.[15]

For his part, in the days after the giddy celebration at the Cooper Institute, Garnet had returned to his work with the African Civilization Society, still unwilling to relinquish his case for leaving the country. But by the spring of 1863, he was also working side by side with those on the other side of the colonization debate, urging Black men to stand fast and enlist as Union soldiers in the Civil War. In doing so, he found some measure of reconciliation with former adversaries. In his effort to gain new recruits, Garnet opened the doors—and offered the pulpit—of Shiloh Church to both Frederick Douglass and George T. Downing. On one April evening, Garnet introduced Frederick Douglass to make the case for the potential recruits in the audience. When Douglass took the pulpit, he sounded a good deal like Garnet had in his controversial 1843 address. Twenty years earlier, Douglass had argued for hours that Garnet's call for open rebellion was too dangerous to publish. Now, he stood next to Garnet and told the Black men before them that the time had come for "retribution." Douglass reminded the audience that until recently a Black man could not so much as raise a hand to a white man without being considered "worthy of death." Now, he told them, "The government has given authority to these same black men to shoulder a musket and kill white rebels."[16] Garnet spoke later in the program, telling the audience that if they did not stand and fight now, "their doom was sealed, as far as this country was concerned."[17]

Garnet's bleak prophesy might well have been inspired by the conversations he heard among the New Yorkers he passed on the way to Shiloh Church each day. His white neighbors were growing increasingly resentful of being called upon to fight a war that many felt did not represent their interests. In spite of a lackluster response from potential white recruits, New York's Governor Seymour refused to allow Black men to sign up for a Colored Regiment stationed in New York. The recruits that Garnet and Douglass convinced to join up would have to travel to Massachusetts to join a regiment there. Those prospective African American soldiers could have helped New York meet its quota of volunteers, and thus stave off a deeply unpopular draft, but Seymour would not budge in his refusal.[18] He decided that he would rather press unwilling white men into service than allow Black men to fight. That decision would, by the end of the summer, have deadly consequences. In March of 1863 Congress passed the Civil War Military Draft Act, requiring enrollment by all eligible men who were citizens, or had filed for citizenship. If one man did not want to serve, he could either pay for a substitute to go in his stead or pay a three-hundred-dollar fine—a huge sum for day workers who earned, when they were able to find work, roughly a dollar a day.[19] Because Black men were not allowed to sign up in New York, the Draft Act conspired to compel only nonwealthy white men to fight in the bloody battles that, by that point in the war, seemed interminable.

James McCune Smith and Henry Highland Garnet had long known to be wary of the heat the summer brought. When the mercury rose, so did, it seemed, the tempers of resentful white men. In July of 1834, riots had devastated many of Garnet's and Smith's childhood haunts. A year later, it was a Fourth of July meeting in New Hampshire that laid the groundwork for the mob that destroyed the Noyes Academy, attended by the young Henry Garnet and Julia. Now, thirty years later, the heat of July brought simmering anger to a boil. Once again, the summer would see New York set aflame.

Local authorities had set the draft selection to begin on Saturday, July 11, and to recommence the next business day. When the sun rose on that following Monday morning, dozens of white New Yorkers woke up with bloodshed on their minds. On July 13, 1863, hundreds of white men attacked the draft office, initiating a wave of brutal destruction that would last for at least three days and nights. Many historians note that governmental organizations were the first to come under attack, as the mob sought to undermine the authority of the draft. The rioters also chose Black children as one of their earliest targets. Within hours of the first unrest, the mob came calling at the Colored Orphan Asylum.

On the morning of July 13, James McCune Smith was not with the children he had worked so hard to keep safe and healthy. In truth, he had not been coming in to the asylum very often that summer. His weakened heart and failing health made it difficult to get to the place where he had invested so many of his working hours. Public transportation often turned away Black people, and he was increasingly unable to make the walk on his own, even on placid days.[20] When the mob turned its sights

RIOTERS CHASING NEGRO WOMEN AND CHILDREN THROUGH THE VACANT LOTS IN LEXINGTON AVENUE.

Rioters Chasing Negro Women and Children, NYC Draft Riots, Black Gotham Archive, circa 1863. New-York Historical Society.

on the main building, there were only a handful of adults in charge of over two hundred children. As witnesses would later recount, "an infuriated mob, which had commenced its ravages in the neighborhood, surrounded the premises of the Asylum and some 500 of them entered the House. . . . despoiling . . . Furniture, Bedding, clothing; etc." They began setting fires in different parts of the building, simply "because it was the home of unoffending colored orphan children."[21] While the mob tore about the asylum, the matron and other women were quickly collecting the children and leading them towards the north exit. They were hoping to exit on Forty-Fourth Street and Fifth Avenue and ask for refuge in the jailhouse on Thirty-Fifth Street. The path would require walking ten city blocks, directly through a surging, murderous mob. As abolitionist and author William Wells Brown would later relate, the streets were filled with an "infuriated band of drunken men, women and children" who sought out "all localities inhabited by the blacks, and murdered all they laid their hands on, without regard to age or sex." But there was nothing for it. Their beloved asylum already in flames, the children had nowhere to go but into the street. Witnesses described how a "long line of trembling, terrified little children filed quietly down stairs and through the halls into the very body of the mob, who literally filled the enclosure, and whose savage yells and inhuman threats thrilled like a death note on every heart." What happened next was remarkable.

At the sight of the frightened children, accounts relate, the "human mass swayed back as though impelled by an unseen power—not a hand was raised to molest them, and without sustaining the slightest injury, children and care-takers reached the station house."[22] There is, quite simply, no easy answer to account for this act of mercy in the midst of unrelenting carnage. If a fictional account depicted the power of childhood softening the hearts of a murderous mob, we would probably write it off as hopelessly unrealistic sentimentality.[23] Perhaps the fact that the children were led by respected white women offered some protection. Perhaps, in this one case, Black children's vulnerability invoked the protective instinct that popular culture insisted that white children deserved as their due.

In any case, the respite was brief, and the children's suffering was far from over. Once they got to the jail, whatever spell had stayed the mob's hand lifted. The children arrived to find they were far from alone. In a particularly wrenching rebuttal of the possibility of true freedom in the North, Black people had been reduced to requesting imprisonment to gain some protection from the gangs roaming the streets outside. Faced with this reality, William Wells Brown would recall, "Hundreds of Blacks, driven from their homes, and hunted and chased through the streets, presented themselves at the doors of jails, prisons and police stations and begged admission."[24] Along with others granted admission, the asylum children were "compactly thrown together, three days and three nights."[25] "The horror of those days and nights cannot be described," recounted one child who survived the experience. "There was only standing room. We could not lie or sit down. The weather was extremely hot." All this time, the mob raged outside, screaming obscenities and trying to set the jail on fire by setting barrels of oil alongside the building. And the children did not just have to share the space with other Black families seeking protection. The police, in an attempt to restore some sort of order, were making arrests, bringing the very people who sought to do them harm within the same building. While there were attempts to keep the children separated from the criminals, it was undoubtedly a terrifying experience. The prisoners would grab at the children through bars and doors, and they tried to flood the rooms where the children stood. In one case, the authorities forgot that a sick child had been laid under a bench in a cell. When the two prisoners found him, they beat him unconscious.[26]

What went on outside the walls of that jail almost defies description. In one case, the mob hung a man in front of his mother. When they were chased off by the authorities, the man was cut down, barely alive. As soon as the authorities left the scene, however, the rioters once again took hold of the man's body, hung it from a lamppost, and mutilated it. There were accounts of infants thrown from open windows, of bodies left in the streets, unrecognizable and unclaimed for days. In one case, the mob pursued a grandmother with an infant and "an invalid boy" of about seven. The child was unable to keep up, and was separated from his grandmother. The mob immediately set upon the "poor sick boy," beating him mercilessly, demanding that he choose whether "he would be hung or have his throat cut." Although the child was rescued by a fireman, the trauma proved fatal, and he died shortly after.[27]

While the children were suffering the fetid heat of a jailhouse basement, Henry Highland Garnet was also constrained behind closed doors while attackers raged all around him. In the very city where, thirty years earlier, Garnet returned from a voyage to find his home attacked and his family on the run, the Shiloh pastor found himself in an eerily similar position. An account by riot survivor William Powell has uncanny echoes of the story of Garnet's father's escape three decades before. In 1829 the senior Garnet had escaped capture by a daring rooftop jump. In 1863, William Powell sat on a rooftop with his family and his neighbors, while the mob pillaged the homes below, wondering if they could "escape from the roof of a five story building, with four females—and one a cripple—besides eight men, without a ladder or any assistance from the outside." In this case help came from a Jewish neighbor, whose mercy, Powell surmised, came from his own knowledge of oppression: "[My relief came] in the person of a little deformed, despised Israelite—who, Samaritan-like, took my poor helpless daughter under his protection in his house."[28] After he had taken in Powell's daughter, the neighbor gave Powell a long rope, which allowed him to escape to the next roof under cover of night.

Back at Garnet's residence, the orator's famous defiance made him a particular target. As James McCune Smith would relate, the rioters "rushed down Thirtieth Street where [Garnet] resided, loudly calling him by name." Once again, Garnet and his family were able to evade the worst-case scenario by a combination of wit and luck. Garnet's daughter, Mary, had thought ahead, and had pried the Garnet name off the door plate. Unable to locate their prey, the rioters did not fulfill their bloody errand. Never one to avoid conflict for long, Henry did take to the streets before the violence had fully subsided. What he saw shook him to his marrow. He would later recount the "demonic" excesses of the mob, describing the fearful desecration of Black bodies to the cheers of onlookers. In his later work ministering to the African American community, he would listen to and record many of the most harrowing stories of the survivors.[29]

Garnet was particularly hurt by the hatred of the Irish with whom he—and many in the abolitionist community—had felt such a kinship. His earlier visions of a global alliance in the 1840s and '50s, in which the starved Irish, the desperate Hungarian peasants, and the oppressed American slaves could all rise together, now seemed to be a naïve dream. On his first trip to Europe, Garnet "had stood in public beside the great [Irish agitator] O'Connell; and we know what his hatred of oppression was." Yet it was undeniable that the Irish had been out in force in New York City, leading some of the worst atrocities against Garnet's community. "He could not tell," he wondered, "how it was that men crossing the ocean should change as much as they."[30]

Eventually, the fury of the mob was spent, and both Henry Highland Garnet and James McCune Smith were faced with the prospect of helping their community recover from unspeakable carnage. Dozens of their neighbors were dead, injured, or in hiding. The Colored Orphan Asylum, an institution that Smith had worked tirelessly to transform into a monument to the future of Black children, was utterly destroyed, its space in the heart of the city forever gone. The managers had hoped to rebuild on the same spot, but their midtown neighbors balked at the chance of bringing such a vulnerable target back in their midst. Doubly homeless, the orphan children were first sheltered on what is now called Randall's Island. They were then shifted first to a dilapidated building on 150th Street in Manhattan, and then to Harlem. The asylum would finally be reinstated in earnest in the Riverdale section of the Bronx, many years after James McCune Smith had passed away.[31]

The children were not the only ones exiled from their place in the heart of New York City. As he approached the end of his life, James McCune Smith came, at last, to fully know the childhood plight of his friend Henry Highland Garnet: he was driven from his home by violent white men. The physician who had returned triumphantly from Europe and put down roots determined to see his work bear fruit in the city he loved, the man who had felt profoundly betrayed by Garnet's insistence that Black people had to leave home to prosper, realized he could not stay where he was. Terrified for the safety of his loved ones, his heart literally failing, Smith decided that his family had to leave Manhattan.[32] The beautiful home that he had built in the hopes that it would—along with the stately Orphan Asylum—stand as a monument to Black industry and excellence, would be sold.[33] He moved his family to Brooklyn. He would spend his final years across the river from his beloved Manhattan, and the Mulberry Street school where it had all begun.

In the days immediately after the riots, a group of New York merchants came forward to try to help with the recovery process. They raised a considerable amount of money to aid the Black community, many of whom had lost everything. When looking for a leader to reach out to these frightened, devastated families, they turned to Henry Highland Garnet, whose "extensive acquaintance among the colored people" rendered him able to establish the necessary trust. As he did when recruiting recipients of Gerrit Smith's land giveaways in the 1840s, Garnet was tasked with talking with prospective beneficiaries so that he could determine their needs and distribute the funds as fairly as possible. Exhausted as he must have been, and as terrifying as it probably was to walk the streets where Black bodies had been hung up mere days earlier, Garnet got right to work. The relief agency was set up across the street from Garnet's own Shiloh Church. He spent his days walking through the ashes to call on devastated families, to ascertain their needs, and to get them the aid they needed. By August, the committee he spearheaded had conducted over eight thousand visits and had paid out relief to over ten thousand people.[34] The report included personal accounts that Garnet and other clergymen had heard and recorded on their calls to Black homes in New York City, making it a document that represents a significant historical record of what the victims endured.

When he had concluded his work, he wrote an eloquent thanks to the white merchants who had sought to ameliorate the devastating consequences of their neighbors' wrath. Garnet's formal thank you is remarkable, especially for anyone who was familiar with the orator's love of fiery rhetoric, and his tendency to find enemies and excoriate them at every turn. This piece, free from anger, was a careful, lovingly written expression of gratitude, presented as a gift. Garnet asked his childhood friend and schoolmate Patrick Reason to engrave his words on fine parchment to present to those who had helped the Black community rebuild. "We were hungry," he wrote to the Merchant's Committee, "and you fed us. We were thirsty and you gave us drink. We were made as strangers in our own homes and you kindly visited us." Garnet was particularly moved by what he assumed were the merchants' motives. Since his days as a schoolboy, Garnet had been told that white people harbored such deep-seated antipathy towards anyone of African descent that no progress could ever be made. His own experiences—being chased and attacked at nearly every resting point he had come to in the United States—certainly supported the idea that much white hatred was universal and immovable. But now, faced with the generosity of these businessmen, Garnet seems to have had a revelation. He had now come to see "by your treatment of us in these days of our mental and physical affliction" that these white pillars of the community had actually "cherished for us kindly and humane feeling of which we had no knowledge."[35]

The response from the merchants was cruel. As if Garnet's acknowledgment of their empathy placed them on the edge of a precipice that might topple their own privileged position, they categorically rejected Garnet's characterization of their "kindly" and "humane" feelings towards African Americans. Instead, they cast the community in precisely the role that Garnet had despairingly portrayed in his speeches. In short, the merchants asserted, they saw Black people not as fellow citizens and brethren but as hungry ghosts to be appeased. "Their condition and their future is a problem to us of momentous importance," they wrote to Garnet. The problem of Black futurity "engages our thoughts, I am well convinced, far more than it possibly can your own; it is the great question of the age. Go where we may the black man does not escape us—when we sit at our tables surrounded by our families—although you are not personally present in bodily shape still you are there—when we retire to our chambers you follow us—and even in the sanctuary of the Most High the question will come without bidding to every heart, what shall be done with the negro?"[36] Here, the chairman seems to share Garnet's vision in which "fathers call from their graves" for justice. These merchants saw the same ghosts at their dinner tables, unmoored from a history or a future beyond the capacity of "human wisdom" to determine.

For the merchants, the reach of these specters had extended into every white home in the nation. "There is hardly a family circle in the North and almost certainly there is not one in the South, where the mother does not mourn over the dead boy or the wife has not been made a widow, and all this has come to us because your people dwelt among us—the innocent cause of untold woes."[37] In the merchants' response, there is an irreconcilable split between the imagined Black bodies that haunt their dining rooms and a future in which actual Black people might sit at their dinner tables. In the void between what was required and what seemed possible, the merchants rested their sights on an imagined Black child—or, to be more specific, on an imagined form of immaturity perpetually unprepared for freedom. "For myself," the reply read, "I had hoped that your race would have been gradually emancipated, first being prepared for the enjoyment of liberty and the discharge of the duties and obligations attendant thereon; but God, who controls all events according as he sees fit, in his own infinite wisdom, seems to our present view to order otherwise, and it is our duty to accept his will as right."

James McCune Smith did not personally participate in the exchange, but he too seemed taken aback by the response. He would quote it at length in a later collaboration with Garnet, without much comment. Perhaps the physician felt that the evidence spoke for itself. In 1852, Smith had critiqued a badly written travelogue of Nicaragua; in that review, he expressed his exasperation with a white ethnologist's inability to accurately describe Black people. Smith had argued that even well-intentioned white men seemed unable to see "an actual physical being of flesh and bones and blood" when faced with a Black person, but would instead conjure "a hideous monster of the mind."[38] That indeed seemed to be the case when this group of altruistic white merchants faced the dignified and courageous Henry Highland Garnet standing before them, making claims on their common humanity. Looking at this charismatic master of oratory, they saw instead a specter, an imagined past coming to claim the future, a figure who, in James McCune Smith's words, "haunts with grim presence the precincts of this republic, shaking his gory locks over legislative halls and family prayers."[39]

The riot offered a set of grim reminders of how little progress has been made, but it did bring about at least one change: the establishment of a Black New York regiment. Faced with the carnage of the riots, federal authorities overrode Governor Seymour's demurrals about establishing a colored regiment for the state. In this endeavor, as in the work of distributing relief funds, Henry Highland Garnet immediately took the lead. He redoubled his efforts to recruit Black soldiers. He also served as a vocal advocate on their behalf once they had enrolled in the army. Nearly every day in the winter of 1863–1864, Garnet, almost certainly stiff and sore, walked on his wooden prosthetic to make his way through the cold, snowy streets of New York to board a ferry to minister to the men who were willing to fight for the Union Army.

Garnet's work ministering to the "colored regiments" would, like so much else in war-torn New York, offer disconcerting echoes of his life as a fugitive slave child. As a fourteen-year-old, Garnet had taken to the streets of New York, armed with a knife, to fight off the "man-stealers" who had preyed on his family. Now, as a forty-eight-year-old man, a respected minister with an international reputation, he found himself accosted by man stealers on those very same streets. One day, he and two friends were attacked while on the Courtlandt Street ferry crossing to Rikers Island, where troops were mustered. Special police protection had to be established at the ferry point, "in order to protect the recruits."[40] The police presence probably dissuaded some of the worst attackers, but in truth, nowhere was safe. When Garnet's young sister had been imprisoned in the 1830s as a "fugitive from labor" by the authorities after her capture by the slave traders, she had wound up in the court of Richard Riker. As greedy "recruiters" sought to meet quotas in 1864, Black children were once again being snatched away from their parents. Now, rather than being brought to the court of Richard Riker, they were dragged to Rikers Island, a plot of land acquired in the seventeenth century by Richard Riker's ancestor, Abraham Riker.[41]

The great war against slavery had, among other things, transformed the practice of kidnapping Black children and collecting slaveholder bounties into the work of kidnapping Black children to collect recruitment bonuses. As one account reports, "Mere boys ranging from fourteen to fifteen, were kidnapped on their way to or from school."[42] Others were accosted, given drugged drinks, and woke up to find themselves "enlisted" and stranded on Rikers Island. As one observer noted, "These runners frequented most of the great highways of travel leading to this city, for hundreds of miles, and so great was the dread of them, that when our agents were sent out with hand-bills offering honest bounties, they were set upon and driven away by the colored men in the districts where these swindlers had previously been."[43] As the *New York Tribune* pointed out, the extent of the runner's predations was almost certainly winked at by military and government officials.[44] Despite the danger to himself, Garnet put himself in the midst of the recruits and worked assiduously to right the wrongs done to them. He gathered statements and penned "remonstrances" to officials. Reforms were made, and the work of recruiting willing soldiers continued. When he was not working directly

Presentation of Colors, 1864. Edward Lamson Henry.

with the recruits, Garnet spoke at pulpits in overflowing Black churches, promising that he would continue to fight for justice on their behalf.[45]

The rigors of the cold winter following the riots eventually gave way to spring, and the time arrived for the soldiers to ship out. On March 5, 1864, the Twentieth Regiment of Colored Troops left Rikers Island. Over a thousand men marched through the streets to a grand reception in Union Square. It was, by all accounts, a thrilling day. Onlookers spoke of the marching columns of Black recruits, resplendent in their "soldierlike appearance, the evenness of their dress, and the carriage of their muskets," garnering an ovation that "had not been seen since the early days of the rebellion."[46] Garnet followed the chief of police and a hundred officers down Broadway to South Ferry and took his place on the platform before the Union League Club house on Seventeenth Street in Union Square with his wife Julia, sitting alongside some of the city's most wealthy and powerful citizens.

Once the troops had finished their march, they stood before the platform, waiting to be formally addressed by, among others, the president of Columbia College. Looking around, they were astounded by what they saw. Mere months after the city had been transformed into a hunting ground for African Americans in the July riots, these Black men saw streets overflowing with New Yorkers who had come to wish them well. The *Tribune* reported a "vast crowd of citizens of every shade and every phase of social and political life" filling Union Square and surrounding streets—every door, window, veranda, tree, and house-top was peopled with spectators.[47] "This don't look like July," remarked one soldier. Another man, clearly thrilled by the huge shift between this warm reception on this early spring day and the hatred that had stalked the streets the previous summer, called out, "How are you, rioters!"[48] They were far from the only ones who were taken aback by the shift in the city's response to armed Black men in their midst. James McCune Smith would later recall the sense of emotional whiplash that permeated the celebration. For Black people, who had "been mobbed, hunted down, hung from the lamp-posts or trees, their dwellings sacked and destroyed, their orphan children turned from their comfortable shelter which was destroyed by fire" now to be "cheered along the same streets" was a turn of events that "put ordinary miracles in the shade."[49]

White participants also noted the remarkable shift between the riots of the summer and the celebrations of the spring. After handing them a flag bestowed by Union League women, and bidding them to "embrace a trust at once so dangerous and so honorable" as the "religion of the flag," Charles King, the president of Columbia College, spoke about the divergence between this proud day and the shameful events that had unfolded in the "fatal month of July." He, like so many in the crowd, felt this was a turning point in the fight for justice and freedom. "No, no my friends," he said to the men standing at attention before him, "you cannot be hindered in your high calling." One need only "look back for a few years—nay, but for a few months in this city—to realize what a forward step has been taken, and to feel quite sure that in such a path there is no step backward." While "prejudice, indeed the rancorous hate of brutalized minds . . . may still throw obstacles in your way, . . . that way is upward and onward and your march cannot be stopped."[50]

As he listened to Charles King give his remarks, Henry Highland Garnet, who had spent much of the past two years devoting himself to making this precise moment come to pass, might have allowed himself to share the belief that now, at last, there was a path "upward and onward" for Black people in the United States. Surely he was too well aware of ongoing inequities in pay and in opportunity for Black troops to be fully convinced that the situation was quite as rosy as King suggested. But he, like the soldiers he had recruited and ministered to, had decided to move a bit closer to embracing the flag and the promise it held. And like his soldiers, Garnet would soon head south. While the troops were headed to New Orleans, Garnet would soon establish himself in Washington, DC, to head the Fifteenth Street Presbyterian Church at the invitation of their board. It was a testament to the national fame he had accrued as an orator that he had received the invitation in the first place. The church board would find that their new minister's reputation was well deserved. Once Garnet arrived, his charisma and eloquence filled the church to the rafters. As one report indicated, the demands for pews outstripped the church's capacity to accommodate them.[51]

The war ground on, but there did seem to be an end in sight—an end that neither Garnet nor James McCune Smith had thought they would ever see in their lifetimes. As the South's demise became more certain, Congress turned to the laws that would govern a nation now, for the first time, wholly free from slavery. Legislators agreed on the final text of the Thirteenth Amendment, declaring that neither "slavery nor involuntary servitude, except as a punishment for crime whereof the party shall have been duly convicted, shall exist within the United States, or any place subject to their jurisdiction." The Senate passed the measure on April 8, 1864, and the House of Representatives passed it on January 31, 1865. On February 1, 1865, Abraham Lincoln approved the joint resolution of Congress that submitted the proposed amendment to the state legislatures. When Georgia ratified the measure on December 6, 1865, slavery was legally abolished in the United States.

On February 12, 1865, just days after Lincoln had submitted the amendment for ratification, Henry Highland Garnet stood before the House of Representatives. He would, on that Sunday, take his place in history as the first Black man to address Congress, an incredible honor. It must have pleased Garnet enormously that he, and not Frederick Douglass, was esteemed to be the "most eloquent black man in the land" and thus the correct choice for the occasion.[52] Garnet invited Martin Delany as his particular guest. Together they had collaborated on a proposed African colonization project in Yoruba. Delany hoped to parlay his visit to Washington into an audience with Lincoln, but Garnet told him not to get his hopes up, noting that it was harder to get into the White House than to mingle with European nobility.[53] Delany insisted that he would keep trying, eventually wearing his friend down. Garnet, turning to his wife Julia, bemusedly declared, "I believe he will do it." Julia's response was quick: "Of course he will." Her words, Delany would later relate, were an act of kind affirmation that came "when most needed."[54]

James McCune Smith was not in Washington, DC, on that day to see his friend, his sometimes rival, and his fellow traveler Henry Garnet stand before Congress. But he was delighted on his behalf. "What a glorious thing about Garnett! [*sic*]" he wrote to Gerrit Smith. The news of his friend's honor, Dr. Smith declared, "cheers me more than the capture of Charleston!" And indeed, it was in some ways a larger victory for the New York African Free School alumni than anything that had taken place on a battlefield. Garnet was asked to preside over a gathering that had voted to end the slavery so many NYAFS children had been born to. It pained Smith to be unable to take part in the celebrations, but his already failing health had taken a turn for the worse in the months after the riots. He could not attend because of "an enlarged heart," he lamented, and "an overworked nervous system; and am compelled to be quiet when there is so much to do."[55]

Still, in many ways, Smith was there beside Garnet, their lifelong friendship undoubtedly an influence on the speech Garnet gave to Congress. Garnet did not mention Smith in the speech itself, but he would, through the elders of his new church in DC, formally request that James McCune Smith write the introduction that would preface its published version. Smith readily agreed, knowing it would probably be one of the last major works he would ever write. James McCune Smith's introductory essay to Garnet's congressional address served as an elegiac remembrance of both of their lives, intertwined as they had been in the forty years since they had met in a classroom on Mulberry Street. Showing no evidence of the rancor that had so often come between them in the past decade, he wrote with love and admiration for his friend Garnet, the boy who was quite the opposite of the "nice, quiet, good little fellow," in whose mouth "butter would not melt." Smith's ode also provides one of the more thorough accounts we have of the New York African Free School. He names their childhood companions as one recites a litany, preserving the names of Black children (several of the students named did not survive to adulthood) and appending them to a document of official government import, one bound to be preserved through history.[56]

As for Garnet's speech, if the assembly expected him to write something similar to the grateful missive he presented to the merchants of New York City, they soon found that they were mistaken. Perhaps the merchants' cold response to Garnet's expression of gratitude the year before had reminded the minister of how often even well-intentioned white promises could be revoked. It was a lesson that he had been taught repeatedly since his childhood, and on that cold Sunday in February, Garnet was determined to remind the nation of what he had learned. He looked out and, addressing the body that had recommended a constitutional amendment abolishing slavery, spoke of "Scribes and Pharisees who rule the State."[57] Indeed, if one came across an undated version of the speech, it would be easy to assume that it had been written well before the Civil War. Although both the Senate and the House had passed the measure to create the amendment, it was still waiting on ratification from southern states. And perhaps it was that lack of finality that led Garnet to portray slavery as a deadly opponent that still needed to be fought on the rhetorical, if not the physical battlefield. He spent much of his speech citing sources ranging from Socrates to Thomas Jefferson to make the case that "slavery is a system of complete injustice."[58] His evidence moved from the great thinkers of the age to his own personal history. His earliest memories as a child, he told the august gathering, "are clouded with [slavery's] wrongs. The first sight that met my eyes was a Christian mother enslaved by professed Christians."[59] Slavery, Garnet reminded the crowd, had "driven troops of women and children into yawning tombs" and had torn countless infants from their mothers in Africa, leaving the "little innocents" to "die on the Middle Passage."[60] But rather than providing an obituary recounting horrors that would now be relegated to the past, Garnet seemed unwilling to believe that those days were over. Slipping between the present tense and the ghost-haunted view of history that had so long marked his political imagination, Garnet looked up from his speech to lock eyes with those in the gallery. In a tone that generations of onlookers had found electrifying, he thundered at the august gathering. "Ye Scribes and Pharisees and hypocrites!" he called out. "Ye blind guides! Ye compass sea and land to make one proselyte, and when he is made ye make him twofold more the child of hell than yourselves. Ye are like unto whited sepulchers, which indeed appear beautiful without, but within are full of dead men's bones, and all uncleanness!"[61]

Garnet, having known for too long how tenacious slavery's grip could be, seemed to have little faith that it would remain in the sepulcher the Congress had built for it. "Its death warrant is signed by God and man. Do not commute the sentence," he exhorted the congressmen before him. For Garnet, slavery was both dead and threatening to reanimate a deadly past. "Give it no respite, but let it be ignominiously executed." "Let the gigantic monster perish," he urged. "Yes, perish now, and perish forever."

Even if slavery were to become legally dead, Garnet warned, its monstrous effects were far from dissipated. Like the ghostly figures the New York merchants imagined sitting among them at dinner, demanding sustenance they had so long been denied, the debt of slavery was far from paid. Garnet told a country that was about to embark—for the first time in its history—on a future free from enslavement that the work had only just begun. "Great sacrifices have been made by the people, great still are demanded ere atonement can be made for our national sins." Always attuned to slavery's close relationship to capitalism, Garnet warned that Americans "have involved ourselves in the sin of unrighteous gain, stimulated by luxury, and pride, and the love of power and oppression." There would be no easy way out of the debts the nation had incurred: "Prosperity

and peace can be purchased only by blood, and with tears of repentance."
To a nation who felt that the Civil War had been a frightful punishment
for the sins of slavery, Garnet insisted, we "may have paid some of the
fearful installments, but there are other heavy obligations to be met."[62]

The publication of Garnet's *Memorial Discourse*, prefaced by James
McCune Smith's introduction, was the final act in a lifetime of friendship
and struggle. In this collaborative publication, Smith lent his gravitas to
confirm Garnet's historic role in the community, and Garnet acknowledged his deep respect for the wisdom of his learned friend. Their lives
together had seen the nation transform alongside their own evolving visions of what the future could hold. James McCune Smith, who had long
believed that evidence of Black excellence would slowly, but surely, move
the race forward, had learned to appreciate his friend's insistence that
history had a daunting habit of imposing the past upon the present. The
riots had taught the comfortably established doctor the pain of upheaval
and of alienation, as a seemingly indestructible prejudice turned the city
streets as bloody as any slave plantation could ever be. He had indeed
made incredible progress, but he had also come to realize that, no matter
how hard one worked, the laws of cause and effect—so powerful in the
science he loved—did not always hold for Black people in the United
States. He had spent years shaking his head at Garnet's impetuosity, his
willingness to wade into any fight at any time. Now, at the end of his life,
he crafted a testimony of his great admiration of his friend's tenacity, his
leadership, and, above all, his courage. In the trying years leading to the
Civil War, Smith wrote, Henry Highland Garnet was

> one black man who neither cowered nor flinched. The tall form of the
> pastor of Shiloh, always in the front, where blows fell thickest, seemed
> rather to dilate with the joys of battle, and his voice became as a trum-
> pet's call; by his eloquence, his high-hearted manhood, his conduct and
> example, he cheered his people, not only his immediate flock, but all who
> heard him throughout the land. Foot to foot with the common foe, so far
> from yielding an inch, he steadily advanced, taking newer and, as he be-
> lieved, broader grounds for our people in whose behalf he claimed perfect
> equality in all things.[63]

At other moments, Smith seemed to be eulogizing his own efforts as well as applauding the work of his friend. He knew his own time was drawing nigh. In one of his final letters to Gerrit Smith, the physician acknowledged that dying just at the dawn of emancipation was beginning to break was a "hard school" indeed. But, he wrote, "It is a satisfaction, nay, a glory to have lived to see this day, even if I know that I cannot live through it." In some respects, James McCune Smith crafted his praise of Garnet as an epitaph that he could also claim for himself as he approached the grave: "He has devoted his life to his people. His hands are clean."[64]

As for Henry Highland Garnet, the wanderer, the exile, the maverick, he would spend much of the rest of his life following a path that his old friend James McCune Smith had long held up as the correct way forward. While he would not relinquish his role in the African Civilization Society—the role that had caused such acrimony between the two friends—Garnet would change its mission. In the years to come, he redirected ACS resources to educating the children of freedpeople in the South. In the end, he made good on the promise that James McCune Smith had accused him of abandoning, spending much of his waning years and resources attending to the needs of vulnerable Black children "in this, the soil which gave them birth."[65]

At the very end of his life, however, almost as if unwilling to let his former critics (like James McCune Smith) get the last word, Garnet would say goodbye to the United States of America, the nation from which he had spent his life demanding justice. In 1880, Garnet's beloved daughter Mary left to do missionary work in Liberia, the land that had so long occupied his dreams. Garnet made up his mind to die in the land of his ancestors. He would do so, however, not as an exile but as a representative of the US government. Even as he left America forever, he would lay claim to national honors due to a citizen and a statesman. He was appointed the US minister and counsel general to Liberia in a post appointed by the president of the United States and approved by the Senate. He left, in failing health, on November 12 and spent the last three months of his life in Africa. He was buried, "like a prince," his friend Alexander Crummell would report, with tributes worthy of someone with the "blood of African chieftains in his veins." The man who had spent his whole life in transit had finally come to rest in the land of the ancestors on behalf of whom he had so long struggled to find justice.

As Garnet came to rest, perhaps he felt he had finally reconciled with the ghosts of a slave past that had dogged his steps throughout his life. He could take satisfaction that so much of his own work, along with that of James McCune Smith, had helped forge a future that neither could have imagined when the two scrawny, impoverished boys had first met at the New York African Free School on Mulberry Street sixty years earlier. Their journey together had been, in James McCune Smith's words, "a hard school." Yet their hard-earned lessons had enabled both men to push the nation in the direction of their own childhood dreams, dreams they had been told would never come to pass. And in truth, while the race of these two friends had been run, the work was far from over. As Garnet himself had told Congress, "the fearful installments" towards freedom had only begun to pay the debt of centuries. "There are other heavy obligations to be met."[66] Future generations—the children that James McCune Smith and Henry Highland Garnet had both spent their lives protecting, advocating for, and educating—faced an uncertain and often painful future ahead. It was, however, undoubtedly a future inextricable from the destiny of the United States.

ACKNOWLEDGMENTS

THIS book began as a lucky archival accident. Unsure of what I was looking for, I stumbled upon the records of the New York African Free Schools and sat transfixed before the humming microfilm machine as I read a skit in which a nine-year-old James McCune Smith chastised his tardy classmate and his inefficient mother. I was hooked. I wanted to know what it was like for those children, standing on that stage, as they sought an education that would qualify them for citizenship in a nation that did not want them to grow up. That question has led me on a long journey, one that has incurred innumerable debts to colleagues, friends, and institutions without whom this project would not be possible.

The moment of archival fascination was the first of many discoveries, aided by the knowledgeable and generous people at historical archives all over the country. I am indebted to the staff at the New-York Historical Society, especially Kathleen Hulser and Jean Ashton, who had faith in this project in its very earliest days. Thanks are also due to the Schomburg Library in New York City, the Beinecke Library at Yale University, the Gerrit Smith Papers archive at Syracuse University, and the Amistad Research Center at Tulane University. I owe particular thanks to the American Antiquarian Society for the generosity and knowledge of its incredible staff. I am especially indebted to Paul Erickson, who has done so much to make this rich archive accessible to the wider public. When Paul invited me to coedit the AAS journal *Common-Place*, I was honored and daunted. Over three years, I had the opportunity to work with incredibly gifted scholars and editors, a process that enriched my thinking immeasurably. Many thanks are due to my coeditor, Walt Woodward, and to Kathy Foley, Catherine Preus, and Rachel Smith. I learned from each one of the editors, who consistently curated some of the most exciting work in early American studies. Many thanks are due to Joseph Adelman, Ellery Foutch, Darcy Fryer, Josh Greenberg, William Huntting Howell, Honorée Jeffers, Justine Murison, and Wendy Woloson. The NEH workshop on "Reading Children" held at the NEH was a model of intellectual collaboration. I am grateful to Pat Crain and Martin Brückner for their invitation to join the fun.

In addition to the "Reading Children" workshop, I am profoundly grateful to two collaborative projects that have taught me to think about slavery studies and youth activism. I owe many thanks to Jessica Pliley, Genevieve LeBaron, and David Blight for their invitation to the Yale Gilder Lehrman Center's Modern Slavery working group. It was a remarkable experience to spend two years in a room with brilliant scholars and activists, including Jean Allain, Kevin Bales, Andrew Crane, Janie Chuang, Grace Delgado, Gunther Peck, Elena Shih, JJ Rosenbaum, Joel Quirk, Zoe Trodd, and Kevin Bales. Tom Thurston and Michelle Zacks were vital to facilitating those remarkable conversations.

I am indebted to Maria Cecire for introducing me to Lainie Castle and the incredible work of the American Library Association Great Story Club. It was a gift to be able to work with so many talented teachers and writers working to empower underserved youth. Their work in the twenty-first century paralleled much of the work James McCune Smith and Henry Highland Garnet sought to accomplish in the nineteenth: helping children to imagine their way into a world that will appreciate their gifts.

Pier Gabrielle Foreman's work on the Colored Conventions Project has been absolutely vital to this project. Because of the organization she created, I had access not only to the treasure trove of activist documents that comprise the colored conventions movement but also to a model of unparalleled scholarly collaboration and generosity. I am grateful to

Gabrielle, Jim Casey, and Sarah Patterson as they helped me integrate these materials into what proved to be one of the most productive graduate classes I have ever had the pleasure to teach. Sarah in particular was a brilliant guide through the intersection of nineteenth-century documents and twenty-first-century digitization.

At the University of Connecticut, I am fortunate to have brilliant colleagues, including Martha Cutter, Jane Gordon, Cathy Schlund-Vials, Shawn Salvant, Chris Vials, and Sarah Winter, all of whom have commented on some aspect of this work. I am especially grateful for the careful readings and sustaining comradery of fellow childhood studies scholars Kate Capshaw and Victoria Ford Smith. Ongoing discussions at the Nathan Hale Inn with Alexis Boylan, Micki McElya, and Kathy Knapp have been a source of both joy and strength.

I am grateful to the University of Connecticut's English Department and American Studies Program for their support. I am especially grateful to the University of Connecticut's Humanities Institute for the year-long fellowship that allowed me to bring the project to completion, and to the tireless work of Michael Lynch and Alexis Boylan in creating such a vibrant environment for humanities scholarship. My writing group is, as always, a source of smart, generous feedback that has improved my thinking and this book enormously. I am grateful for the years-long conversation I have been able to enjoy with Jeff Allred, Sophie Bell, Sarah Chinn, Joseph Entin, Hildegard Hoeller, Meg Toth, and Jennifer Travis.

Robin Bernstein has always been a model of impeccable scholarship and of generosity. I have spent much of my scholarly career being inspired by—and hoping to emulate—the work of Karen Sánchez-Eppler. Her friendship and collaboration are gifts. I am grateful to Rachel Adams for her wisdom and friendship. Many thanks are due to Lenny Cassuto for his unwavering support of this project since its genesis in graduate school. I owe thanks to Karen Kupperman for many things, including an introduction to Clara Platter at NYU Press, whose enthusiasm for this project has inspired me. I have been sustained and enlightened by the larger scholarly community of Americanist scholars, and owe much to the conference panels, Facebook messages, happy-hour conversations, and several combinations of these with Sarah Adelman, Sari Altschuler,

Hester Blum, Natalia Cecire, Sari Edelstein, Corrine Field, Brigitte Fielder, Nat Hurley, Lucia Hodgson, Holly Jackson, Catherine Jones, Elizabeth Marshall, Philip Nel, Britt Rusert, Marion Rust, Rebekah Sheldon, Jonathan Senchyne, Kyla Wazana Tompkins, Crystal Webster, Nazera Wright, and Xine Yao. I am thankful to Sarah Blackwood and Sarah Mesle for their impeccable editorship on work that helped me think through many of the issues in this book. Emily Wright's keen copyediting has sharpened and clarified my work.

Matthew Larson has been a source of immeasurable support as I struggled through this labor of love. My sisters Susie and Helen have always provided fun and strength in equal measure. In many ways, my son, Connor, has grown up alongside this project, and I am grateful for how joyful he made my present, and how urgent he rendered my thinking about the future. My mother and father taught me how powerfully legacies of courage and love can sustain and shape our path forward.

Finally, I am profoundly grateful for the experience of getting to know the lives and work of Henry Highland Garnet and James McCune Smith. I hope that this book invites much more study into their courageous lives and groundbreaking work. I have spent many years since I first "met" James McCune Smith researching the lives of the schoolchildren whose words leapt off the page that day. I know now, after many years of tracing their words—and deeds—that I will never be able to fully do them justice, though I do hope to have paid them homage.

NOTES

INTRODUCTION

1. I capitalize "Black" when referring to Black people throughout the manuscript to reflect the viewpoint of many scholars in the field that, in the words of Lori L. Tharps, when "speaking of a culture, ethnicity or group of people, the name should be capitalized. Black with a capital B refers to people of the African diaspora. Lowercase black is simply a color." Lori L. Tharps, "The Case for Black with a Capital B," *New York Times*, November 18, 2014.

2. Over the course of its history, there were six school buildings affiliated under the term "New York African Free School." The students I discuss throughout this book attended New York African Free School #2 on Mulberry Street. I refer to that school as NYAFS throughout, in keeping with the usage of Smith, Garnet, and their contemporaries, who referred to their alma mater as the New York African Free School. For a record of the different schools and their locations, please see "Examination Days," curated by Anna Mae Duane and Tom Thurston, at https://www.nyhistory.org. I am indebted to Amanda Greenwell and Daniel Pfeiffer, whose work on this archive has convinced me that the subject's name is Margaret Odle, rather than Addle, as I had originally imagined. New-York Historical Society & Museum, New-York African Free-School Records (hereafter, NYAFS Records), 3: 40–41.

3. NYAFS Records, 3: 34.

4. NYAFS Records, 3: 34–38.

5. This book would not be possible without the pioneering work of historians and scholars who have excavated the work of these two men, and the world of Black abolitionism that they lived in. John Stauffer's work on James McCune Smith has been truly groundbreaking, and is an inspiration for much of what follows. John Stauffer, *The Black Hearts of Men* (Cambridge, MA: Harvard University Press, 2009) and *The Collected Works of James McCune Smith: Black Intellectual and Abolitionist* (Oxford: Oxford University Press, 2006). For an analysis of Black New York, Carla Peterson and Leslie M. Harris have been indispensable. Carla Peterson, *Black Gotham: A Family History of African Americans in Nineteenth-Century New York* (New Haven, CT: Yale University Press, 2012); Leslie M. Harris, *In the Shadow of Slavery: African Americans in New York City, 1626–1863* (Chicago: University of Chicago Press, 2004). Britt Rusert's work on science as a site of Black creativity is a necessity for understanding the work

of James McCune Smith. Britt Rusert, *Fugitive Science: Empiricism and Freedom in Early African American Culture* (New York: NYU Press, 2017). Robin Bernstein's magisterial *Racial Innocence* has helped me better understand the racial logics of childhood in the nineteenth century. Robin Bernstein, *Racial Innocence: Performing American Childhood from Slavery to Civil Rights* (New York: NYU Press, 2011). I am indebted to Graham Russel Gao Hodges for his work on Black New York. Graham Russel Hodges, *Root and Branch: African Americans in New York and East Jersey, 1613–1863* (Chapel Hill: University of North Carolina Press, 1999) and *David Ruggles: A Radical Black Abolitionist and the Underground Railroad in New York City* (Chapel Hill: University of North Carolina Press, 2010). The works of Earl Ofari Hutchinson, Joel Schor, and Martin Pasternak have been integral to my understanding of Henry Highland Garnet's life. Joel Schor, *Henry Highland Garnet: A Voice of Black Radicalism in the Nineteenth Century* (New York: Greenwood, 1977); Earl Ofari Hutchinson, *Let Your Motto Be Resistance: The Life and Thought of Henry Highland Garnet* (Boston: Beacon, 1972); Martin Pasternak, *Rise Now and Fly to Arms: The Life of Henry Highland Garnet* (New York: Routledge, 1994). I am especially indebted to P. Gabrielle Foreman, Sarah Patterson, Jim Casey, and others for their tireless work collecting and posting the proceedings of the nineteenth-century Colored Conventions. Colored Conventions: Bringing Nineteenth-Century Black Organizing to Digital Life, coloredconventions.org.

6. For a fascinating discussion of youth and political activity in early America, see Jon Grinspan, *The Virgin Vote: How Young Americans Made Democracy Social, Politics Personal, and Voting Popular in the Nineteenth Century* (Chapel Hill: University of North Carolina Press, 2016).

7. See Corrine Field, *The Struggle for Equal Adulthood: Gender, Race, Age, and the Fight for Citizenship in Antebellum America* (Chapel Hill: University of North Carolina Press, 2014). For a take on age as an organizing principle of nineteenth-century life, see Sari Edelstein, *Adulthood and Other Fictions: American Literature and the Unmaking of Age* (New York: Oxford University Press, 2019).

8. A recent (though far from exhaustive) list of such work in the nineteenth century includes Brigitte Fielder, "'No Rights That Any One Is Bound to Respect': Pets, Race, and African American Child Readers," in *Who Writes for Black Children? African American Children's Literature before 1900*, ed. Kate Capshaw and Anna Mae Duane (Minneapolis: University of Minnesota Press, 2017); Manisha Sinha, *The Slave's Cause: A History of Abolition* (New Haven, CT: Yale University Press, 2016); Derick Spires, *The Practice of Citizenship: Black Politics and Print Culture in the Early United States* (Philadelphia: University of Pennsylvania Press, 2019); Britt Rusert, *Fugitive Science: Empiricism and Freedom in Early African American Culture* (New York: NYU Press, 2017); Pier Gabrielle Foreman and the work of the Colored Conventions Project (ccp.org); Nazera Wright, *Black Girlhood in the Nineteenth Century* (Chicago: University of Illinois Press, 2017).

9. James McCune Smith to Gerrit Smith, May 12, 1848. Gerrit Smith Papers, Syracuse University, box 34 (hereafter, Smith Papers).

10. Although other scholars use "McCune Smith" as a last name, I have opted to follow the usage of his peers, who universally referred to him as Dr. Smith, not Dr. McCune Smith, indicating that they considered Smith his last name. I shall do the same throughout.

11. Some of the most compelling work in this vein includes Greg Grandin, *The Empire of Necessity: Slavery, Freedom, and Deception in the New World* (New York: Metropolitan Books, 2014); Caitlin Rosenthal, *Accounting for Slavery: Masters and Management* (Cambridge, MA: Harvard University Press, 2018); Walter Johnson, *River of Dark Dreams: Slavery and Empire in the Cotton Kingdom* (Cambridge, MA: Harvard University Press, 2013); Edward E. Baptist,

The Half Has Never Been Told: Slavery and the Making of American Capitalism (New York: Basic Books, 2016).

12. In many ways, Garnet's philosophy finds echoes in the theoretical framework of Christina Sharpe and other Afro-pessimist scholars. Christina Sharpe, *In the Wake: On Blackness and Being* (Durham, NC: Duke University Press, 2016).

13. See, for instance, Dorothy Roberts, *Shattered Bonds: The Color of Child Welfare* (New York: Basic Books, 2002); Erica Meiners, *For the Children? Protecting Innocence in a Carceral State* (Minneapolis: University of Minnesota Press, 2016).

CHAPTER 1. THE STAR STUDENT AS SPECIMEN

1. Stanley J. Idzerda, Anne C. Loveland, and Marc H. Miller, *Lafayette, Hero of Two Worlds: The Art and Pageantry of His Farewell Tour of America, 1824–1825; Essays* (Corona, NY: Queens Museum, 1989); Marian Klamkin, *The Return of Lafayette, 1824–1825* (New York: Scribners, 1975); Sylvia Neely, "The Politics of Liberty in the Old World and the New: Lafayette's Return to America in 1824," *Journal of the Early Republic* 6, no. 2 (1986): 151–71; Edgar Ewing Brandon, ed., *Lafayette, Guest of the Nation: A Contemporary Account of the Triumphal Tour of General Lafayette through the United States in 1824–1825, as Reported by the Local Newspapers*, vol. 1 (Oxford, OH: Oxford Historical Press, 1950).

2. "My First Reading—Lafayette," in Walt Whitman, *The Complete Prose Works of Walt Whitman* (New York: Putnam's, 1902), 17.

3. Dennis C. Kurjack, "Evolution of a Shrine," *Pennsylvania History: A Journal of Mid-Atlantic Studies* 21, no. 3 (1954): 193–200.

4. For sources that discuss the years after the War of 1812 as the breeding ground for American nationalism and the emphasis on Manifest Destiny that would grow from it, see Donald R. Hickey, *The War of 1812: A Forgotten Conflict* (Urbana: University of Illinois Press, 1990). As Hickey writes in the 2012 edition of the above volume, "As America's second and last war against Great Britain it echoed the ideology and issues of the American Revolution" (2–3). For contemporary arguments that the War of 1812 was a second American Revolution, see the *National Intelligencer*, July 8, 1812, and the New York *National Advocate*, particularly the issues of December 15, 1812, and May 22, 1813.

5. As quoted in a letter by Thomas Clarkson (October 3, 1845), published in *The Liberty Bell: The Friends of Freedom* (Boston), January 1, 1846, p. 58. This quotation was printed in broadsides. Also quoted in William C. Nell, *The Colored Patriots of the American Revolution* (Boston: Robert F. Wallcut, 1855), 388.

6. Qtd. in Thomas Morgan, "The Education and Medical Practice of Dr. James McCune Smith (1813–1865), First Black American to Hold a Medical Degree," *Journal of the National Medical Association* 95, no. 7 (2003): 606; Carla Peterson, *Black Gotham*, 114; and Stauffer, *Collected Works*, xx. Stauffer attributes this quotation to Henry Highland Garnet, which I have not been able to verify.

7. His entries in *Fredrick Douglass' Paper*, both in the "Heads of Colored People" series and as "The New York Correspondent," feature fond remembrances of the school and schoolmates. Also see James McCune Smith, "Introduction," Henry Highland Garnet, *A Memorial Discourse* (Philadelphia: Joseph M. Wilson, 1865); Smith writes about Ira Aldridge in the *Anglo-African Magazine*, January 1, 1860, 27–32.

8. McCune Smith, "Introduction," 20.

9. See Joseph Lancaster, *Improvements in Education, as It Respects the Industrious Classes* (London: Darton and Harvey, 1803); *The British System of Education: Being a Complete Epit-*

ome of the Improvements Practised by Joseph Lancaster (Washington, DC: Joseph Milligan and William Cooper, 1812); also Patricia Crain, "Children of Media, Children as Media: Optical Telegraphs, Indian Pupils, and Joseph Lancaster's System for Cultural Replication," in *New Media, 1740–1915*, ed. Lisa Gitelman and Geoffrey B. Pingree (Cambridge, MA: MIT Press, 2003), 70. Of course, the Lancasterian system is only part of the story of Black education in the nineteenth century. There is a rich body of work detailing other schools and strategies that unfortunately fall out of the purview of this study, but deserve extended attention. See Susan Paul, *Memoir of James Jackson: The Attentive and Obedient Scholar, Who Died in Boston, October 31, 1833, Aged Six Years and Eleven Months*, ed. Lois Brown (Cambridge, MA: Harvard University Press, 2000); Heather Andrea Williams, *Self-Taught: African American Education in Slavery and Freedom* (Chapel Hill: University of North Carolina Press, 2009); Edward Mabee, *Black Education in New York State: From Colonial to Modern Times* (Syracuse, NY: Syracuse University Press, 1979).

10. The ship's given name was *Elizabeth*, and it sailed in 1820. Joseph Crane Hartzell, *The Africa Mission of the Methodist Episcopal Church* (New York: Board of Foreign Missions, 1909), 27.

11. I use the term "self-emancipated" rather than "runaway" to describe Smith's mother, in accordance with Smith's own usage, which recasts the criminal act of running away as a radical act of liberation. For more on preferred terminology, please see the following document prepared by senior scholars in the field: https://docs.google.com/document/d/1A4TEdDgYslX-hlKezLodMIM71My3KTNozxRvoIQTOQs/mobilebasic.

12. As Thomas Morgan and John Stauffer relate, the only mention of Smith's father's name is found in the University of Glasgow Matriculation Album for 1832, which lists "James M'Cune Smith" as "filius natu maximus Samuelis, Mercatoris apud New York" (first natural son of Samuel, merchant, New York), 20, 21. In a letter to Rev. Orville Dewey, DD, Smith characterized himself as "the son of a slave, owing my liberty to the emancipation act of the State of New York, and having kindred in a southern State; some of them slaveholders, others slaves." "Freedom and Slavery for Africans," *National Anti-Slavery Standard*, February 1, 1844. Morgan, "Medical Practice of James McCune Smith," 605. Stauffer, *Collected Works*, xix. In a letter to Gerrit Smith, McCune Smith referred to "the Old Puritan blood in me that leaps at fair and faithful blows laid on regardless of anything but their bare truth," suggesting that his father had descended from a family with deep roots in American soil. Letter to Gerrit Smith, March 31, 1855, Smith Papers, box 34.

13. Smith, "Introduction," 21.

14. *Anglo-African Magazine*, January 1860, 27–32.

15. *Frederick Douglass' Paper*, March 18, 1852.

16. Charles C. Andrews, *History of the New York African Free Schools* (New York: Mahlon Day, 1830), 119–20.

17. Leslie M. Harris, *In the Shadow of Slavery: African Americans in New York City, 1626–1863* (Chicago: University of Chicago Press, 2004), 141. Quotation from *Minutes of the Proceedings of the Fifteenth American Convention for Promoting the Abolition of Slavery* (Philadelphia: Merritt, 1817), 30–31.

18. See Benjamin Quarles, *Black Abolitionists* (New York: Da Capo Press, 1991), 12.

19. There is a competing story for why Andrews was fired. One account contends that Charles Andrews whipped a young student for the audacity of referring to a Black man as a "gentleman." The evidence for such outrage at its occurrence is slim, particularly in light of James McCune Smith's fond remembrances of regular "flagellations" at the hand of the

schoolmaster. The primary source for this story appears as a recollection in the 1921 proceedings of the Prince Hall Lodge of Masons, nearly a hundred years after its occurrence. The story is cited by Edward Mabee in *Black Education in New York State: From Colonial to Modern Times* (Syracuse, NY: Syracuse University Press, 1979), 22. Leslie Harris also discusses the alleged incident in *The Shadow of Slavery*, 142–44.

20 Records, *New York Manumission Society*, 8:78. At the New-York Historical Society. The records have been digitized and can be accessed at the following address: https://cdm16694. contentdm.oclc.org.

21. Records, *New York Manumission Society*, 8:78.

22. "Dr. J. McCune Smith," *Colored American*, June 9, 1838.

23. "Eulogy on the Life and Character of Dr. John Brown," *Colored American*, March 28, 1840.

24. "Extract 3," *Colored American*, December 16, 1837.

25. For more on this adaptation, see Martha Cutter, "The Child's Illustrated Antislavery Talking Book: Abigail Field Mott's Abridgment of Olaudah Equiano's *Interesting Narrative* for African American Children," in *Who Writes for Black Children? African American Children's Literature before 1900*, ed. Kate Capshaw and Anna Mae Duane (Minneapolis: University of Minnesota Press, 2017); and Valentina K. Tikoff, "Role Model for African American Children: Abigail Field Mott's *Life and Adventures of Olaudah Equiano* and White Northern Abolitionism," in *Who Writes?*

26. As John Stauffer indicates, the journal is no longer extant. While it seems likely that he kept the journal throughout his time abroad, the last entry known to scholars is September 15, 1832, just as he prepared to leave Liverpool for Glasgow. Stauffer, *Collected Works*, 8.

27. "Extracts," *Colored American*, November 11, 1837.

28. "Dr. Smith's Journal," *Colored American*, November 11, 1837.

29. James McCune Smith mentions both an 1809 and an 1827 parade in "Introduction."

30. "Extract 4," *Colored American*, February 3, 1838.

31. For more on Aldridge's life and work, see Herbert Marshall and Mildred Stock, *Ira Aldridge: The Negro Tragedian* (London: Rockliff, 1958); Bernth Lindfors, ed., *Ira Aldridge, the African Roscius* (Rochester, NY: University of Rochester Press, 2007); Krystyna Kujawinska Courtney, "Ira Aldridge, Shakespeare, and Color-Conscious Performances in Nineteenth-Century Europe," in *Colorblind Shakespeare: New Perspectives on Race and Performance*, ed. Ayanna Thompson (New York: Routledge, 2006), 121–40.

32. "Extract 6," *Colored American*, June 30, 1838.

33. Morgan, "Medical Practice of James McCune Smith," 603.

34. "The Turpin Legacy," *Colored American*, December 30, 1837.

35. "First Annual Report of the Association for the Benefit of Colored Orphans," *Colored American*, December 30, 1837.

36. Thomas Robert Moseley, *A History of the New-York Manumission Society, 1785–1849* (New York: NYU Press, 1963). The story of the origins of the New York Colored Orphan Asylum can be found in *From Cherry Street to Green Pastures: A History of the Colored Orphan Asylum at Riverdale-on-Hudson, 1836–1936*, in *Records of the Association for the Benefit of Colored Orphans. Series X: Centennial Booklet, 1936*, New-York Historical Society. Also see Harris, *In the Shadow of Slavery*, 145; and William Seraile, *Angels of Mercy: White Women and the History of New York's Colored Orphan Asylum* (New York: Fordham University Press, 2013), 9.

37. *From Cherry Street*, 5.

38. Seraile, *Angels of Mercy*, 9.

39. "Slavery and Its Effects," *Colored American*, September 9, 1837.

40. "Reception of Dr. Smith by the Colored Citizens of New York," *Colored American*, October 28, 1837.

41. There is no evidence that Garnet was in the audience the day of James McCune Smith's welcome reception, but Thomas Sidney, who had accompanied Garnet and Crummell on an ill-fated trip to a school in New Hampshire, was among those who spoke proudly of Smith's accomplishments.

42. "Reception of Dr. Smith by the Colored Citizens of New York."

43. For more on the remarkable interracial coalition among Smith, Frederick Douglass, Gerrit Smith, and John Brown, see Stauffer, *The Black Hearts of Men*.

44. According to the *Black Abolitionist Papers*, "In 1837 Smith, Henry Highland Garnet, George T. Downing, Charles L. Reason, John J. Zuille, and other local Black leaders formed the Colored Young Men of New York City to flood the state legislature with petitions asking for equal suffrage." Peter C. Ripley, ed., *The Black Abolitionist Papers* (Chapel Hill: University of North Carolina Press, 1992), 106. Smith referred to this meeting years later in a published exchange in the *Weekly Anglo-African*, December 30, 1860.

45. *Colored American*, December 23, 1837.

46. "The Turpin Legacy," *Colored American*, December 30, 1837.

47. Seraile, *Angels of Mercy*, 12–14.

48. *Weekly Advocate*, January 14, 1837.

49. *Colored American*, November 3, 1838.

50. *Colored American*, January 26, 1839. Also, *Minutes of the December 9, 1837 Annual Meeting; Text of the First Annual Report of the Association*, in *Records of the Association for the Benefit of Colored Orphans, 1836–1972*, vol. 1.

51. *Colored American*, January 26, 1839.

52. *Colored American*, October 28, 1837.

53. *Colored American*, January 26, 1839.

CHAPTER 2. SHIFTING GROUND, LOST PARENTS, UPROOTED SCHOOLS

1. Perhaps this lovely drawing was the handiwork of Henry Highland Garnet's schoolmate Patrick Reason, who would go on to become one of the nation's top engravers. Certainly Reason's artistic prowess was a subject of pride among the students and teachers. When Charles C. Andrews, the NYAFS schoolmaster, published his *History of the New York African Free Schools*, he featured Reason's depiction of the school prominently. Charles C. Andrews, *History of the New-York African Free Schools* (New York: Mahlon Day, 1830).

2. "H.H. Garnet," *Emancipator and Republican*, March 21, 1844.

3. Alexander Crummell, "Eulogium," in *Africa and America: Addresses and Discourses* (New York: Wiley, 1891).

4. "H.H. Garnet," 184.

5. James McCune Smith, "Sketch of the Life and Labors of Rev. Henry Highland Garnet," in *Memorial Discourse*, 19. Because it seems highly unlikely that Garnet did not have some input—and a modicum of editorial control—over this biography attached to his own speech, this is one of the more reliable resources on Garnet's early life.

6. In a letter written to Garnet, James McCune Smith recalls their neighborhood as a place where the students "often fought our way to school and from school." Letter, James McCune

Smith to Henry Highland Garnet (Document 19) in *Black Abolitionist Papers*, ed. Peter Ripley (Chapel Hill: University of North Carolina Press, 1992), 100. Hereafter, *BAP*.

7. W. E. B. Du Bois, "Of Alexander Crummell," in *The Souls of Black Folk* (Seattle: Amazon Classics, 2017), 172.

8. Crummell, "Eulogium," 298.

9. Smith, "Sketch of the Life," 21.

10. "Practical Anti-Slavery," *Liberator*, July 25, 1835. Garnet's passport lists him as five feet, eleven inches tall. Henry Highland Garnet, Passport application, August 24, 1861. National Archives and Records Administration (NARA), Washington, DC; Roll 098—22 Jul 1861–26 Aug 1861. Accessed via Ancestry.com.

11. Crummell, "Eulogium," 274.

12. Crummell, "Eulogium," 25.

13. See, for instance, Russ Castronovo's discussion of Washington as the adoptive father of an orphan nation in *Fathering the Nation: American Genealogies of Slavery and Freedom* (Berkeley: University of California Press, 1996), 33.

14. Frederick Douglass, "What Is the Slave to the Fourth of July?" in *My Bondage and My Freedom* (New York: Miller, Orton & Mulligan, 1855), 441.

15. Crummell, "Eulogium," 275. Also mentioned in James McCune Smith, "Sketch," 25.

16. Crummell, "Eulogium," 276.

17. *Emancipator and Republican*, March 21, 1844, 184.

18. *First Annual Report of the American Anti-Slavery Society* (New York, 1834), 56. Also see "'Chronicles of Kidnapping in New York': Resistance to the Fugitive Slave Law, 1834–1835," *Afro-Americans in New York Life and History* 8 (Jan. 1984): 7–15.

19. This evidence could be read in several ways—she may well have offered evidence proving that she was living in New York City during the time when she did actually live there. She may also be "proving" that she was living in New York City during the time she was, in fact, enslaved in Maryland. By all accounts, the slave catchers were working on behalf of the Garnets' former owner, who would have had a valid legal claim on her, regardless of when she left the plantation. Smith, "Sketch," 25. For more on the connection between Richard Riker and Rikers Island prison, see Anna Mae Duane, "The Shame of Rikers," *Slate*, July 2017, http://www.slate.com.

20. Eric Foner, *Gateway to Freedom: The Hidden History of the Underground Railroad* (New York: Norton, 2015), 52.

21. Smith, "Sketch," 27.

22. Smith, "Sketch," 26.

23. Garnet was apprenticed to Captain Epenetus Smith of Long Island. Smith, "Sketch," 26.

24. Smith, "Sketch," 26.

25. Smith, "Sketch," 28.

26. *Liberator*, April 19, 1834.

27. Herbert Aptheker, *A Documentary History of the Negro People in the United States* (New York: Citadel, 1951), 151–52; *Liberator*, April 19, 1834.

28. "A Delightful Token of Personal Regard," *Liberator*, April 19, 1834.

29. "A Delightful Token of Personal Regard."

30. *Report of the Proceedings at the Formation of the African Education Society Instituted at Washington*, December 28, 1829 (Washington, DC: JC Dunn, 1830).

31. James Forten, "To the Humane and Benevolent Inhabitants of the City and County of Philadelphia," 1818, in *Early Negro Writing: 1760–1837*, ed. Dorothy Porter (Baltimore, MD: Black Classic Press, 1995), 264.

32. See William Lloyd Garrison, *Thoughts on African Colonization; or, An Impartial Exhibition of the Doctrines, Principles, and Purposes of the American Colonization Society* (Boston: Garrison and Knapp, 1832).

33. Craig D. Townsend, *Faith in Their Own Color: Black Episcopalians in Antebellum New York City* (New York: Columbia University Press, 2012), 89. Carla Peterson, *Black Gotham*, 105.

34. "Constitution of the Phoenix Society," *Liberator*, June 29, 1833. The Phoenix Society was dedicated to increasing educational opportunities for both boys and girls. From the evidence I have seen, women were not given many speaking roles at the gatherings held by Garnet and his cohort.

35. "Minutes and Proceedings of the First Annual Convention of the People of Colour Held by Adjournments in the City of Philadelphia from 6–9 June, 1831" (Philadelphia, 1831).

36. "From the New Haven Palladium," *Connecticut Courant*, September 9, 1831; also reprinted in *College for Coloured Youth: An Account of the New-Haven City Meeting and Resolutions: With Recommendations of the College, and Strictures upon the Doings of New Haven* (New York: Publ. by the Committee, 1831), 5.

37. *Connecticut Journal*, September 9, 1831.

38. *Liberator*, March 16, 1833.

39. *Liberator*, March 16, 1833.

40. *Liberator*, March 16, 1833.

41. Andrew T. Judson et al., "Appeal to the American Colonization Society," March 22, 1833, published in "Fruits of Colonizationism!" (Boston: American Antiquarian Society, 1833).

42. Samuel J. May, *Some Recollections of Our Antislavery Conflict* (Boston: Fields, Osgood, 1869), 47.

43. Andrew T. Judson, "Argument of Andrew T. Judson, in the Case of the State of Connecticut vs. Prudence Crandall [excerpt]." Delivered before the Supreme Court of Errors of the State of Connecticut, July 1834 (Boston: Garrison and Knapp, 1834).

44. Susan Strane, *A Whole Souled Woman: Prudence Crandall and the Education of Black Women* (New York: Norton, 1990), 90. Also Donald E. Williams, Jr., *Prudence Crandall's Legacy: The Fight for Equality in the 1830s, Dred Scott, and* Brown v. Board of Education (Middletown, CT: Wesleyan University Press, 2014), 377. I am indebted to Yale's Gilder Lehrman Center for its open access document collection of materials relating to this incident. "The Black Law of Connecticut (1833)—Citizens ALL: African Americans in Connecticut, 1700–1850." Yale University, Gilder Lehrman Center for the Study of Slavery, Resistance, & Abolition, 2017. http://glc.yale.edu.

45. Edwin G. Burrows and Mike Wallace, *Gotham: A History of New York City to 1898* (New York: Oxford University Press, 1999), 556–57.

46. "More Riots in New-York," *Salem Gazette*, July 15, 1834.

47. "More Riots in New-York."

48. William Allen Wallace, *The History of Canaan, New Hampshire* (Concord, NH: Rumford Press, 1910), 255.

49. Circular printed as a result of Trustees Meeting, September 11, 1834. Reprinted in Wallace, *History of Canaan*, 264.

50. Crummell, "Eulogium," 279.

51. Crummell, "Eulogium," 285.

52. "Practical Anti-Slavery in Plymouth, N.H.," *Liberator*, July 25, 1835.

53. "Practical Anti-Slavery in Plymouth, N.H.," *Liberator*, July 25, 1835.

54. Wallace, *History of Canaan*, 294–95; *Liberator*, July 4, 1835.

55. Wallace, *History of Canaan*, 268. *The Granite Monthly: A Magazine of Literature, History, and State Progress* 48 (Concord, NH: Granite Monthly, 1916), 274.

56. Crummell, "Eulogium," 13.

57. Crummell, "Eulogium," 13.

58. Smith, "Sketch," in *Memorial Discourse*, 31.

59. Beriah Green, "A Sketch of the Condition and Prospects of the Oneida Institute by the Board of Instruction and Government 1834." Republished in *The Miscellaneous Writings of Beriah Green* (Whitesboro, NY: Oneida Institute, 1841), 262.

60. Green, "A Sketch," 266.

61. Crummell, "Eulogium," 284.

62. Letter, Garnet to Alexander Crummell, May 13, 1837. Alexander Crummell Papers at Schomburg Library, NYC.

63. Letter, Garnet to Alexander Crummell. May 13, 1837.

64. Letter, Garnet to Alexander Crummell. May 13, 1837.

65. Letter, Garnet to Alexander Crummell. May 13, 1837.

66. *Colored American*, August 2, 1837; *Colored American*, September 9, 1837; James McCune Smith refers to the meeting in a letter to Garnet published in the *Weekly Anglo-African*, December 30, 1860. See also *BAP*, document 100.

67. *Colored American*, February 18, 1837.

68. Matthew Lewis, "Alonzo the Brave, and Fair Imogine," in *The Monk* (New York: Routledge, 1907), 250. See also Jared Hickman, *Black Prometheus: Race and Radicalism in the Age of Atlantic Slavery* (New York: Oxford University Press, 2017); Schor, *Henry Highland Garnet*, 17–19; Pasternak, *Rise Now and Fly to Arms*, 10–15.

69. Beriah Green, "A Sketch," 249–59. Pasternak suggests that Garnet also studied African history at the institute, but I have been unable to confirm this. Pasternak, *Rise Now and Fly to Arms*, 28.

70. "Anniversary of the American Anti-Slavery Society," *Liberator*, May 22, 1840.

71. "Minutes and Proceedings of the First Annual Convention of the People of Colour," 5; Colored Conventions: Bringing Nineteenth-Century Black Organizing to Digital Life. coloredconventions.org.

72. "Minutes and Proceedings of the First Annual Convention of the People of Colour," 20. The original quotation is from Lord Byron, "Childe Harold's Pilgrimage," canto ii, stanzas 73–77. See Lord Byron, "Childe Harold's Pilgrimage," in *The Works of the Rt. Hon. Lord Byron*, vol. 1 (Philadelphia: Pomeroy, 1824), 72.

73. Lord Byron, "Childe Harold's Pilgrimage," 71.

74. See Stauffer, *Black Hearts*, especially 70–88.

CHAPTER 3. ORPHANS, DATA, AND THE AMERICAN STORY

1. NYAFS Records, 3: 54.

2. *Colored American*, September 30, 1837.

3. *Colored American*, September 30, 1837.

4. Edward Jarvis, "Statistics of Insanity in the United States," *Boston Medical and Surgical Journal* 27 (1842): 116–21. To his credit, once he realized the figures were falsified, Jarvis worked strenuously to refute the assumptions based on this erroneous data.

5. "Reflections on the Census of 1840," *Southern Literary Messenger* 9 (1843): 340–52.

6. John Calhoun to Richard Pakenham, April 18, 1844. Reprinted in *The Library of Original Sources: 1833–1865*, vol. 9, ed. Oliver Joseph Thatcher (Milwaukee: University Research Exten-

sion, 1915), 115. Also see William Stanton, *The Leopard's Spots: Scientific Attitudes toward Race in America, 1815–1859* (Chicago: University of Chicago Press, 1966), 58–63.

7. Samuel Morton, *Crania Ægyptiaca; or, Observations on Egyptian Ethnography* (Philadelphia: John Penington, 1844), 60.

8. Morton, *Crania Aegyptiaca*, 59.

9. Morton, *Crania Aegyptiaca*, 59–60.

10. Morton, *Crania Aegyptiaca*, 59–60.

11. For the increasing investment in the child as a site of progress, see Sari Edelstein, *Adulthood and Other Fictions* (New York: Oxford University Press, 2019).

12. James McCune Smith, "A Dissertation on the Influence of Climate on Longevity" (New York: Office of Merchants' Magazine, 1846). Held at the Beinecke Library, Yale University.

13. James McCune Smith, "The Destiny of the People of Color," 1843, in Stauffer, *Collected Works*, 49.

14. McCune Smith, "The Destiny of the People of Color," 53.

15. See Britt Rusert, *Fugitive Science: Empiricism and Freedom in Early African American Culture* (New York: NYU Press, 2017); and *W.E.B. Du Bois's Data Portraits: Visualizing Black America*, ed. Whitney Battle-Baptiste and Britt Rusert (Princeton, NJ: Princeton Architectural Press, 2018).

16. *Liberator*, February 23, 1844.

17. Bryan Edwards, *The History, Civil and Commercial, of the British Colonies in the West Indies*, 3 vols. (London, 1807), 3: 99.

18. "Lecture on the Haytien Revolutions," 1841, in Stauffer, *Collected Works*, 27.

19. "Lecture on the Haytien Revolutions," 1841, in Stauffer, *Collected Works*, 27.

20. "The Bosjesman—Trade with South Africa—Cultivation—Introduction of the New England Plough," *New-Hampshire Gazette*, April 18, 1848.

21. "The Bosjesman." Although we do not know exactly where Omo was born and raised, or what language he spoke, it is worth noting that Omo means "baby" in Yuroba, a language spoken in the general area where Omo was found (according to the source cited in this note, "a thousand miles Northeast of Capetown along the equatorial line").

22. *National Anti-Slavery Standard*, February 22, 1849.

23. *National Anti-Slavery Standard*, February 22, 1849.

24. "The Bosjesman."

25. "Letters from Perley Washington," *Daily Atlas*, published as the *Boston Daily Atlas*, March 4, 1848.

26. "Letters from Perley Washington."

27. See Rosemarie Garland Thomson, *Extraordinary Bodies: Disability in American Literature and Culture* (New York: Columbia University Press, 1997), especially chapter 2.

28. "Great Curiosity," *Trenton State Gazette*, November 13, 1847, 1.

29. Samuel G. Morton, "Some Observations of the Bushman Hottentot Boy," *Academy of Natural Sciences of Philadelphia Proceedings* 4 (1848): 5–7. William Stanton uses the incident of Morton examining the "Bushman" boy to lead off his study of the American School, in *The Leopard's Spots*, 1–2; Stanton does not mention the New York meeting. "Annual Meeting of the Colored Orphan Asylum," *National Anti-Slavery Standard*, February 22, 1849. The *Standard* also ran a copy of a letter about Henry's history that Chase sent to the Lyceum of Natural History in New York City (later the New York Academy of Sciences). See also Bruce R. Dain. *A Hideous Monster of the Mind: American Race Theory in the Early Republic* (Cambridge, MA: Harvard University Press, 2002).

30. Morton, "Some Observations of the Bushman Hottentot Boy."

31. *National Anti-Slavery Standard*, February 22, 1849.

32. *First Annual Report of the Governors of the Alms House, New-York, for the Year 1849* (New York: George F. Nesbitt, 1850), 65.

33. "Annual Meeting of the Coloured Orphan Asylum," *National Anti-Slavery Standard*, February 22, 1849. My reading of this moment is influenced by Bruce Dain's analysis in *Hideous Monster of the Mind*.

34. "Annual Meeting of the Coloured Orphan Asylum," *National Anti-Slavery Standard*, February 22, 1849.

35. Saidiya Hartman, "Venus in Two Acts," *Small Axe* 12, no. 2 (2008): 1–14. I am indebted to Cristobal Silva for pointing me to this article.

36. *Colored American*, January 26, 1839.

37. James Janeway, *A Token for Children, to Which Is Added a Token for the Children of New England* (Worcester, MA: Isaiah, Thomas, 1795), 9.

38. *First Annual Report of the Governors*, 59.

39. *First Annual Report of the Governors*, 57.

40. Harriet Beecher Stowe, *Uncle Tom's Cabin* (Cambridge, MA: Harvard University Press, 2009), 386.

41. Thomas Jefferson, "Notes on the State of Virginia," in *Thomas Jefferson: Writings*, ed. Merrill Peterson (New York: Library of America, 1984), chapter 14.

42. *National Anti-Slavery Standard*, February 22, 1849.

43. *National Anti-Slavery Standard*, September 29, 1855.

CHAPTER 4. THROWING DOWN THE SHOVEL

1. NYAFS Records, 3: 42–43.

2. Pasternak, *Rise Now and Fly to Arms*, 55.

3. Crummell, "Eulogium," 301.

4. Crummell, "Eulogium," 301.

5. Garnet to George Whipple, July 10, 1850, American Missionary Association Archive, Tulane University, box 106; *The North Star*, April 13, 1849.

6. Garnet's poetry is published in *The North Star*, March 30, 1849; "Progress in Geneva," *The North Star*, April 13, 1849.

7. Henry Highland Garnet to Gerrit Smith, September 16, 1848. Smith Papers, box 20.

8. James McCune Smith to Gerrit Smith, December 28, 1846. Smith Papers, box 34.

9. *The North Star*, December 8, 1848.

10. *Minutes of the National Convention of Colored Citizens, Held at Buffalo* (New York: Percy and Reed, 1843), 13.

11. For more on Julia and Henry's collaboration, see Derrick Spires, "'Flights of Fancy': Rereading Henry Highland Garnet's 'Address to the Slaves' through Reception History and Print Culture," in *Colored Conventions in the Nineteenth Century and the Digital Age*, ed. P. Gabrielle Foreman, Sarah L. Patterson, and Jim Casey (Chapel Hill: University of North Carolina Press, forthcoming).

12. *Christian Recorder*, January 22, 1870. The Colored Conventions Project, headed by P. Gabrielle Foreman, is doing groundbreaking work to illuminate the obscured roles of women in the convention movement. For a touchstone text in the scholarship chronicling the role of Black women in the abolitionist movement, see Carla Peterson, *Doers of the Word: African-American Women Speakers and Writers in the North, 1830–1880* (New Brunswick, NJ: Rutgers University Press, 1998).

13. In this way, Garnet's political imaginary reflects an understanding of time theorized by twenty-first-century scholars like Christina Sharpe, who sees Black life as existing in the wake of the slave ship, living in a climate of white supremacy that renders Black precarity a state of being. Christina Sharpe, *In the Wake: On Blackness and Being* (Durham, NC: Duke University Press, 2016).

14. For rich critical analysis of the gothic/spectral in Black thought, see Ivy Wilson, *Specters of Democracy: Blackness and the Aesthetics of Politics in the Antebellum U.S.* (Oxford: Oxford University Press, 2011).

15. *Herald of Freedom*, November 18, 1839, 149. Also in Schor, *Henry Highland Garnet*, 21–22.

16. *Emancipator and Free American*, July, 7, 1842. Garnet signs the call as chairman.

17. *Emancipator and Free American*, July, 7, 1842.

18. Henry Highland Garnet, "A Letter to Mrs. Maria W. Chapman," *Emancipator and Republican*, November 30, 1843, 124, reprinted in *Liberator*, December 8, 1843. As Derrick Spires suggests, it is notable that Garnet publicly acknowledged his intellectual debt to Julia, even as he glossed over the specifics of its extent. Spires, "'Flights of Fancy.'"

19. *Minutes of the National Convention of Colored Citizens*, 13.

20. *Emancipator and Republican*, also published as *Emancipator and Weekly Chronicle*, August 6, 1845, 60.

21. Amos Beeman, Scrapbook, 2: 3. James Weldon Johnson Collection in the American Literature Collection, Beinecke Rare Book and Manuscript Library, Yale University, boxes 2 and 3.

22. William Wells Brown, *The Black Man: His Antecedents, His Genius, and His Achievements* (Boston: James Redpath, 1863), 150.

23. *Minutes of the National Convention of Colored Citizens*, 12.

24. Crummell, "Eulogium," 282.

25. David Blight's magisterial biography of Douglass offers a fascinating study of Douglass's rise to fame. David Blight, *Frederick Douglass: Prophet of Freedom* (New York: Simon & Schuster, 2018).

26. William Lloyd Garrison, "Preface," in Frederick Douglass, *Narrative of the Life of Frederick Douglass* (Boston: Anti-Slavery Office, 1845), iv.

27. Garrison, "Preface," iv.

28. Letter from James McCune Smith to Gerrit Smith, July 28, 1848. Smith Papers, box 34.

29. To be precise, the quotation opens the speech as it is published in 1848. Since we have no reproduction of the speech as it was given in 1843, this is the best indication we have. Recall that Garnet had used this quotation as early as 1840 in the Antislavery Anniversary Convention.

30. Peter P. Hinks, *To Awaken My Afflicted Brethren: David Walker and the Problem of Antebellum Slave Resistance* (University Park: Pennsylvania State University Press, 2006), xxxix.

31. Walker's *Appeal, with a Brief Sketch of His Life. And also Garnet's Address to the Slaves of the United States of America* (New York: Printed by J. H. Tobitt, 1848), vii.

32. *Walker's Appeal*, 31.

33. *Walker's Appeal*, 17, 67.

34. Garnet, "Address to the Slaves," 95.

35. Garnet, "Address to the Slaves," 96.

36. Garnet, "Address to the Slaves," 96.

37. Gayatri Chakravorty Spivak, "General Strike," *Rethinking Marxism: A Journal of Economics, Culture & Society* 26, no. 1 (2014): 9–14.

38. Henry Highland Garnet, *The Past and the Present Condition of the Destiny of the Colored Race* (Troy, NY: Steamless of J.C. Kneeland, 1848), 20.

39. For Dana Luciano, the prevalence of grief throughout the nineteenth century can be read as a physical bulwark against the cruel dictates of progress. For Luciano, the "affective residue of the vanished past in the present tense" permits the "mournful body to assess the ongoing significance of the past in a culture speeding ever more rapidly toward the attainment of its historical destiny." Dana Luciano, *Arranging Grief: Sacred Time and the Body in Nineteenth-Century America* (New York: NYU Press, 2007), 2. On different modes of nineteenth-century time, see Lloyd Pratt, *Archives of American Time: Literature and Modernity in the Nineteenth Century* (Philadelphia: University of Pennsylvania Press, 2011).

40. Thomas Jefferson, "Notes on the State of Virginia," 264.

41. *The North Star*, January 26, 1849.

42. See Reinhard O. Johnson, *The Liberty Party, 1840-1848: Antislavery Third-Party Politics in the United States* (Baton Rouge: Louisiana State University Press, 2009).

43. *The North Star*, January 26, 1849.

44. "Colonization and Emigration . . . H.H. Garnet's Reply to S.S. Ward," *The North Star*, March 2, 1849.

45. "Colonization and Emigration."

46. It is possible, of course, that the reference to Chartist rebellion was added between the spoken version of the address and the version published in 1848. The actions, chronicled in both British and American periodicals, would also feature in Friedrich Engels's 1845 *Conditions of the Working Class.* While it is highly unlikely that Garnet had read Engels's text, I mention it here as an indicator of how Garnet was coming to conclusions that were emerging in what would become Marxist analyses of a global labor struggle. Friedrich Engels, *Conditions of the Working-Class in England*, ed. David McLellen (London: Oxford University Press, 2009), 224. By 1849, periodicals like the *National Era* were discussing the tactics of the Chartists. "Sketches of Modern Reforms and Reformers, in Great Britain and Ireland," *National Era*, July 23, 1849.

47. *NY Daily Tribune Dispatch*, January 1848.

48. "France: All Eyes Continue Fixed upon France and Her Infant Republic," *The North Star*, April 28, 1848.

49. *The North Star*, April 28, 1848. For more on the influence 1848 had on Douglass and others see Benjamin Fagan, "*The North Star* and the Atlantic, 1848," *African American Review* 47, no. 1 (2014): 51–67.

50. Henry Highland Garnet, "Model Republic," *The North Star*, April 28, 1848. Douglass mentioned that he clipped the piece from the *Troy Daily Post.*

51. The family's name was also spelled "Weems" in many articles. I have chosen to follow the spelling favored by most historians.

52. *Anti-Slavery Reporter*, December 1, 1852.

53. 1850 Census for the Town of Seneca, NY. (Geneva was considered part of Seneca at this time.)

54. "Atrocious Outrage on Henry H. Garnet," *The North Star*, July 7, 1848.

55. *The North Star* (Rochester, NY), June 23, 1848; July 7, 1848; August 25, 1848. Also Bryan Prince, *A Shadow on the Household: One Enslaved Family's Incredible Struggle for Freedom* (McClelland & Stewart, 2009). Kindle edition, location 928.

56. Letter from Garnet to Arthur Tappan, August 25, 1849. AMA Collection, Tulane University, box 106.

57. *The North Star*, July 27, 1849.

58. "Communications: The Disgraceful Proceedings in Zion Church, N.Y.," *The North Star*, June 22, 1849.

59. "'Calling Him Out' and He Comes," *The North Star*, September 7, 1849.

60. *The North Star*, July 27, 1849.

CHAPTER 5. PUMPING OUT A SINKING SHIP

1. NYAFS Records, 3: 45–47.

2. *Emancipator*, November 16, 1837.

3. "B'hoy" was a common term referring to a street tough.

4. *Frederick Douglass' Paper*, March 25, 1852.

5. Letter to Gerrit Smith, March 31, 1855. Smith Papers, box 34.

6. *Frederick Douglass' Paper*, March 25, 1852.

7. Green, "Extracts from a Pamphlet," 252.

8. Proceedings of the Colored National Convention, Held in Rochester, July 6th, 7th, and 8th, 1853 (Rochester, NY: Office of Frederick Douglass' Paper, 1853), 19. Colored Conventions: Bringing Nineteenth-Century Black Organizing to Digital Life. coloredconventions.org.

9. Letter to Gerrit Smith, July 7, 1848. Smith Papers, box 34.

10. Letter from the Editor, *Frederick Douglass' Paper*, May 27, 1853. My interpretation of the tension between Frederick Douglass and James McCune Smith about the content of "Heads" is indebted to Stauffer's analysis. Stauffer, *Collected Works*, 187–89, 233.

11. "Heads of the Colored People: The Inventor," *Frederick Douglass' Paper*, September 9, 1853.

12. James McCune Smith to Gerrit Smith, March 31, 1855. Smith Papers, box 34.

13. William Lloyd Garrison, "Preface," in *Narrative of the Life of Frederick Douglass* (Boston: Anti-Slavery Office, 1845), viii. Garrison's vouching for Douglass had followed a longstanding formula in which Black stories were framed and validated by white writers, a formula John Sekora has characterized as a "Black message in a white envelope." John Sekora, "Black Message/White Envelope: Genre, Authenticity, and Authority in the Antebellum Slave Narrative," *Callaloo* 32 (1987): 482–515.

14. James McCune Smith to Gerrit Smith, July 28, 1848. Smith Papers, box 34.

15. As John Stauffer writes, "Women are the greatest heroes" in many of McCune Smith's writings for *Frederick Douglass' Paper*. Stauffer, *Black Hearts*, 223. For more on "The Washerwoman" sketch, see Rachel Banner, "Thinking through Things: Labors of Freedom in James McCune Smith's 'The Washerwoman.'" *ESQ: A Journal of the American Renaissance* 59, no. 2 (2013): 291–328.

16. "The Washerwoman," *Frederick Douglass' Paper*, June 17, 1852.

17. *Frederick Douglass' Paper*, June 17, 1852.

18. Frederick Douglass, *Narrative of the Life of Frederick Douglass* (Boston: Anti-Slavery Office, 1845), 57.

19. "The Washerwoman."

20. 1860 Census: New York Ward 5, District 2, New York, New York; Roll: M653_790; Page: 585; Family History Library Film: 803790. Accessed via ancestry.com.

21. By the time he published "The Schoolmaster" in November of 1854, he had lost his three remaining children, Anna Gertrude Smith, Frederick Douglass Smith, and Peter Williams Smith, all in the space of four weeks. Stauffer, *Collected Work*, 224.

22. "The Arctic," *Boston Courier*, October 19, 1854.

23. *Daily Globe* (Washington, DC), October 18, 1854; *Daily Alta California*, November 15, 1854.

24. "Horoscope," *Frederick Douglass' Paper*, March 7, 1865.

25. "No. X: The Schoolmaster," *Frederick Douglass' Paper*, November 3, 1854.

26. James McCune Smith, "The Destiny of the People of Color," 1843, in Stauffer, *Collected Works*, 49.

27. Ralph Waldo Emerson, "Self-Reliance," in *The Essential Writings of Ralph Waldo Emerson* (New York: Modern Library Classics, 2000), 133.

28. *Moby-Dick* did not enjoy its current status or popularity in the 1850s, but Melville certainly saw himself as part of this larger conversation about navigating the obligations between the individual and society.

29. Henry David Thoreau, *Walden*, 1854 (New York: Crowell, 1910), 6.

30. Proceedings of the Colored National Convention, Held in Rochester, NY, 35.

31. "Our Leaders," *Frederick Douglass' Paper*, September 21, 1855.

32. Frederick Douglass, *My Bondage and My Freedom* (New York: Miller, Orton & Mulligan, 1855), 361. (Hereafter *MBMF.*)

33. *MBMF*, 362.

34. Frederick Douglass, *The Life and Times of Frederick Douglass, Written by Himself* (Hartford, CT: Park, 1882), 568.

35. *MBMF*, xviii.

36. *MBMF*, xviii.

37. *MBMF*, xviii.

38. See David Blight, *Frederick Douglass: Prophet of Freedom* (New York: Simon and Schuster, 2018), especially the chapter "A Childhood of Extremes," 19–35.

39. *MBMF*, 118.

40. *MBMF*, 108.

41. *MBMF*, 133.

42. *MBMF*, 48.

43. *MBMF*, 52.

44. It is important to note that while Prichard himself was antislavery, his own work and his admiration for works like Morton's *Crania Americana* lent support to arguments insisting that the white and Black races were inherently separate, and far from equal.

45. Smith, "Introduction," *MBMF*, xxx.

46. *MBMF*, 24.

47. Here Smith builds upon Douglass's own expanded attention to his mother's influence on his life and legacy. In Douglass's first *Narrative*, his mother was a ghostly, silent figure, but in *My Bondage*, Douglass reveals that his mother somehow had acquired literacy, even while working as a field hand, an extraordinary achievement that he attributes to her "earnest love of knowledge." *MBMF*, 24: 39.

48. *MBMF*, 24.

49. *Frederick Douglass' Paper*, July 6, 1855.

50. Stauffer, *Black Hearts*, 24.

51. *Minutes of the National Convention of Colored Citizens, Held at Buffalo* (New York: Percy and Reed, 1843), 16.

52. *National Anti-Slavery Standard*, November, 14, 1844.

53. *Frederick Douglass' Paper*, July 6, 1855.

54. Stauffer, *Black Hearts*.

55. *Frederick Douglass' Paper*, September 21, 1855.

CHAPTER 6. FOLLOW THE MONEY, FIND THE REVOLUTION

1. In June, the gains of the French laboring class had been rolled back in brutal fashion. In what would later be called the June Days, protesting workers were slaughtered by government forces. Still more devastating to those who wanted to believe in a global uprising of the common people against authoritarian tyrants and monarchists, the killing orders came from liberal

middle-class republicans, unwilling to lose their status to what they saw as an increasingly demanding working class. In the end, over ten thousand people were dead, and four thousand insurgents were deported to Algeria. For an overview of the June Days revolt and the aftermath see Mark Traugott, *Armies of the Poor: Determinants of Working-Class Participation in the Parisian Insurrection of June 1848* (New York: Routledge, 2017); Robert John Weston Evans and Hartmut Pogge Von Strandmann, eds., *The Revolutions in Europe, 1848–1849: From Reform to Reaction* (Oxford: Oxford University Press, 2002); Karl Marx, Friedrich Engels, and Clemens Palme Dutt, *The Class Struggles in France, 1848–50* (London: Martin Lawrence, 1895); Roger V. Gould, *Insurgent Identities: Class, Community, and Protest in Paris from 1848 to the Commune* (Chicago: University of Chicago Press, 1995).

2. American diplomats eventually negotiated his release and travel to the United States. For more on Kossuth, see Tim Roberts, "Lajos Kossuth and the Permeable American Orient of the Mid-Nineteenth Century," *Diplomatic History* 39, no. 5 (2015): 793–818.

3. "Extract 4," *Colored American*, February 3, 1838.

4. William Wells Brown, *Three Years in Europe* (London: Oliver and Boyd, 1852), letter 1, July 28, 1849, 7.

5. Brown, *Three Years in Europe*, 7.

6. Reception Speech at Finsbury Chapel, Moorfields, England, May 12, 1846, and Dr. Campbell's Reply, in *MBMF*, 408.

7. Christopher Brown, *Moral Capital: Foundations of British Abolitionism* (Chapel Hill: University of North Carolina Press, 2006).

8. "American Slavery: The Free-Labour Movement," *Anti-Slavery Reporter* 5, no. 58 (1850): 160–61. As they did with so much of Garnet's rhetoric, antislavery activists soon picked up on the powerful effect of Garnet's phrasing. A report from a Free Produce meeting in Rochester in 1851 both cites a letter from Garnet as their opening inspiration and goes on to connect the iron collar to allegedly innocent acts of consumption: "The *iron collar*, the hand-cuff, the knotted-lash and branding-iron, to the quivering flesh of the unfortunate who have fallen among thieves, and all the rest of the paraphernalia of human torture which the ingenuity of the most inhuman tyrant can invent, depend almost, if not exclusively upon the consumption of the produce of the labor of the slave." "Free Produce Convention," *The North Star*, January 23, 1851.

9. William Wells Brown, *The Anti-Slavery Harp: A Collection of Songs for Anti-Slavery Meetings* (Boston: Bella Marsh, 1848), 30.

10. See Nathan Hans, *Dan Emmett and the Rise of Early Negro Minstrelsy* (Norman: Oklahoma University Press, 1962). For conventions of early American theater and audience interjections, see Sarah Chinn, *Spectacular Men: Race, Gender, and Nation on the Early American Stage* (Oxford: Oxford University Press, 2017).

11. Sarah Meer, *Uncle Tom Mania: Slavery, Minstrelsy, and Transatlantic Culture in the 1850s* (Athens: University of Georgia Press, 2005).

12. "H.H. Garnet," *Anti-Slavery Reporter*, January 1, 1851. The speech had been given in November of 1850.

13. Karl Marx, *The Poverty of Philosophy: A Reply to M. Proudhon's* Philosophy of Poverty (New York: International Publishers, n.d.), 94–95.

14. For just a few examples, see Edward E. Baptist, *The Half Has Never Been Told: Slavery and the Making of American Capitalism* (New York: Basic Civitas Books, 2014); Walter Johnson et al., "Race Capitalism Justice," *Boston Review* forum 1 (Winter 2017). Stephanie Smallwood, "Turning African Slaves into Atlantic Commodities," in *Saltwater Slavery: A Middle Passage from Africa to American Diaspora* (Cambridge, MA: Harvard University Press, 2007), 33–64; W.

E. B. Du Bois, *Black Reconstruction in America, 1860–1880*, 1935, ed. Henry Louis Gates (New York: Oxford University Press, 2014).

15. *The North Star*, January 26, 1849.

16. *New York Daily Tribune*, April 14, 1848. The piece was reprinted from *Northernstar*, a Chartist newspaper out of Yorkshire, Britain.

17. Henry Highland Garnet to Samuel Ringgold Ward, September 4, 1850, *Impartial Citizen*, October 5, 1850.

18. Letter to Gerrit Smith, Esq., from H. H. Garnet, September 28th, 1850, *Impartial Citizen*, October 26, 1850.

19. *Frederick Douglass' Paper*, June 26, 1851, reprinted from the *British Banner*.

20. *Impartial Citizen*, October 26, 1850.

21. *Impartial Citizen*, October 26, 1850.

22. Seventeen of these parishioners had to move to Canada in the act's aftermath. *Frederick Douglass' Paper*, June 26, 1851, reprinted from the *British Banner*.

23. Samuel Rhodes to Gerrit Smith, November 21, 1850. Smith Papers, box 31.

24. Julia Garnet to Gerrit Smith, February 14, 1851. Smith Papers, box 19.

25. Julia Garnet to Gerrit Smith.

26. *Geneva Gazette*, March 7, 1851.

27. *Frederick Douglass' Paper*, March 11, 1852; also Prince, *A Shadow on the Household*, loc. 1008–9.

28. *Frederick Douglass' Paper*, December 31, 1852.

29. *Sketch of the Life of Charles B. Ray* (New York: J.J. Little, 1887), 35–36. The description of their collaboration follows:

> We had here, on one occasion, a party of twenty-eight persons of all ages, from the old grandmother to a child of five years. We destined them for Canada. I secured passage for them in a barge, and Mr. Wright and myself spent the day in providing food, and personally saw them on the barge. I then took the regular passenger boat to the foot of Cortland Street and started. Arriving in the morning, I reported to the Committee at Albany, and then returned to Troy and gave Brother Garnet notice, and he and I spent the day in visiting [a] friend of the cause there, to raise money to help the party through to Toronto, Canada, via Oswego.

30. Jeffrey Brackett, *The Negro in Maryland: A Study of the Institution of Slavery* (Freeport, NY: Books for Libraries Press, 1969), 179. Also see Prince, *Shadow on the Household*, loc. 201.

31. "The Weims Family: Illustration of American Slavery," *Anti-Slavery Reporter*, December 1, 1852.

32. Garnet to Charles B. Ray, *BAP* 1: 327. Also in *Antislavery Reporter*, December 1, 1852.

33. Garnet to Charles B. Ray.

34. *Slave*, no. 23, 92.

35. Garnet to Charles B. Ray.

36. Anna Richardson to Charles B. Ray, December 10, 1852, in *Sketch of the Life of Rev. Charles B. Ray* (New York: J.J. Little, 1887), 41–42.

37. *BAP*, 1: 327.

38. *Anti-Slavery Advocate*, December 1852.

39. "Interesting Narrative: The Weems Family," *Frederick Douglass' Paper*, February 1856, 1–2.

40. *Anti-Slavery Reporter*, January 1853, 28–29.

41. *Christian News*, January 20, 1853.

42. *Inquirer*, April 23, 1853.

43. Schor, *Henry Highland Garnet*, 125. These activities are recorded in the *Missionary Records of the United Presbyterian Church*, May 1854, 84–85.

44. *Inquirer*, April 23, 1853.

45. *Inquirer*, April 23, 1853.

46. *Frederick Douglass' Paper*, September 2, 1853.

47. I have made silent corrections to the spelling of Garnet's name. *Frederick Douglass' Paper*, September 2, 1853.

48. "Rev. Wm. H. Bishop," *Frederick Douglass' Paper*, September 21, 1855. I have made silent spelling and punctuation corrections.

49. *Frederick Douglas' Paper*, April 13, 1855.

50. *United Presbyterian Missionary Records*, March 1, 1856, 36–37.

51. *Frederick Douglass' Paper*, March 21, 1856; *Voice of the Fugitive*, reprinted in Schor, *Henry Highland Garnet*, 129–30. Prince, *A Shadow on the Household*, loc. 4239–41.

52. Garnet to Gerrit Smith, March 25, 1856, Smith Papers, letter 277, box 20.

53. Schor, *Henry Highland Garnet*, 137.

54. Harriet Beecher Stowe, *Uncle Tom's Cabin* (Cambridge, MA: Harvard University Press, 2009), 564.

CHAPTER 7. BITTER BATTLES, AFRICAN CIVILIZATION, AND JOHN BROWN'S BODY

1. *Weekly Anglo-African*, January 5, 1861.

2. "Speech at an Enthusiastic Meeting of the Colored Citizens of Boston," *Weekly Anglo-African*, September 10, 1859.

3. "African Civilization Society," *Douglass Monthly*, February 1859.

4. Henry Louis Gates and Jennifer Burton, eds., *Call and Response: Key Debates in African American Studies* (New York: Norton, 2011), 76.

5. Benjamin Coates to Ralph R. Gurley, Philadelphia, January 13, 1859. In *Back to Africa: Benjamin Coates and the Colonization Movement in America, 1848–1880*, ed. Emma J. Lapsansky-Werner and Margaret Hope Bacon (University City: Pennsylvania State University Press, 2005).

6. Ousmane K. Power-Greene, *Against Wind and Tide: The African American Struggle against the Colonization Movement* (New York: NYU Press, 2014), 7. See also James Oliver Horton and Lois E. Horton, *In Hope of Liberty, Culture, Community, and Protest among Northern Free Blacks, 1700–1860* (New York: Oxford University Press, 1997).

7. *Weekly Anglo-African*, March 14, 1863. Also in *Apropos of Africa: Sentiments of American Negro Leaders on Africa from the 1800s to the 1950s*, ed. Adelaide Cromwell Hill and Martin Kilson (London: Frank Cass, 1969), 160.

8. T. H. Barnes, *My Experience as an Inmate of the Colored Orphan Asylum, New York City* (New York: Crawford Family, 2005), 7. Manuscript at the Schomburg Center for Research in Black Culture; Seventh Annual Report (1843), 6–10, 13, 15, 16. Eighth Annual Report (1844), 4–7, 9, 10, 12, 19, 20. Twelfth Annual Report (1848). All found in *Association for the Benefit of Colored Orphans Records, New-York Historical Society*, series 1. Also cited in William Seraile, *Angels of Mercy: White Women and the History of New York's Colored Orphan Asylum* (New York: Fordham University Press, 2011), 233.

9. According to COA Admission Records, Thomas Henry Barnes was admitted on June 22, 1860, when he was six years of age. *Records of the Association for the Benefit of Colored Orphans, 1836–1972*, series 3: Admission Records, 1837–1937, vol. 23, p. 354. New-York Historical Society.

10. T. H. Barnes, *My Experience as an Inmate*, 10.

11. T. H. Barnes, *My Experience as an Inmate*, 8.

12. *Frederick Douglass' Paper*, August 8, 1856.

13. For an excellent account of how Garnet was one in a long line of Black activists who inspired white abolitionists, see Manisha Sinha, *The Slave's Cause: A History of Abolition* (New Haven, CT: Yale University Press, 2016), esp. 231, 418–19.

14. According to James McCune Smith, Brown raised funds for the publication of the 1843 address, though historians have been unable to confirm this. Smith, "Sketch," *Memorial Discourse*, 52.

15. Stephen B. Oates, *To Purge with Blood: A Biography of John Brown* (Boston: University of Massachusetts Press, 1984), 62.

16. Frederick Douglass, *The Life and Times of Frederick Douglass*, new rev. ed. (Boston: De Wolfe & Fikse, 1892), 337.

17. Their friendship is chronicled in Stauffer, *Black Hearts*.

18. Stauffer, *Black Hearts*, 247.

19. For a particularly powerful account of how Garnet was one in a long legacy of Black leaders who inspired white abolitionists, see Sinha, *The Slave's Cause*.

20. *Appeal, with a Brief Sketch of His Life. And also Garnet's Address to the Slaves of the United States of America* (New York: Printed by J. H. Tobitt, 1848), 96.

21. "No Union with Slaveholders," *Liberator*, December 9, 1859.

22. David Reynolds, one of Brown's recent biographers, calls Brown the "Man Who Killed Slavery, [and] Sparked the Civil War," in the subtitle of his book. David Reynolds, *John Brown, Abolitionist: The Man Who Killed Slavery, Sparked the Civil War, and Seeded Civil Rights* (New York: Vintage, 2005).

23. As David Reynolds points out, wild rumors followed the attack, including stories asserting that the raid had been carried out by "250 whites and 600 Black people." Few could imagine that Brown's small party was behind such a daring foray. David S. Reynolds, *John Brown, Abolitionist*, 334–36.

24. *New York Herald*, November 2, 1859.

25. "Requisition for the Arrest of Frederick Douglass," Douglass, *The Life and Times*, 379.

26. "Letter to the Wife of John Brown," *Weekly Anglo-African*, December 17, 1859. Also in *Blacks on Brown*, ed. Benjamin Quarles (Urbana: University of Illinois Press, 1972), 16–17.

27. Franny Nudelman, *John Brown's Body: Slavery, Violence, and the Culture of War* (Chapel Hill: University of North Carolina Press, 2015), 29.

28. "The Great Balloon," *New York Tribune*, published as *New-York Daily Tribune*, November 2, 1859, 8.

29. "Will Brown Be Sustained Now?" *Plain Dealer*, October 25, 1859, 2.

30. "Will Brown Be Sustained Now?" 2.

31. The "Irrepressible Conflict," *Weekly Houston Telegraph*, published as the *Weekly Telegraph*, November 16, 1859, 3.

32. New York City lawyer and philanthropist Hiram Ketchum—who had written many of the speeches performed by Garnet and McCune Smith's classmates in the 1820s—was a supporter of the Colored Orphan Asylum. He was also a supporter of colonizationist ideals. In 1846, Ketchum introduced the colonizationist Henry Clay to an audience in New York City, and took the time to declare "at considerable length, that the *Asylum* had no opinion to express in regard to Slavery," insisting that "with the exciting topics of the day it [the Asylum] had no concern." *Anti-Slavery Standard*, January 22, 1846.

33. *Twenty-Third Report of the Colored Orphan Asylum (1859)*, 31. In Association for the Benefit of Colored Orphans Records, New-York Historical Society. For information about Anna Marie's age and status see "Admissions, 1837–1866," also in Colored Orphan Records, Series 3. Piner's letter is quoted in William Seraile, *Angels of Mercy: White Women and the His-*

tory of New York's Colored Orphan Asylum (New York: Fordham University Press, 2011), Kindle edition, 63–64.

34. *New York Daily Tribune*, April 13, 1860.

35. "The Phoenixonian Literary Society," *Colored American*, July 8, 1837.

36. *New York Daily Tribune*, April 13, 1860.

37. *Weekly Anglo-African*, December 30, 1860.

38. *Weekly Anglo-African*, December 30, 1860.

39. *Weekly Anglo-African*, January 19, 1861.

40. *Weekly Anglo-African*, January 19, 1861.

41. Martin Delany, *Official Report of the Niger Valley Exploring Party* (New York, 1861), 10; Victor Ullman, *Martin R. Delany: The Beginnings of Black Nationalism* (Boston: Beacon, 1971), 226–46.

42. *Scott v. Sandford*, 60 U.S. 19 How. 393 393 (1856).

43. *Frederick Douglass' Monthly*, November 1861; *Anti-Slavery Reporter*, October 1, 1861; *Weekly Anglo-African*, September 7, 1861.

44. "Amusements," *Weekly Anglo-African*, November 30, 1861.

45. *Weekly Anglo-African*, September 7, 1861.

46. *Weekly Anglo-African*, September 7, 1861.

47. "Henry Highland Garnet Re-visits England," *Douglass Monthly*, September 1861.

48. "Rev. H.H. Garnet's Speech at Birmingham," *Weekly Anglo African*, November 16, 1861.

49. "Rev. H.H. Garnet's Speech."

50. "Rev. H.H. Garnet's Speech."

51. As Sven Beckert writes, "By paralyzing the dominant producer of one of the industrial world's most important commodities, the Civil War brought to a climax the tensions within global capitalism as it had evolved during the first half of the nineteenth century and led to a paradoxical result: the liberation of 4 million slaves in North America and the extension and intensification of imperial control over potential cotton-growing regions in Asia and Africa." Sven Beckert, "Emancipation and Empire: Reconstructing the World Wide Web of Cotton Production in the Age of the American Civil War," *American Historical Review* 109, no. 5 (2004): 1406.

52. James McCune Smith to Henry Highland Garnet, *Weekly Anglo-African*, December 30, 1860; *New York Herald*, May 18, 1857.

53. HHG to SS Jocelyn, September 14, 1859; November 29, 1859; December 14, 1860; American Missionary Association Archive, Tulane University, boxes 106–7.

54. *Weekly Anglo-African*, January 18, 1862.

55. Their pressure had apparently persuaded the Shiloh trustees, who reinstated Garnet as pastor.

56. *Weekly Anglo-African*, February 22, 1862.

CHAPTER 8. THE WAR'S END AND THE NATION'S FUTURE

1. *New York Daily Tribune*, May 14, 1862.

2. *New York Daily Tribune*, May 14, 1862.

3. *New York Daily Tribune*, May 14, 1862.

4. An act "releasing certain persons held to labor in the District of Columbia" and providing one hundred thousand dollars for colonization became law on April 16, 1862. On July 16, another act freed slaves in the hands of the army and granted five hundred thousand dollars for colonization. *New York Daily Tribune*, August 15, 1862.

5. As Kate Masur points out, Benjamin Quarles's initial assertion that Lincoln's associate had chosen recently freed slaves to come to the White House has been proven false. Instead,

the men came from the Black Washington elite. Kate Masur, "The African American Delegation to Abraham Lincoln: A Reappraisal," *Civil War History* 56, no. 2 (2010): 117–44.

6. "Address on Colonization to a Deputation of Negroes," in *Collected Works of Abraham Lincoln, 1809–1865*, vol. 5, ed. Roy P. Basler (New Brunswick, NJ: Rutgers University Press, 1953), 371, 372.

7. "Address on Colonization," 373.

8. "Address on Colonization," 371–72.

9. Kyle Volk, *Moral Minorities and the Making of American Democracy* (New York: Oxford University Press, 2017), 148.

10. "Important Meeting of the Colored People of Boston," *Boston Liberator*, August 1, 1862. In 1852, Smith was invited to be a founding member of the New York Statistics Institute.

11. Masur, "The African American Delegation," 126.

12. "Important Meeting of the Colored People."

13. Henry Highland Garnet to Editor [of *Weekly Anglo-African*], *Pacific Appeal*, October 11, 1862.

14. Masur, "The African American Delegation," 138; *New York Times*, September 2, 1862.

15. Masur, "The African American Delegation," 140–42.

16. "A Great Meeting at Shiloh Church," *Frederick Douglass Monthly*, June 1863.

17. "A Great Meeting at Shiloh Church."

18. Bernet Schecter, *Devil's Own Work: The Civil War Draft Riots and the Fight to Reconstruct America* (New York: Walker, 2005), 99.

19. Adrian Cook, *Armies of the Streets: The New York City Draft Riots of 1863* (Lexington: University Press of Kentucky, 1974), 8; Alice Rutkowski "Gender, Genre, Race, and Nation: The 1863 New York City Draft Riots," *Studies in the Literary Imagination* 40, no. 2 (2007): 111–32, 174.

20. See 11th Annual Report of the Colored Orphan Asylum, *Minutes of Board Meetings, 1836-1936*, vol. 1. Records of the Association for the Benefit of Colored Orphans Manuscript Collection at the New-York Historical Society.

21. *Minutes of the Board Meetings*, vol. 3, July 25, 1863. Records of the Association for the Benefit of Colored Orphans Manuscript Collection at the New-York Historical Society. Also "The Mob in New York," *New York Times*, July 14, 1863.

22. 1868 Report of the NY Colored Orphan Asylum. *Minutes of Board Meetings, 1836-1936*, vol. 3. Sarah Mulhall Adelman provides a useful and thorough analysis of the mob's sparing of the asylum's children. Sarah Mulhall Adelman, "'Permitted to Proceed Unmolested': Childhood and Race in the Burning of the Colored Orphan Asylum," *Common-place* 17, no. 2. http://common-place.org.

23. There are several, often contradictory, accounts of what stayed the mob's hands. Some newspaper accounts attribute the crowd's restraint to the efforts of a heroic white fireman. "The Rioters Burning and Sacking the Colored Orphan Asylum," *Harper's Weekly*, August 1, 1863, 493.

24. William Wells Brown, *The Negro in the American Rebellion: His Heroism and His Fidelity* (Boston: Lee and Sheperd, 1867), 194.

25. Barnes, *My Experience as an Inmate*, 18.

26. Barnes, *My Experience as an Inmate*, 18.

27. *Report of the Committee of Merchants for the Relief of Colored People, Suffering from the Late Riots in the City of New York* (New York, 1863), 14, 16, 18–19. As the primary agent of the committee, Garnet was almost certainly the one who had heard and recorded many of the stories preserved in the report.

28. Letter to the *New Bedford Standard*, reprinted in the *Pacific Appeal*, August 22, 1863.

29. *Report of the Committee of Merchants*.

30. *Proceedings of the National Convention of Colored Citizens and Their Friends, Held in Syracuse, October 1864.* Available via the Colored Conventions Project. http://coloredconventions.org.

31. *Minutes of the Board Meetings,* July 25, September 11, October 9, 1863. Also in Seraile, *Angels of Mercy,* 75.

32. 1860 Federal Census. New York Ward 5, District 2, New York, New York. Via Ancestry.com.

33. 1860 Federal Census. New York Ward 5, District 2, New York, New York. Via Ancestry.com.

34. *Report of the Committee of Merchants,* 11.

35. *Memorial Discourse,* 63. Also found in *Report of the New York Relief Commission for Colored People* (New York: Whitherone, Steam Printer, 1863), 3; and *Anti-Slavery Reporter,* November 2, 1863.

36. *Report of the Committee of Merchants,* 36.

37. *Report of the Committee of Merchants,* 36.

38. "Nicaragua," *Frederick Douglass' Paper,* January 8, 1852.

39. "Nicaragua."

40. *New York Union League Club Report Committee on Volunteering* (New York: Union League, 1864), 36, 12.

41. Martha Bockée Flint, *Early Long Island: A Colonial Study* (New York: Putnam's, 1893), 82.

42. "Report of Mr. Vincent Coyler, General Superintendent of Recruiting," in *New York Union League Club Report Committee on Volunteering* (New York: Union League, 1864), 36.

43. "Report of Mr. Vincent Coyler," 36.

44. *New York Tribune,* February 17, 1864.

45. "Report of Mr. Vincent Coyler," 37–38.

46. *New York Examiner,* March 5, 1864, qtd. in Henry O'Reilly, *First Organization of Colored Troops in the State of New York, to Aid in Suppressing the Slave-holders' Rebellion: Statements concerning the Origin, Difficulties, and Success of the Movement, including Official Documents, Military Testimonials, Proceedings of the "Union League Club," etc., Collated for the "New York Association for Colored Volunteers"* (New York: Baker & Godwin, 1864), 16; *New York Times,* March 6, 1864.

47. *New York Tribune,* March 5, 1864. O'Reilly, *First Organization,* 16.

48. O'Reilly, *First Organization,* 19.

49. McCune Smith, "Introduction," 58.

50. *New York Tribune,* March 5, 1864; O'Reilly, *First Organization,* 17.

51. *Weekly Anglo-African,* June 14, 1865.

52. *Weekly Anglo-African,* June 14, 1865.

53. Frank A. Roll, *Life and Public Services of Martin R. Delany, Sub-Assistant Commissioner Bureau Relief of Refugees, Freedman, and of Abandoned Lands, and Late Major 104th U.S. Colored Troops* (Boston: Lee & Shepard, 1883), 167.

54. Roll, *Life and Public Services.*

55. James McCune Smith to Gerrit Smith, January 13, 1864. Smith Papers, box 34.

56. James McCune Smith, "Introduction," 26–28, in *Memorial Discourse.*

57. *Memorial Discourse,* 71.

58. *Memorial Discourse,* 79.

59. *Memorial Discourse,* 73.

60. *Memorial Discourse,* 76.

61. *Memorial Discourse,* 80.

62. *Memorial Discourse,* 88.

63. *Memorial Discourse,* 57.

64. *Memorial Discourse*, 57.

65. James McCune Smith, *Weekly Anglo-African*, January 5, 1861. For more on Garnet's work with schools in the South, see *Weekly Anglo-African*, September 9, 1865; "Appeal of the African Civilization Society on Behalf of the Education of the Freedmen and Their Children" (New York, 1865). Garnet would have a short stint as president of Avery College in Pittsburgh, and would also have some input with schools in New York City, marrying a New York school administrator, Sarah J. Tompkins, after Julia died in 1879.

66. *Memorial Discourse*, 88.

INDEX

ABOUT THE AUTHOR

ANNA MAE DUANE is Associate Professor of English at the University of Connecticut. She is the author and editor of five books exploring the relationship between conceptions of childhood and race. Her work has been supported by Fulbright and NEH grants, and has appeared in scholarly journals and mainstream venues, including *Slate*, *Salon*, Avidly. com, and PBS's *History Detectives*.